THE *DISCIPLINA CLERICALIS* OF PETRUS ALFONSI

A VOLUME IN

THE ISLAMIC WORLD

SERIES

FOUNDED BY G.E. VON GRUNEBAUM

Published under the auspices of the
NEAR EASTERN CENTER
UNIVERSITY OF CALIFORNIA
LOS ANGELES

The
Disciplina Clericalis
of Petrus Alfonsi

Translated and edited by

EBERHARD HERMES

Translated into English by
P. R. Quarrie

UNIVERSITY OF CALIFORNIA PRESS

Berkeley and Los Angeles

First published in the United States by
The University of California Press
Berkeley and Los Angeles, California
Translated from the original Latin
and from the German: *Die Kunst, vernünftig
zu Leben (Disciplina Clericalis)*
Copyright © 1970 Artemis Verlags-AG, Zürich
This translation © Routledge & Kegan Paul Ltd 1977

Library of Congress Catalog Card Number 73-94434
ISBN 0-520-02704-3

Printed in Great Britain

CONTENTS

v

TRANSLATOR'S NOTE

The translation of the *Disciplina Clericalis* itself, and that of any passages quoted from other works of Petrus Alfonsi in the body of the introduction, has been made anew from the original Latin, with reference to the German version of Herr Hermes. The text used for the *Disciplina Clericalis* was the Heidelberg, 1911 edition of Hilka and Söderhjelm.

A brief note of some of the early printed editions of the work has been added after the Bibliography.

P. R. Quarrie

The Jews have ... always been a minority, and a minority is always forced to think for itself; that is the fortunate part of their fate. The knowledge of the fact that they were sufficiently protected against the majority and its rulers by their particular power and success must always be kept in the forefront of a Jew's mind, despite any thoughts to the contrary, The power of persuasion over the majority is the most telling possession of this small minority, and is due to their elasticity and readiness to adapt.

(Leo Baeck, *Das Wesen des Judentums*, Cologne, 1960, p. 3)

Because I was a Jew, I found myself free from many prejudices which constrict others in the use of their intellect, and as a Jew I found myself always prepared to be in opposition, and disclaim any agreement with the 'compact majority'.

(Sigmund Freud, *Brief an die Mitglieder des Vereins Bnai Brith*, 6 May 1926)

Part One

THE AUTHOR AND HIS TIMES

by

Eberhard Hermes

1 'TO HAVE THE EXPERIENCE OF A JEW'

The 'Sincere Friends' was a group of Muslim men of learning working in Basra in the tenth century A.D. They held the view that a man should not exclude from the sphere of his interest any book, advice, or any foreign pattern of existence, when his wish was to be really educated.[1] It is completely in agreement with this point of view that they attempt to outline the ideal man in whom, in accordance with their ideas, they emphasise the characteristic of every group that is to be found in the Islamic Middle Ages:[2]

> The ideal and morally blameless man should be of East Persian extraction, an Arab in his beliefs, a follower of the Hanafi school of law. His education should be Iraqi in its form, he should be a Jew from the point of view of experience of the world, a young Jesus in his habits, and holy as a Syrian monk. In self-knowledge, he should be as a Greek, and as an Indian in the interpretation of secrets. Lastly he should be a Sufi in the totality of his spiritual life.[3]

From this catalogue in which 'with unusual clarity are laid out the real elements of Islamic education for true consciousness',[4] the thing that interests us more than all else is the characterisation of the Jew as a man of particular experience. Is this peculiarity of the Jews provable in other places and at other times? What kind of experience is meant? How does it come about that, by virtue of being men of experience, the Jews are cut off from other groups?

To provide proof for this impression that the learned men of Basra had of the Jews, men who lived with them in the empire of the caliph, is not difficult. There is found in Europe in the Middle

3

Ages a land where Jews were able to live for centuries in free inter-course with other groups of society, so that through a comparison and consideration of the particular contribution made by them, one can establish what was the effect of the Jews on the common culture of the former group.

This question of the Jewish experience is based not on a glance backwards into the recent past, and the fate that this people met with, a unique happening, but on the fact that they deserve consideration for being the only people in history to have been obliged, so to speak, for more than two thousand years, to live as a minority in a society, distinguished by speech, religion and character from them, and to have been forced to preserve their own identity. This sort of condition for existence provides a meaningful model for the spiritual and interior tension, which man has to cope with in modern pluralistic society, which because of the incomparable paraphernalia of power and the intricacy of higher mental activities, makes demands on a man such as have never been demanded of him in history. In this open society one must acquire one's independence at a critical and rational distance, and this activity must be accomplished from the point of view of some role or other in society. 'Personal maturity presumes Adaptation.'[5] So man must be both critical of himself in his own personal identity, and know himself, and be able to understand and attune himself to the values of foreign groups, when he wishes to assert himself in this pluralistic society, and at the same time he must provide his contribution to the preservation of this society.[6]

In the light of the fact that the social accomplishments that modern society demands from an individual are only with difficulty attained, and that in the past mankind has scarcely been ready for them, it is worth everyone's while to enquire of those people who were able to exist throughout their quite long history by both self-assertion and adaptation.[7]

2   AN OUTSIDER IN EUROPEAN LITERATURE

The West is generally considered as a synthesis of Greco-Roman antiquity, the world of the barbarian invaders and Christianity. It is upon this scheme that all the investigations, summaries and surveys of intellectual history are based. In their systematic endeavours to bring order into the wide variety of dates, periods, and important personages, they favour the typical, while overlooking a few quite straightforward phenomena.[1] The closed system has no place for the 'outsider'. Such an outsider is the oldest collection of novelle in the Middle Ages, the *Disciplina Clericalis* of Petrus Alfonsi, which the Romance scholar Karl Vossler described in the following charming manner:[2]

How easy and swift is ... success in world literature (a success of the first rank) such as befell this prosaic edifying and didactic conversation book, the *Disciplina Clericalis*! No wonder. In these lively sayings Eastern wisdom for the conduct of life combines with Christian piety in a manner that is witty, pious, and that delights in stories. A Jewish doctor and man of learning, Rabbi Moses Sefardi, from Huesca in Aragon, was in 1106 converted to Christianity, and adopted the name of Petrus Alfonsi. He wrote this book, first, it appears, in Arabic, and then in easy Latin. It filled him with joy to confirm his new beliefs, and the Christian way of thinking, and to demonstrate their truth in a manner both witty and cautious, using proverbs, verses, examples, fables, anecdotes and tales of men's fates, and to present in a significant way distant stories through the voice of a father who speaks to his son. This charming little work has been transmitted to us in more than sixty old manuscripts. In the twelfth century it was done into French verse and later again into prose. In the course of the fifteenth and sixteenth centuries adaptations appeared in Spanish, Catalan, Gascon, Italian, German, English and even Icelandic. In all the countries of Europe, moralists and preachers, society groups and story-tellers like Chaucer, Boccaccio, Steinhöwel, used for their different purposes, motifs, judgments and Arabesques from the treasure chest of the Christianized Spanish Jew. If we wished to hunt after the particular details of this material we would have to search in all of world literature, so overmastering is the success of the author. His presentation is both convincing and to the point. Both in the general and the particular it appears that the shaping of the various materials cost him little trouble. Providentially, the author found himself right in the middle of that very land where Eastern and Western styles and philosophy of life were in opposition on the broadest front. What did it matter to him that the land was Spain? One could imagine a similar book springing up either in Southern Italy or anywhere in the Mediterranean area. For the author, the Semite of Arabic and Jewish education who had converted to Christianity, the literary synthesis took place without additions. His equanimity assured him of a broad success, like that theatre director in the prologue to Faust: 'Whoever brings much, will bring more; if there is one act, others will be added! Like a stew, it must please you. . . . What's the use, you offer them a whole meal, the public will still pull it to pieces.'

With this little book there springs from a world that lay in the distance, the old Greco-Roman culture which as if by considering its own antiquity, as had done Western Christianity,[3] produced a new way of looking at mankind and the world in the Latin Middle Ages. In this the merchant plays a role which he had not before achieved, at least in the West,[4] whereas the knight scarcely makes an appearance.[5] At the high-point of the Middle Ages which so loved marvels, we have here a work in which there is no miracle. Although during the twelfth century the Virgin Mary stood at the central point of piety,[6] in this book she is not even mentioned; we find in a work written at the same time and of the same provenance as the *Cantar del mio Cid*, no mention of the tourney, of knightly journeys, of the beautiful titled lady. Rather as a matter of course we find assumed a society of towns and townsmen unknown to the West before that time.[7]

The active interest of the Spanish kings in the Arabic and Jewish literature paved the way for the appearance of such a book in the Latin world. The most famous of these Christian kings, who were interested in oriental culture, is Alfonso the Wise of Castile (ruled 1252–84). He caused a translation to be made into Spanish of the books of proverbs of the Arabic doctors Ḥunayn b. Isḥâq (808–73) and al-Mubashshir (*c.* 1100), and also the Qur'an, the Mishna and the Talmud.[8] He organised, so to speak, the spiritual culture of his country.[9] His brother was responsible for the translation of the Arabo-Indian story of 'The Seven Wise Men' into Castilian.

In the foreword to the *Libro de los Engannos et los Asayamientos de las Mujeres (Book of the Wiles and Contrivances of Women)*, which dates from 1253, he is called

The infant Don Fadrique, son of the great and glorious king, Don Fernando and of the holy, modest and admirable queen, Dona Beatrice, has brought this about so that the fame of his name may not pass away ever, for he has learned from the teaching of the sages that the fame of a wise man who has done good never passes away, and he knows that nothing is better suited to help one attain the eternal life than good works, and knowledge,[10] for indeed knowledge is a sound ship in which to bring a person on without any danger, and together with good works, it causes the person to attain eternity. Life, however, is short, and knowledge is both difficult to attain and requires much time for its attainment,[11] and because of this, man cannot learn more than has been granted to him by God's grace, which is bestowed upon him and sent down from heaven. Therefore, the prince has wished that this book be translated from Arabic into Castilian to be a warning of the wiles and guile of women in the desire to make progress, do good, and also to reward these people who desire the same end.[12]

There may be also a little irony at play, but at all events the justification of the translation of those novelle which were diffused in the East bears witness to a programme for education set out by the Spanish king, the basis of whose thought was: 'Through knowledge is life mastered.' We know of another such statement of cultural policy, also from the Middle Ages, in the example of the *Capitularia* of Charlemagne. But in what respect? What, however, distinguishes the efforts of the Spanish king from those of the Carolingian Renaissance is that they do not grasp at their unique heritage to 'organise the spiritual culture of their country', but rather make use of the underlying Arabo-Judaic culture that they found in their immediate neighbourhood. Thus they introduced into the treasury of European tradition an un-classical cultural element.

Petrus Alfonsi used the following three Arabic works, which later were so beloved in their Spanish translation, for his *Disciplina Clericalis*, the collections of proverbs made by Hunayn and al-Mubashshir, as well as the *Book of the Wiles and Contrivances of Women*.[13] Even though it is only hinted at in the prologue, it can be assumed that behind the compilation of the *Disciplina Clericalis* lies the wish of a king to acquaint himself with oriental wisdom of life, and to provide useful guidance and training for his subjects. It is possible that this king Alfonso of Aragon was affected in the same way as was the English Count Rivers who in 1473 journeyed by sea to Santiago de Compostela, and then remained in Spain a little to recuperate. As he had a great deal of time for reading, he took the advice of a farmer and devoted himself to a reading of the French translation of the book of sayings of al-Mubashshir. This Arabic work fascinated and astonished him: he could not believe that there could exist such a wonderful mirror for Christians and such a refreshing draught for all thinking men. There by means of examples and precepts were all conditions thoroughly dealt with; virtue and knowledge praised, stupidity and vice roundly condemned. As he saw that the book would be an indispensable aid for the training and education of men, he therefore began to translate it into English.[14]

Because of the peculiar circumstances under which the book took its genesis, and the author lived, preoccupation with the *Disciplina Clericalis* and its author rests from the outset on a theme which is not guaranteed to impress itself very firmly on matters of literary history. A work that attempts to interpret the average human life and transfers such an interpretation from one culture to another, given the fact that the author of the book belongs to neither culture, but to a third that is a guest amongst the others and whose people for centuries have busied themselves with matters of translation and mediation in matters of cultural exchange, such a work must necessarily mirror something of the existence of those men who are to be found on the fringes of closed societies, and must equally give some idea of the interchanges between the naïve conformism of those who give unquestioning adherence to tradition, and the critical spirit that has immeasurably greater fields of experience to draw on.

3   A MUCH TRAVELLED STORY

The *Disciplina Clericalis* occupies a very important position on the caravan route of the transference of oriental tales to the West, and is a fruitful sphere of activity for researchers into the history of these tales. Most of these stories have a very interesting and much travelled background, and even now in the literature of our century, traces are still to be found. In chapter 31 of Thomas Mann's novel

Doctor Faustus, we have an example of this. There, the chronicler, Serenus Zeitblom, describes how the composer Adrian Leverkühn one day came upon the collection of exempla put together in the thirteenth century, generally known as the *Gesta Romanorum*:

I am of the opinion that the *Gesta*—in their historical uninstructedness, pious, Christian didacticism and moral naïveté, with the eccentric casuistry of parricide, adultery and complicated incest; their undocumented Roman emperors, with daughters whom they fantastically guarded and then offered for sale under the most hair-splitting conditions—it is not to be denied, I say, that all these fables presented in a solemn, latinising and indescribably naïve style of translation, concerning knights in pilgrimage to the Promised Land, wanton wives, artful procuresses, clerics given to the black arts, do have an extraordinarily diverting effect. They were in the highest degree calculated to stimulate Adrian's penchant for parody, and the thought of maturing a condensed musical dramatisation of them for the puppet theatre occupied his mind from the day he came across them. There is the completely immoral tale that anticipates the *Decameron*, of the 'godless guile of the old woman', in which an accomplice of guilty passion, under the mask of sanctity, succeeds in persuading a noble and even exceptionally decent and honourable wife, that she has sinful desires on a youth who is eaten up by passion for her, while her trustful husband is away on a journey. The witch makes her little bitch puppy fast for two days, and then gives it bread with mustard to eat, which causes the little beast to shed copious tears. She then takes it to the virtuous lady, who receives her with all due honour, as she, as does everyone else, considers her to be a saint. When, however, the lady sees the weeping puppy, and surprised, asks the cause of this, the old woman gives the appearance of not wishing to reply. When pressed, she tells that the little dog was once her own daughter, who was too chaste, and who because of the fact that she spurned a young man on fire with love for her, had caused his death. For this she had been punished by metamorphosis into this shape, and consequently weeps continually despairing of her doggy nature. Telling these deliberate lies, the old bawd weeps too, but the lady, horrified at the similarity of her own case, and that of the dog, tells the woman of the young man who is ill with love of her. At this, the old woman earnestly urges her to imagine what an irretrievable pity it would be if she too should be turned into a puppy. She is then commissioned to bring the groaning suitor that he may slake his lust in God's name, so that the two by means of a godless trick, celebrate the sweetest adultery.

This story of 'The Weeping Puppy', which is the title of Hans Sachs's carnival piece for the year 1554,[1] is still found today in oral transmission. This is clear from a glance at Aarne-Thompson's catalogue of the types of the folk-tale.[2] It harkens back to considerable antiquity, and has been widely transmitted. The transformation motif leads us back to India where the idea of metempsychosis was well established in antiquity. The young woman never doubts for a moment that the bitch puppy was once a girl. Obviously this naïve belief is simply demanded by the story itself, but basically this was something related to an audience which entertained the possibility of such a metempsychosis, and later still, to an audience which was so informed in such matters, that there were people who actually believed in it. How the comic development of the story was received by a sceptical public is difficult to say.[3]

The next trace of our tale is in the Indian *Sukasaptati*, *The Book of Parrots*, a 'framework' story, in which a parrot keeps on edge a woman determined on adultery, and prevents her from fulfilling her immoral designs before her husband returns.[4] Our story is also to be found in another 'framework' story of Indian origin, namely 'The Tale of the Seven Wise Masters', where the narration of stories has exactly the same purpose—the postponement of some immoral act until there is some decisive change. In this work a king condemns his son to death because of the accusations of a favourite concubine, whose love the son had rejected, and who was, because of this, full of hate. Seven wise men attempt to make the king doubt the truth of these accusations by relating stories on the malice of womankind, and the concubine responds by using seven evil men who also tell stories to persuade the king to take the woman's part. Eventually truth triumphs, the son is saved, and the accuser condemned to death herself.[5] The most widely known form of this 'Sindbad' story is the late Arabic *Arabian Nights*,[6] where the motif of the 'delaying story' appears in two guises, for Scheherazade also, who is the narrator of the whole tale, struggles to arrest the progress of her own proposed execution by ensnaring the king in stories.

The main medium for the transmission of Indian story material to the West was Persia. The stories were translated into Persian in India itself at the courts of the Muslim princes, and were further transmitted in this linguistic form until their arrival in Baghdad or elsewhere, where they were translated into Arabic by one of the many arabicised Persians living in Arab lands.[7] The journey then continued to Spain where the stories were translated from Arabic— sometimes through the medium of Hebrew versions—into Latin and then into the various vernaculars, thereby becoming 'at home' in Europe.

In all this travel, our story occupies a special position. In a collection of the thirteenth century, comparable to the *Gesta* and known as the *Compilacio singularis exemplorum*, a work which provides the preacher with edifying similes which enliven and illustrate Christian teaching, we find in the immediate vicinity of the story of 'The Weeping Puppy', the following story:[8]

> Another old woman arranged a rendezvous for a married
> woman with a 'clerk'. After she had brought the woman into
> her house, the old woman sent for the clerk, but he was not
> to be found. The old woman, however, saw a good-looking
> young man in the street, who appealed to her, and so she said,
> 'What would you give me if I were to bring you a beautiful
> wife from Paris?' The young man named a particular sum, and
> went with her. The wife however recognised in him her own
> husband; she jumped on him, boxed his ears, pulled his hair
> and cried, 'Now I see what a liar you are, you thief! I wanted
> to put you to the test, and now I've caught you!' He tried to
> exonerate himself, and pointed out that he had never done
> anything like that before. In such a way did the wife through
> her wickedness escape all shame, whereas the husband was
> left to bear all the blame.

If one looks at the two stories together, and sees them next to each other, the impression is quickly formed that they have some- thing to do with each other. In most versions of the story of 'The Seven Wise Men', the two are found together, and also in the Syriac *Sindbad*, Greek *Syntipas*, Hebrew *Mischle Sendabar*, the Spanish *Libro de los Engannos*, and also in the *Arabian Nights*, where the transference acts as a link:[9]

> So the woman adorned herself, and prepared a meal while the old woman went out to await the youth. He, however, did not come, and the old woman, look as she might, found no trace of him. She said to herself, 'What's to be done? Shall that delicious feast, which has been prepared for him, be wasted? And what about the money I was promised? No, I'll not allow my cunning plan to be spoiled. I'll look for another to take his place, and take him to her!' So she searched the streets and suddenly saw a handsome, charming young man who had obviously just returned from a journey. She went up to him, greeted him and said, 'Do you long for food and drink and a beautiful woman, who already is prepared for your coming?' The man asked, 'Where is this to be had?', and the old woman replied, 'At my house.' So he went with her, but she did not know that he was the woman's husband.

In the *Sukasaptati* and the Persian *Sindibād-Nāmeh*, the two stories are separate, and this quite clearly shows that basically the two tales existed singly, and had nothing to do with each other. The explanation for the joining of the two is that a narrator had at some juncture the need to rearrange the two stories to obtain a proportionate distribution.

The narrator who introduced into the Arabic version the story of the burned veil, was obliged to make room for this by joining together two other stories. The result is a similar unification of the tales that were originally separate.[10] For example, in the Hebrew *Mischle Sendabar*, the story of Ghula the ghost-maiden,[11] and that of the spring that changed sex,[12] are made into one story,[13] in order to arrive at a proportionate distribution of stories. Such is the scope of enquiries and investigations into folk stories.[14]

It is however established that the joining together of these two stories is not just a matter of straight composition: the tale of 'The Weeping Puppy' gains far more from the continuation in another story, extraordinary in its effect. The woman comes to grief not only in spite of her chastity, but also because she knows that the shame will transfer itself from her to her husband. The theme is not just the weakness, but rather the wickedness of women. The young woman learns the 'tricks of women' in the school of the cunning old woman. Is it not perhaps for this reason that a narrator has joined together the two stories, and on this basis, sought a new story for an empty space? Is it not perhaps because of this further possibility of intensifying the theme of feminine cunning, that he took it upon himself to change the composition of the whole work?

We must of course see in this story-teller an attitude that is no longer content with merely handling the age-old motif of 'criticism of women' in the traditional way, but which is beginning to treat the theme in a witty and ingenious way, so that it is not with Thomas Mann's character, Adrian Leverkühn, that the spirit of parody makes its first appearance.

The use, adaptation and transmission of an old story is something that gives rise to human motifs. Whoever tells a story, has a point of view and an interest. In enquiring after this point of view and this interest lies the sole charm of bothering about an old story and its transmission.

Basically the transmission of stories of the type of *The Wiles and Contrivances of Women* goes back to the primitive motif of 'criticism of women' which is the need to 'give women a knock'. Criticism of women is a common topos in world literature. In the Babylonian 'Conversation between master and servant', it is already found:[15]

Woman is a pit—a pit, a hole, a watery grave; woman is a
sharp sword of iron that cuts through man's neck.

Ancient literature—Hesiod, Simonides, Euripides[16]—is full of such remarks. In Arabic there are two verses of the Qur'an which assert that not even the devil with all his wiles could succeed against the tricks of women:[17]

Be mindful of the word of God the most high: verily your
feminine guile is great! And compare with this the words of the
most High and most Praised: verily, Satan's guile is weak.

In the Latin Middle Ages, woman was characterised as 'a sweet poison' ('dulce venenum'), and the opinion was firmly held that she was by nature inclined to evil ('semper prona rei/quae prohibetur ei').[18] This evaluation of women had considerable effects on girls' education, which in some parts is even today not entirely accepted. A thirteenth-century text enjoins that only nuns should be taught to read and write; as far as the rest of women are concerned, the attitude is that they need no more poison, as the serpents already have too much.[19] In 1787 an Italian lady complained to Goethe:[20]

> We are not taught to write because man is afraid that we will
> use our pens to write love letters; we would not be allowed to
> read, if it were not that we are obliged to occupy ourselves
> with a prayer book.

One should not however consider 'criticism of women' as an institution, but rather one should attempt to find out what causes someone to speak thus of women, and whether he merely repeats parrot-fashion what has already been said. We know, for example, that after the death of the physician, al-Mubashshir of Cairo, his wife hurried into his library together with her maids and threw armfuls of books through the window into a bowl of water in the courtyard. The apparent reason for this was that the husband during his lifetime had never managed to convince his wife of the value of his literary work. The anti-feminist proverbs that al-Mubashshir had put into the mouth of Socrates in his *Book of Worldly Wisdom* may have been his revenge.[21] The later translation into English made from the French version by Count Rivers, and the trànslation of the famous printer Caxton (*c.* 1421–91) show surprisingly, when examined, that these Socratic proverbs are missing. A 'fayr lady' had obviously succeeded in removing the criticism of her fellows, or he was so in love with her that he had written nothing inimical to women; either that, or he was one of those few men who had had only good experiences of women. Caxton inserts into his translation passages where he says that only a Socrates could have told the truth, with the ironical remark, however, that in these proverbs women should not be considered worse than they are in reality;[22] from which remark readers of anti-feminist proverbs should receive some enlightenment!

4   THE ANSWER OF THE PHYSICIAN AND THE THEORY OF THE NOVELLA

How did the story of 'The Weeping Puppy' find its way into the *Gesta Romanorum*? The compiler used the *Disciplina Clericalis*, as a comparison[1] of the texts shows and an explicit citation of the source testifies.[2] His intention was of a purely didactic nature. He wished by the use of individual stories to stress the demands and prohibitions of Christian morals. How these stories were understood, can be excellently illustrated from the allegory of the chess game taken from the *Gesta*:[3]

> The queen is our soul, which can never learn to wage war abroad, but is driven to do good works from within the body. For our soul, that is reason, should direct our body, like the rider his horse, towards virtue, and teach the body not to go beyond the bounds of the church's teachings. It must proceed from the square of one virtue to that of another. So too must the queen go forwards on the chess board for a long period and not jump, but remain within the bounds fixed for it. Dyna, the daughter of Jacob, preserved her maidenhead so long as she kept quietly within her brother's house, but as soon as she, driven by curiosity, took herself off to foreign parts, she was dishonoured herself.[4]

Without undue trouble the moves of chess are shown in the text in terms of spiritual advice; the basic reality is clear to the pious glance, and important as a sign, as regards other understanding. The world of things is conceived as a schoolbook.[5] How easily the shift from the basis of the story to the allegorical meaning is accomplished is shown by the transference from the lady in danger in the game of chess to the Old Testament story of abduction. This style of allegory only holds if the interest of the story-teller remains entirely given over to spiritual instruction. It will by necessity cease to be as soon as what is told, and thus the story itself, or the relating, and thus the relation between the narrator and his public, becomes the centre of awareness; in short, if pedagogic naïveté ceases to exist in order to make room for a critical awareness.

However novelle were related during the Middle Ages, whether in Latin or in the vernacular, the narrator could always draw on exempla, short humorous stories, facetiae and anecdotes which stretched back in an unbroken literary tradition to the ancient world, which obliged him to act, as did the compiler of the *Gesta Romanorum*, in a didactic manner, and to stress the useful portions of their stories as a stimulant or deterrent to the correct conduct of life. This tradition is so undisputed, that even the superior intelligences amongst these story-tellers follow the rule to the letter and conduct themselves, at least in the prologue or in the stories within a frame, as teachers.[6] Boccaccio was the first openly to take up arms against this tradition, and to stress the social function of story-telling as against the didactic.[7]

In Islam also the realistic story which deals with human life, was treated purely as a didactic exemplum. Pure delight in story-telling or psychological interest in the colourful world of man was taboo. This is why so many masterly tales like those in the *Arabian Nights*, remain anonymous. The authors did not dare to allow them to appear under their names.[8]

This attitude that the value of literature lies in its educational worth is still widespread even today. It seems to betray a naïve, uncritical attitude to the world, and plays an important role in questions of censorship, literary criticism or the form of school textbooks in which writers of just average ability, because of the positive form of their work, are preferred to masters of language, because they express the attitude proper to the didactic end of literature.[9] The consequence of this attitude is the demand that the guidance of the literary life come 'from above', as a modern presentation of that early period of the European novella accepted as self-evident:[10]

> We recognise the basic undertone in such stories, which has spread itself to the people under the official class with their formal ostentation and splendour, their outward dignities, and foreign models of imitated literature. It is an impudent, democratic tone, that values wit and cunning most highly and takes great pleasure in solidly sensual joys. Later it would fashion for itself a more important hearing. The fact that it is an undertone which gradually becomes prominent, is evidence to us of a general observation that naturally has nothing surprising in it. Culture lies in the form of transmitted learning tiresomely acquired in school; education penetrates from above to below. Occasionally the lower classes reacted and desired an expression that was much more joyful and jolly when compared with such high seriousness. To keep this tendency correctly in check was the task that fell to the church at that time as the wise educator of the people. It was not easy, and there were many false starts, in which much was omitted, indeed assumed, or on the other hand repressed too strongly, when it should have been more carefully cherished.

The weapon used by the superior spirits amongst these story-tellers in their struggle for liberty in the face of the compulsion of tradition, was irony.[11] They could not because of their rank give way to the 'guidance from above', but were obliged to stand on their rights, to bring their contribution to the literary life through free discussion with the existing powers.

The author of the *Disciplina Clericalis* possessed from the very beginning a certain superiority in the matter of the theory of the novella, in as much as he was at home in three different worlds, and was able, by comparison, to recognise the limitations of didactic demands. He treated these demands as something human, and employed the weapon of irony not only to protect his liberty in the formation of his work, but also to unmask by irony men's attitudes to erotic tales and thereby the hypocrisy of that particular theory of the novella.

In the *Disciplina Clericalis*, the story of 'The Weeping Puppy' is found, with four other erotic exempla, in the framework of an exchange between teacher and pupil, the theme of which is the blame of women. At the beginning the teacher expresses his fear that the readers will consider him an immoral person if he tells stories about evil women. The pupil, however, calms him by pointing out that the stories are related with an educational purpose in view. The master allows his young listener to experience for himself that mankind never understands such stories in an educational sense, and that it is more true that the moral justification of such a narrative is a pure fiction. After the first story the pupil is not angered by the wickedness of women, but rather filled with enthusiasm for what he has learned which, he says, he would not exchange for all the wealth of the Arabs. He asks for a second tale giving as the reason that in his later professional life he would be able to utilise it to advise those under his care. It can, however, be seen that this is said only in the theoretical sense, in order to conceal his true desire which is to retell this novella at some jolly gathering.

After the second story his enthusiasm is even greater, and after the third, the master becomes angry, because the pupil would like to hear even more:

What? Are you still not satisfied? I have told you three stories, and you still won't stop asking for more!

The pupil replies that the three stories were very short, and he wanted to hear a longer one. In answer to this request, the master tells the story of the countryman who had to convey 2,000 sheep across a river, and was allowed only one small skiff in which to do this, which could only take two sheep at a time. Just as the royal story-teller wanted by the use of this story to gain some respite, so too the master wants respite. The pupil objects to this, saying that the relationship between the king and his story-teller bears no resemblance to that between pupil and master which is a personal relationship based on love. Here narration is clearly divided off from education, although in theory it is true that every narrative must have a didactic aim. The narrative element is shown to be entertainment whereas the didactic element appears to be bound up with the hypothesis that a popular personal relation exists between narrative and the hearer.

When the teacher suggested that the listener would take the narrator of erotic novelle for an immoral person, he already knew that the listener did not wish to be instructed but to be entertained. The pupil clearly corroborated this estimation of the listeners through his reaction. For if listeners consider the didactic pretensions of the narrator to be unworthy of belief, they thereby betray that they are not really eager to learn, but are merely curious and eager for entertainment. The narrating physician shows in this framework of ironic exchange how men are made up in reality, whereas the proponents of the didactic theory of the novella base themselves on how men ought to be, namely eager to learn and ready to change their lives. It is as a contrast to their abstract idealism that Petrus Alfonsi sets up his clearheaded notion of human experience.

At the end of the series of the true erotic exempla, the pupil reacts as the didactic theory expects him to: 'I will not marry.' He is a good pupil, who observes the rules of the game, and gives those answers which he thinks the master would like to hear. The epistle that goes under the name of St Jerome called 'Valerius to Rufinus, to dissuade him from marriage',[12] which was a favourite in the Middle Ages, states that the success of such teaching on the wickedness of women is to be found in the decision of the pupil to adopt celibacy. The master now proceeds to show that not all women are wicked, and that this doctrine is based on an inadmissible generalised judgment, and is therefore inadequate for a decision on celibacy. Further the correction of prejudice succeeds through an ironic expression, when the pupil remarks that praise of women is a 'res nova', i.e. something completely new.

Petrus Alfonsi is not against literary didacticism; he wishes only to put in its right perspective the relation between education and entertainment. How man is made up is not a question that should be laboured. Man must from his own nature develop an attitude that needs education as much as recreation. When that is forgotten, as in the case of the theory of the novella, man reacts by fulfilling at least superficially the demands of the pedagogues, but in secret satisfies his own needs. Petrus Alfonsi did not forget this fact. Therefore in his little book we find alternation of didacticism and entertainment; for example, he proceeds directly from his section on table manners to the jokes on Maimundus on the same subject. This he does in a free and easy manner. The strain of the lesson is followed by amusement, the recreational aim leads one gently back to the end of the Maimundus story in a new, pointed didactic passage.[13]

The physician knows what human nature does when in need. His view as a story-teller is diatetic; he will not only tell men what they must know (in his opinion) in order to live in a rational manner, but he will say it in such a manner that they will be able to accept it, because it is with pleasure that they hear it:[14]

> I have also considered the infirmity of man's physical nature which makes it necessary to break up instruction into small sections so that boredom does not set in. Also I have been mindful of the fact that in order to facilitate remembrance of what has been learnt, the pill must be softened and sweetened by various means, because man is by nature forgetful and has need of many tricks which will remind him again of those things he has forgotten.

The physician sets his experience against the self-deception of errors of human nature and its needs, and with his diatetic foundation of story-telling makes a particular contribution to the rational solution of that old antinomy that exists between the didactic and recreational function of literature, so often formulated as irreconcilable alternatives.[15]

His contribution founded a new tradition: the consideration of the diatetic importance of the story-telling became a topos.[16] In the preface to the *Count Lucanor* the exempla were used as sweeteners for the bitter medicine of learning. The *Cento Novelle Antiche* were related to liven up and comfort mankind in his physical life.[17] Hans

Sachs, too, ends the foreword to the second volume of the first folio edition of his work with the words:[18]

> But, my good hearted, friendly best of readers, thou wouldst take this second book of my poems as a common garden of delight that stands on roads open to all men. There can be found not only a few trees that bear sweet fruit to be the food of those in health, but also roots and cabbage, nasty and bitter to the taste, which purge the sick of their evil humours, and drive out the rotting dampness of vice. In the same way fragrant violets and lilies can be used to distil powerful oils, colognes and essences which will cure the weak and feeble spirits overcome with trouble: indeed there are many other wild flowers, of less nobility perhaps, which can still be used for this purpose—as clover, thistle and cornflowers. Thereby are melancholic and bilious humours made joyous and light-hearted by the use of pretty, colourful flowers.

5   EASTERN FORMS OF WISDOM

The perusal of a systematically constructed work is a strain. The execution of a complicated, closely reasoned and compact train of thought could with difficulty help to remove melancholy from a 'weak' mind. On the other hand, those works, like the *Disciplina Clericalis*, which are unified by such a diatetic point of view, are loose and unsystematic in form, as well as rich in variety. They proceed in a manner where one association follows another, and they expressly avoid abstract concepts in favour of an illustrative approach.

It is a well-established fact that a percipient example excites more thought than a theoretical instruction. This was known to the Indian God Pakka, when he saw that an adulterous woman had had her husband murdered by her lover, but that she was now being deserted by him because he feared a similar fate might befall him too. The god changed himself into a jackal, took two helpers, a fish and a bird, and demonstrated to the woman an apposite fable. The jackal approached with a piece of meat in his mouth. The fish leapt out of the water and fell down before him. At this the jackal dropped the meat and snapped at the fish, which rushed back into the water while the bird made off skywards with the meat. The jackal wanted both things, and ended up with neither. The woman saw her own case in this fable and shame and repentance seized her.[1]

The same type of story occurs in the Arabic example of the qadi of the caliph, who helped a widow who had been dispossessed because the caliph's palace was being enlarged. He appeared before the caliph with an ass and a large sack, and asked the caliph, for he wondered not a little, if he could fill the sack with soil from the palace garden. Moved by curiosity, the caliph consented, and helped to load the full sack onto the ass's back. He found the sack too heavy to lift alone. 'Master', said the qadi, 'you find this burden too heavy, and it contains but a small part of the land that you have unlawfully taken from a poor widow. How will you be able to carry all that stolen land if the judge of the world places it upon your shoulders at the great day of judgment?' The caliph understood and gave the widow back her piece of ground.[2]

It is also the case that allegory is not presented as such, but that the allegorical style is best served by interchange: the king once rode through his country disguised, and found pleasure in a beautiful woman, in that she would not allow herself to be seduced. She told her husband of the visit of the noble unknown person, and he realised that this could have been the caliph, and so he did not dare to allude to this any more, as he was worried. His family reported him to the court in the following words:

> May God strengthen the power of the king! This man has received a piece of land from us to sow; he tilled it for a while, but now he has let it lie fallow. And now he does not allow us to lease it out to anyone who will cultivate it. But he himself does not sow it. Now the field is coming to harm, and we fear that it will be completely lost because it is fallow, for when land is not cultivated, it is ruined.

The king asked the man: 'What is stopping you from sowing your land?' He answered:

> May God strengthen the power of the king. I was told that a lion had entered the field, and I was afraid of it, and did not dare to approach the field any more. For I know that I have bequeathed nothing to the lion and I am afraid of him.

The king however understood the allegory and said to him:[3]

Indeed the lion has indeed not trodden upon your land: it is still good for sowing; therefore sow. God bless you! The lion does not harm.

This illustrative type of approach always appears to the Western mind as something typically oriental, but in fact it is found amongst all peoples at a particular stage of their intellectual development. Oriental descent is however to be attributed to a literary form which has developed from a predilection for a pictorial approach, and has reached the West through the medium of Petrus Alfonsi: that form of instruction for life in which proverbs and exempla alternate, and which is often found either as the speech of a father with his son, or the advice given by a master to a pupil. In Hebrew it is called 'meschalim' (the title of the Proverbs of Solomon in which we find at 7: 6 ff. a story explained) and in Arabic 'amṭāl'.[4] In English the meaning is 'proverbs' or 'allegories'.

Proverbs and exempla are not different forms; they come from the same root. In the classical Arabic *Book of Proverbs* of Abû 'Ubayd (770–838), which later became canonical, we find, for example, the proverb: 'Two swords go not into one scabbard.'[5] The famous Seljuk chancellor, Niẓām-al-Mulk (ob. 1092), explains this sentence in his *Book of Statesmanship*, which is written in exactly this mixed form, and gives the following story as explanation:[6]

The king of the Romans, Parwiz, was very fond of his chancellor, Bahrâm Tschubin and was very generous towards him. One day he heard that Bahrâm had punished his page with twenty lashes. He called the chancellor to him and ordered him to bring thither 500 swords from the armoury, and said: 'Bahrâm, select the best of these?' And he chose 150 of them. The king then said: 'Find the ten best of these.' And Bahrâm obeyed. Then he was ordered to select the two best from these ten, and when he had done this, the king said: 'Now put these two swords into one scabbard.' The chancellor replied: 'O King, two swords go not into one scabbard.' Then Parwiz asked: 'Can there be two people giving orders in one land?' When Bahrâm heard this, he realised his own fault, and prostrated himself before the king. The king continued: 'Leave such things to us! For the almighty and sublime God has given us judgment over the earth, not you.'

It can be seen quite clearly that this story is based on the proverb. The process that the narrator has used to develop a realisation of the proverb is as simple as possible: he has guided it by means of a chain of numbers (500–150–10–2) to the decisive point where the point of the allegory strikes the chancellor and he realises his guilt. It is as if the story had been previously fixed in the proverb.

Conversely, a story can be shrivelled up to a saying. The fable of the mule from the *Disciplina Clericalis* (Ex. IV)[7] is, for example, found today as a proverb in Cairo:[8]

The mule was asked: 'Who is your father?' He said: 'My uncle is the horse.'

A parallel to the story of the thankless serpent (*Disciplina Clericalis*, Ex. V) is still told today in this form:[9]

The raven was asked 'Why do you steal the soup?' It answered: 'This lack of virtue is my nature.'

Such proverbs are basically stories which have either been shrunk or expanded. It is the same with the proverbs, explanatory exempla and fables of an allegorical character. Moreover one form is always potentially contained in the other, and this has meant that their adoption into the corpus of Western proverbs was the most natural thing in the world.[10]

In the introduction to his book Abû 'Ubayd characterises allegory and proverbs as 'a byroad in linguistic terms', and considers that with the help of these indirect methods of expression three things can be attained: Abbreviation of expression, accurate delineation of what is meant, and beauty of comparison.[11] When indirect expression accurately portrays what is meant, this is then shown by the fact that mankind always understands a situation by use of a model sooner than it does by a concrete, individual case, because the model banishes inessential but confusing individual facts, and is free from the actual excitement that in the two actual situations fosters confusion in judgment. It is for this reason that al-Mubarrad (ob. 898) defines allegory as: 'a common saleable expression, in which a secondary happening is compared with a primary.'[12] The case of the model will here be seen, so to speak, as the prototype of all individual cases:[13]

Before wasting many words over a rich man who, one knows, through pure avarice has done nothing with his wealth, one imagines a portrait: one should compare his hoarded riches, which thereby are useless to himself and others, to green fodder that loses its value, if it is not used as fodder. Thus it is said shortly and concisely—green fodder, no camel.

Al-Fârâbî (ob. 950) in his definition brings forward two other important signs of illustrative expression: ability to be understood by all, and 'psychiatric' effect:[14]

Allegory is an expression by which common folk as well as well educated, by means of common speech effect mutual understanding, with the result that it has become the everyday medium of expression between them, and springs to their lips in both joy and sorrow. It is a tool that enables them to express things that previously they could not express, and also to construct far-reaching thought structures. It is also used to free one from trouble and worry.

The abstract systematic clarification of series of objects would be too much for uneducated persons and would allow the educated no rest or recreation. It is further true that what a systematic logically arranged work describes, exists in a sense, but not in reality. Reality should be clothed with rather more force, because the arrangement of the real world, that we live in, is colourful and varied and not at all systematic. In books of proverbs, reality is mirrored, as it shows itself to be to the reporters of human day-to-day existence, and not as it appears to an organised system of thought. The form of 'oriental lessons for life' has something to do with non-interference and a certain *laissez-faire* attitude.

The need to 'free oneself of worry and trouble' and 'liven up the heart'[15] by reading, talk and interchange of ideas is clearly demonstrated by the fact that the Arabs were so keen to parody their own sayings and stories. Man will not always tolerate earnestness in lessons for life; sometimes a tale must be told and listened to that will merely amuse and entertain. An example of this is the famous story of the 'Surety' which al-Bakrî of Cordoba (ob. 1094) tells to illustrate the proverb 'After this no more misery and no further day of misery':[16]

Because of bad weather the king an-Nu 'mân returned from

hunting without his entourage and was put up for the night by
a man of the tribe of Ṭajj. On the following day, when the
splendid entourage arrived, the man knew with whom he had
been dealing. The king invited him to court saying: 'Come to
me and I will make you rich.' Eventually at the insistence of his
wife, the man started out on the journey, and came upon the
king on a day of unhappiness. The king ordered him to be
executed, at which the Ṭajjit protested: 'I am the man who took
you in on that stormy night. I have come here that you may
fulfil your promise.' An-Nu 'mân welcomed him, and wished to
grant his every wish, except that he would not be able to free
him from death. 'Good', said the man, 'but I have a debt to
settle, namely I must return some money that was entrusted
to me, and so I must draw up my bill.' The king gave him
leave to do this, as long as someone stood surety for him.
The cousin and brother-in-law of the king Sarik ibn 'Umair,
stood surety. The Ṭajjit returned to his family in order to
arrange everything, and then he started on his journey back
clad in his shroud and anointed like a corpse. The morning
set for the execution he had still not returned and the king
demanded that the man who had stood surety be put to death.
Finally, however, the man from the tribe of Ṭajj appeared at
the right time, and the king wondered at this and said: 'I do
not know which of you two is the nobler. Tell me, Ṭajjit, what
made you fulfil your promise when you knew that you must
die?' He answered: 'My religion obliged me.' The king asked:
'What is your religion?', and he answered: 'I am a Christian',
and described his beliefs to the king. Nu 'mân saw the light,
and became a Christian and said: 'After this no more misery
and no day of misery.' He rewarded the Ṭajjit richly. This
experience was the cause of Nu 'mân's ascetic life, and why he
abdicated and set out as a pilgrim on his journeyings.

Connected with this story of the day of fate is another story
that can be told: a king once in a rage had both his best friends put
to death.[17] In sorrow at this, he had two obelisks put up and every
year he spent two days there. On the first of these days, the day of
fortune, he rewarded those who had come there, but on the second,
the day of misery, the first man to approach was put to death.[18]
This series of facts is also the first to be parodied, and in this parody

the new motif is that those who are passing by, have to greet the tombs of the friends. One day the watchmen bring a fuller who has not carried out this order. The king has to put him to death, but he first awards him two wishes before death. The first is: 'I wish that I could give the king a blow on the nape of the neck with this mallet.'

The ministers could find no way out, and were unable to prevent the fuller from carrying out his wish. Thus the king received his blow and lay in a fever for six months. Then he let the fuller out of prison to hear his second wish, and after that to execute him. The second wish was: 'If I am really going to be put to death, then I have made up my mind to give you another blow on the other side of your neck.' Horror seized the king, and he toiled ceaselessly to dissuade the fuller. Finally, he had to annul the sentence of death, and allow that the fuller had in fact saluted the tombs, and had been slandered by the watchmen.[19] This dénouement sharply satirises the through-going legal formalism that had to be used in order to justify the illegal by means of 'ingenious twists of inter-pretation'.[20]

A further adjunct to the unsystematic free-association structure of oriental books of wisdom is the mixture of prose and verse, such as we find in the *Disciplina Clericalis*. This had already found its way into European literature in Hellenistic times through the so-called Menippean satire.[21] However it is very alien to a classical feeling for form. A better characterisation is that found in the Haggadah, the narrative part of the Jewish Talmud, which can be classed as a 'cumulative species of poetry'.[22]

This form cannot be understood, if attempts to explain it are made by reference to its unfitness for explanation on a classical configuration. It is rather the expression of an entirely determined view of the word. One of the most famous examples of this mixture of prose and poetry in proverbs, exempla and meditations is the Old Testament Book of *Ecclesiastes* (Qohelet), the favourite book of the author of the *Disciplina Clericalis*. There one can see a deep scepticism against plain speaking, a closed system:

> When I applied mine heart to know wisdom, and to see the
> business that is done upon the earth: (for also there is that
> neither day nor night seeth sleep with his eyes:)
> Then I beheld all the work of God, that a man cannot find
> out the work that is done under the sun: because though a man

labour to seek it out, yet he shall not find it; yea farther;
though a wise man think to know it, yet shall he not be able to
find it. (Ecclesiastes 8: 16–17)

It has been realised that mankind cannot attain full knowledge
(7: 23–4), but rather that through knowing he becomes more
wonderful:

For in much wisdom is much grief: and he that increaseth
knowledge increaseth sorrow. (1: 18)

Some are of the opinion that the sentence on the fear of God
(12: 13) with which Petrus Alfonsi also closes his little book is not
really suited to the deep pessimism of which Ecclesiastes is full,
and is an appendix of the 'pious editor'. Clearly, however, the
preacher has himself experienced this tension between belief in
God's righteousness and the daily experience of the 'vanity' of
human existence. His piety has not made him a solitary. He is a
believer and a realist.[23]

God's activity is not denied but rather human formulae
concerning divine action.

Scepticism and provisos 'stem from an attitude that is not
prepared to admit the mysterious in favour of an ostensible understanding of divine workings'.[24] The preacher is unwilling to impose
anything upon himself; 'redemption does not come from the toil
and senselessness of human work here in this world'.[25] He 'belongs
to those who withstand the everlasting attempt made by man to
bring together into one system God and the world, a system which
through its methodical arrangement obscures the incalculable
elements of life and history'. Qohelet knows well, and expresses, the
fact that human life is a paradox.[26]

This conception of the world cannot be expressed by a 'classical',
well balanced and carefully weighed form: its instrument is that
mixed sequential form of expression which contains the paradoxical
nature of the human reality, by means of a varied and unsystematic
intertwining of the motifs found in this reality, and manages to do
this without entirely neglecting every form of verbal discipline.

It is not by chance that the great revolution from which our
modern world has arisen, does not have oriental ideas and thoughts
as its basis but Western. That sceptical conception of the world,
which prefers to leave things as they are, instead of changing them,

has become incapable of great plans and their execution. That 'disappointing emptiness that borders on cynicism', which an al-Ghazzâlî uses to remind himself of the fact that for none of the corresponding Islamic principles is there a follower of the prophet and that there is no other alternative than to put up with the existing relationships, which ensure that not everything becomes topsy-turvy,[27] would not in itself have brought forth the ideas and impulse of modern socialism. To occupy itself with such a conception of the world could be healthy for the West, because it could there-by learn the regulator which permits knowledge of the dangers of too fundamental an interference with the actual.

The emptiness of human life that is commonly demonstrated in the form of Eastern proverbs should not be stamped merely as 'fatalism'. It springs from a powerful will to learn and a considerable readiness to experience life, and it is thus an active conception, if viewed at an even greater distance in time, which attempts to see happiness in an ever-changing transformation of relationships.

This will to learn is to be found demonstrated in a charming manner by a modern chassidic story, in which Jews, who are our contemporaries, confront the achievements of modern technology with the basic religious texts handed down to them, and do this to a background of humour:[28]

> 'Above all else man has the power to learn', the Rabbi of Sadagora said to his Chassidim, 'and everything induces us to learn. We are induced to learn about not just everything that God has made, but everything made by man too'. One of the Chassidim who doubted said: 'What can we learn from the railway?' 'That at the whim of a moment, man can miss everything.' 'And from the telegraph?' 'That every word can be counted and reckoned up.' 'And from the telephone?' 'That what is heard there, we say here.'

6 EVERYTHING IS TWO-SIDED (CONTENTS AND PLAN OF THE *DISCIPLINA CLERICALIS*)

The *Disciplina Clericalis* begins and ends with advice on the fear of God. The ending repeats verbatim the closing section of

Ecclesiastes in the Old Testament (12: 13, 14). The passage in which this motif is to be found in both works, deserves closer comparison. In Ecclesiastes we find:

> Keep thy foot when thou goest to the house of God, and be
> more ready to hear, than to give the sacrifice of fools; for
> they consider not that they do evil.
> Be not rash with thy mouth, and let not thine heart be hasty to
> utter any thing before God: for God is in heaven, and thou
> upon earth: therefore let thy words be few.
> For in the multitude of dreams and many words there are also
> divers vanities: but fear thou God. (5: 1, 2, 7)

Here the theme appears in a double aspect. The absolute is confronted with the essentially human. The counsel given to fear God is added as a warning against pious self-deception: 'for God is in heaven, and thou upon earth.' To reach God is difficult, it is easier to succeed through 'dreams and vanities'.

Petrus Alfonsi handles the motif in the same way. He has already prepared the way in the prologue:

> On the other hand, I decided that, within the capabilities of my
> senses, everything must be avoided in this book that might
> be found contrary to our beliefs.

It is furthermore clear that the reader should first of all 'sense' the book, and then accept it. The proviso as to his senses arouses doubt in the reader's mind too. Therefore there follows a tactful piece of information concerning what it means to criticise a book.

> If, however, anyone should flick through this work with a
> human and therefore superficial eye, and see something in it
> where human nature has not been sufficiently on its guard, I
> advise him to re-read it again and again, and I propose that he,
> and all others who are perfect in the Catholic faith, correct
> what is wrong. For in anything invented by man, there is no
> perfection, as the philosopher says.

The author thus realises that men always criticise before they have looked sufficiently hard. He shows himself to be ready to accept correction, but names the condition that anyone who wishes to set him right, must expend the energy of reading him intently. It is ironic that he suggests such correction should come from those who are perfect in their beliefs, while remarking at the same time that there is no perfection on earth. To believe oneself perfect in one's beliefs, is an indirect method of demonstrating one's error. It is thus that we arrive at the theme of pious self-deception in which there occur also the sayings on the fear of God:

> If you disobey God, do what you may to appear to love him,
> it is still not worthy of belief.

Then there follows the first dialogue of the book in which Socrates expresses, as it were, 'a phenomenology of religious conformism':

> Imagine a man who both openly and secretly shows himself
> obedient to God, that he may be considered holy by men, and
> thereby be more honoured by them. Another man, more subtle
> than the first, disregards this type of hypocrisy in order that
> he may be aided in a greater, for when he fasts or gives alms,
> and is asked if he has done this, he answers: 'God knows!',
> or rather: 'No', in order that he may be viewed with greater
> reverence, and that it may be said of him that he is no
> hypocrite, because he does not wish to brag about what he has
> done before people. Also I believe that there are few who do
> not share in this hypocrisy in some way.

Here it can be seen for the first time that if a man tries to play a role that he wants to play, and this to the exclusion of all others, he is still evading a proper understanding of himself, and it is clear also that a man cannot separate a proper self-knowledge and an adaptation of roles. The individual is just 'bound on all sides by identification' and can only rebel by means of a spot of self-under-standing and originality.[1] Independence for the man who will not boast or display himself, is only apparent or imaginary. In fact these attempts at independence are part and parcel of the concept of identification. Indeed our author shows himself to be self-critical in his 'phenomenology' when he points out that no one at all is free from self-deception.

The closing section of the work also displays the confrontation between fear of the Lord and the excessively human illusion and self-deception. From Exemplum XXX onwards we are told of the manner and ways in which mankind views death, and his attitudes thereto. These attitudes must continue to exist, as is customary. As a contradiction to these illusions however, the advice is given to think of the end at the right time. As regards this end, the fear of the Lord appears as fear of God's judgment on men.

This 'dialectical' treatment of a theme is a component basic consideration of the *Disciplina Clericalis* and at the same time an expression of the author's critical approach to knowledge. The story of the 'half-friend' mirrors what is generally so in reality. The story of the 'perfect friend' is told here, in order to set this reality against an ideal yard-stick. In the section entitled 'Silence' the ideal proportion of spiritual explanation and correct learning is outlined. In a following section, entitled 'True Nobility' the sober estimation of real relationships is discussed, relationships in which success belongs to the man who agrees with what everyone says. Between these two is the pair of stories (Exempla III and IV) in which the boaster is contrasted with the real expert.

The basic component idea that lies as a foundation for all ideas of experience of life, is that everything is two-sided. This is not, as in classical works, treated as a rational principle on which to build, but operates in our book, in a loose form that relies on association. The operation is unobtrusive with the result that the individual motifs are always being taken up again, and contrasted with one another in a dialectical manner. In 'Intelligence' an example is given of the connection and antithesis between friend and foe, wisdom and stupidity, liberty and necessity, talent and education. This last antithesis is assumed in the disposition of Exempla XV and XVI, where in one the natural intelligence of the wife meets with success, and in the other it is the 'technical' know-how of the wise man gained through scientific study that decides the issue. These two stories are contrasted, for in XV it is the man with whom the money has been deposited who is the imposter, whereas in XVI it is the one who entrusts. Exempla XVI and XVII belong together in as much as in one the philosopher displays his knowledge of men. In XVIII the voyagers are deceived as regards the road they have taken, and in XIX they give a false estimate of their companion. The young man in XXIX knows that the only imperishable treasures are to be amassed in heaven. In XXX the thief slips into the error of thinking that nevertheless he could begin something on this earth with his stolen goods.

In a composition that is loosely articulated like the links of a chain, there is still a unity that runs through the whole work. The most important theme is the problem of leading a proper life in the society of one's fellow-men. At the very beginning even piety is viewed as a socio-psychological problem. The first pair of Exempla deal with friendship. 'Secrecy' raises the important question of whether everything should be disclosed to one's fellows. In 'Silence' the subject of real conversation is evaded. 'Lying' is dealt with entirely from the point of view of how one injures one's fellow-man, if one is not open with him.

In the stories that deal with women who are blameworthy, the subject of life-companions is dealt with, and in Exempla XV, XVI and XVII, the subject is 'helping one's fellow in distress'. The epilogue to XVI places alongside friendship and matrimony the third intimate social relationship, namely neighbourliness. The treatment given to fellowship in travelling is that of an indispensable human relationship in the world of the Eastern trader. 'The Generous Man, the Miser and the Spendthrift' shows how even in material matters men are dependent on each other and in 'The Taking and Approving of Advice' it is demonstrated that men use each other's advice. The necessity of the suitable ordering of all these various social interconnections is demanded by the author in the introduction to 'Eating Customs',[2] where he remarks that the forms and styles of fellowship at table are not just a matter for the court, but must everywhere be maintained.

How strictly the author keeps a check on the direction of the motif is shown by the surprising use of the marriage motif in 'The Utilisation of High Roads'. Here the author gives meaning to the criticism of the whole series of motifs: a man should take as his wife a chaste girl, even if she is already older. It is right for him to observe custom and stick to the main roads; a man succeeds, if he goes alone, only in hopelessness; in spite of all the disappointments that lie in wait for one in one's dealing with one's fellows a man journeys better when he sticks with them, and gets on with them as well as possible. Here the average, typical man is viewed with an affection that has no illusions.

Petrus Alfonsi too sticks to the main road with his little book. It is not affectation that makes him use popular speech, and the popular form of wisdom literature, that makes him relate stories known to everybody, use proverbs known to every man and cite the Bible. But still he brings his own highly personal treatment and estimation of things to the fore, at least certainly for the person who notices the underlying order, and perceives the irony, with which well-known materials are used in an entirely special way that illuminates them, and the person who has an ear for the individual tone that the author produces from the old instrument of the book of proverbs.

This procedure of writing for a double public at one and the same time has as its foundation the renunciation of any attempt to change people. So most of those who plagiarised those sections on the 'seven liberal arts' that Petrus Alfonsi had written elsewhere, in which he thoroughly discussed his proposals for a revision of the basic concepts of science, have merely indicated by the sequence of subjects that they understood these in their own way, and that they once again had re-established the traditional canon. People's interest in the *Disciplina Clericalis* was of an exclusively materialistic sort. This is clearly demonstrated by the history of the text. Of the sixty-three manuscripts only a small part have the complete text; most of them have only those parts that were of interest, either the stories or the sententiae, or a selection from both. In common with similar writings, Cicero's *De Amicitia*, various books of fables, the Proverbs of Solomon, or the *Legenda Aurea*, the plagiarisers betray the fact that they are seeking exempla and proverbs for their own ends, and are not concerned with what the author meant. They have noticed that the author of the *Disciplina Clericalis* belongs to a foreign world. The comparison of the work with Alexander's letter on the marvels of India, or with the *Historia Alexandri Magni*, which describes the amazing lands and peoples of the East, or with a section from another work by Petrus Alfonsi, the so-called *De Machometo*, bears testimony to the active desire of Western man to learn and know something about that distant foreign world that had suddenly attained such importance in the age of the Crusades.

The affection of the author of the *Disciplina Clericalis* for the average, ordinary man can be admitted, because he views mankind extremely critically. The chain of motifs that deal with human relations is intimately connected with a further leitmotif, namely the constant reference to the gullibility of men, and their tendency to fool themselves. This motif is introduced in 'Hypocrisy'. In Exempla XXII–XXIV, it is explicitly made the theme. The beginning and end of the book link the theme of the fear of God and that of human self-deception. The motif is always being referred to additionally, as, for example, in the conversation between father and son in the introduction to Exemplum I, in 'Books That Are Not To Be Believed' or in 'The Taking and Approving of Advice'.

The two Exempla VII and VIII connect this theme of human illusion with the death-motif. In VII, the comrade succumbs to the temptations of 'la dolce vita', runs into evil company, and is sentenced to death. In VIII, where the companion does not succumb to seduction, the story suddenly makes the transition from the sweet song of the woman to the raucous cry of the owl that presages death. The hidden connection between sinful temptations and the death-cry has been explained as follows by Thomas Mann:[3]

> The birds of death and the hens of death are generally held
> by common belief to be the smaller types of owl or screech-owl,
> which, so the story goes, bang themselves at night against the
> windows of the mortally ill, and cry 'Come with me', thereby
> calling the sick soul to freedom. Is it not surprising that this
> formula is also used by the sisterhood of the streets when they
> lurk under the street-lights, and insolently and familiarly invite
> men home to bed? . . .
>
> They try to take your arm and lead you off the pavement:
> they look at you out of the corner of their eyes, in which the
> street-lights are mirrored: they twist their lips in a lurid and
> obscene smile, and whisper with the hasty, stolen cry of the
> bird of death: they give short sideways movements of the head
> with looks of complete uncompromising stupidity, as if there
> lurked waiting for the brave fellow who follows the hint and
> obeys the summons, some tremendous, priceless and unlimited
> treasure.

The peculiar illusion of seduction is here well expressed. The exaggerated, boundless and fantastic element of human expectation and eagerness to live is so portrayed that there is therein a presentiment of disappointment and disillusionment.

The allusion to death explains, as in the stories in Petrus Alfonsi, that man's eagerness to live is directed towards something that exists only in his imagination, whereas only the end is a matter of strict fact for the man who is determined not to fool himself.

This is what the preacher in Ecclesiastes had thought when he said of mankind:

> For he knoweth not that which shall be: for who can tell him
> when it shall be? (8: 7)

Only this is always so:

> This is an evil among all things that are done under the sun,
> that there is one event unto all. (9: 3)

The preacher knows that mankind does not realise its expectations:

> All things are full of labour; man cannot utter it; the eye is
> not satisfied with seeing, nor the ear filled with hearing. (1: 8)

But man does not despair of the 'vanity of things' but rather returns comforted to life:

> Go thy way, eat thy bread with joy, and drink thy wine with a
> merry heart. (9: 7)

In the same way Petrus Alfonsi adopts an earnest tone at the end of Exemplum VIII in a quick volte-face, faithful to his basic idea that a man should be able to lighten for mankind the heavy loss of his final existence:[4] the little owl is the image of the man who continually has joy in his song, his poetry and his son, be they ever such failures. One must allow such pride. In a certain sense, illusions are as necessary for mankind as the poisons that a doctor prescribes for the healing of a sick man.

7 THE LIFE OF THE AUTHOR

While the *Disciplina Clericalis* was copied out and translated all over Europe, and grew quickly in popularity, there is another work by the Spanish doctor that remains reading for specialists, namely the theologians. This work is the *Conversations of Petrus Alfonsi*, who from a Jew became a Christian, in which are refuted the false views of the Jews by means of theological and philosophical arguments, and some misunderstood passages explained. Vincent of Beauvais (flor. 1264), the well-known librarian of Count Ludwig IX the Holy, terms it a 'clever book'.[1] The Romance scholar Gröber terms it 'the most important literary apologia for Christian, as opposed to Jewish, beliefs ever written'.[2] Manitius praises the 'distinguished repose of its oriental powers of reasoning and persuasion'.[3] An indirect reference to the esteem in which this book was held in the Middle Ages, is a matter of some little interest; it is often mentioned in the most widely read book of that period, the *Legenda Aurea* (thirteenth century), as providing trustworthy information on the customs of the Muslims.

In the life of Pelagius (ch. 178) there are found amongst others, the following details that originate in the work of the Spanish Jew:[4]

> Indeed even before they perform their prayers, they wash (so as to be completely and utterly pure), their anus, genitals, hands, arms, face, mouth, nose, ears, eyes and hair. They do this most earnestly, and close with their feet. When they have done this, they confess out loud together their beliefs, that there is only one God, that he has no similar or equal, and that Mohammed is his prophet.
>
> Each year they fast for the duration of one whole month, and during this time of fasting, they eat only at night, as during the day they abstain from food completely. Thus it is that no one from that hour of the day, when a man can distinguish with the naked eye a black from a white thread, until the sunset, either drinks or has intercourse with his wife. But from sunset until the first light of the next day, they may eat, drink, have sexual intercourse with their wives, as pleases each.

This information is quite exact. The unacknowledged use of this in the *Legenda Aurea* is proof that Petrus Alfonsi was used because of the excellence of his information, and because he was considered an authority on the Islamic world. In view of the distortion of the picture that later Christian writers made for apologetic reasons, the fact that such information is to be found in a defence of Christian beliefs against Judaism and Islam[5] in the year 1100 should be highly valued.

This Islamic scholar was a Rabbi brought up in the traditions of Jewish religious learning, who later, in the year 1106, converted to the Catholic faith. He describes this step in the preamble to his *Conversations* in the following words:

> The almighty has illumined me with his spirit, and has shown me the path of righteousness, in which he first freed my eyes from their dimness, and drew away the veil from my heart that laboured in error. He opened for me the doors to the understanding of the prophets, and their secrets became intelligible to me, and I gained thereby the ability to attain the

correct understanding of their truth, and I have since busied
myself in increasing this understanding. Thus I have arrived at
their meaning, and at what a man must believe, namely that
there is only one God in the trinity of persons, none of whom
precedes the others in time, and none of whom
is separated from the others in any way; they are called the
Father, Son and Holy Spirit; and that the blessed Mary
conceived by the Holy Spirit without intercourse with any man,
and bore the Messiah by giving him a body and soul that should
be the home of his incomprehensible Godhead. Further, I
believe that Christ was created from three substances, body,
soul, and Godhead, and that God and man are one in him. I
believe that the Jews, as he had himself ordained and desired,[6]
crucified him, in order that he who was the creator, might also
become the saviour of the whole of Holy Church—for such is
the name given to the believers who preceded him and who
followed him. I believe that, his body being dead and buried, he
rose from the dead on the third day, and ascended into heaven,
and remains with the Father. I believe also that he will come on
the day of Judgment to judge the living and the dead, as was
foretold by the prophets and has been ordained by them for
the future order.

As I now by reason of God's mercy have arrived at such a
high peak of belief, and have put off the mantle of error,
and driven out the garment of sin, I have been baptised and
purified from sin in my place of living, the town of Huesca,
at the hands of the most glorious and righteous bishop
of the town, Steven. When I was baptised I further
realised that which I have already mentioned, namely my belief
in the Holy Apostles and the Holy Catholic church. This
baptism took place in the year 1106 of the birth of Our Lord, in
the forty-fourth year of my life, in the month of June, on the
feast of SS. Peter and Paul. It is for this reason that I took the
name Peter in veneration and memory of the Apostle. My
father[7] was Alfonso the famous ruler of Spain. It was he who
introduced me to the springs of heaven,[8] and for that reason
I added his name to my adopted name of Peter, and am
therefore called Peter the son of Alfonso. The Jews who had
known me previously, and had acknowledged me as learned in
the books of the prophets and the sayings of the masters, and

also possessed of a good education in the seven liberal arts, when they heard that I had adopted the law and beliefs of the Christians, and become one of them, thought that I had done this by spurning God and the Law, and by putting off all shame. Others held the opinion that I had acted in this way because I had not understood correctly the sayings of the prophets. There were others who held that I had done it for vain glory, and slanderously alleged that I had done it for secular honours, because I saw that Christian society was superior in power to all others. It is because of all this, that I have written this little book, so that everyone can learn my intentions and the reasons I had for my action. I intend to expose the false views of all other religions, and then to show that the Christian law is superior to all. At the end I have placed all those objections that might be raised by an enemy of Christ's law and I have demolished them with reasoned and well-founded arguments. I have given the whole book the form of a dialogue, so that the reader's mind may be quicker to understand. In the role of the defender of Christian principles, I have placed the name which I now have as a Christian, and in the role of the person speaking for the opposition, I have placed the name Moses, which was my name before baptism. I have divided the book into twelve parts so that the reader may find what he desires more quickly.[9]

This autobiographical text is completely lacking in any bitterness towards the members of that faith which the convert had left because of his baptism. The prejudices that came from that quarter are gently and objectively dealt with. Apparently meaningful expressions like 'the mantle of error' are rarely indulged in; Jewish scholarship is not seen as an expression of obduracy, which is generally so in Christian writings on apologetics, but rather as the foundation for Christian religious knowledge. The approach is made clear if one reads the methodological introduction to the *Conversations*:[10]

From my earliest childhood I had a particularly good friend who always stuck by me; his name was Moses. From the beginning he was my fellow student and companion. When he received the information that I had left the beliefs in which I had been brought up and had adopted Christian beliefs, he

left the town where he was living, and came quickly to me. As
he approached one could see on his face all the signs of
indignation and he greeted me not as a friend but as a stranger.
He began as follows: 'Ho there, Petrus Alfonsi, it is many years
since I was wont to come and see you to talk with you in all
the fullness of detail, and my desires to see you again have
long remained unfulfilled, until today, when I now see
you—God be thanked—standing in front of me with cheerful
face. I ask you to explain your reasons for leaving the old
beliefs, and taking up new ones. I know well that you were
learned in the books of the prophets, and that even as a lad you
excelled all your contemporaries in the interpretation of our
Law with the words of our teachers: I know that you, whenever
there was an opponent, always took up the shield to defend
our beliefs, and that you preached in the synagogues that the
Jews should never desert their beliefs. I know, too, that you
taught scriptural learning to many of your fellow believers, and
that you furthered the scribes in their knowledge. Therefore,
now I am completely at a loss to know why I now see you so
changed, and cut off from the path of righteousness. It seems
to my heart that this has come about solely through error.'

I answered him: 'It is the way of uneducated and
inexperienced people to make a protest if they see someone do
something which is contrary to their own custom, even if that
action is completely correct. They declare it to be incorrect
according to their standards and prejudices. You, however,
have been brought up in the cradle of Philosophy, nurtured at
the breasts of Wisdom; how can you accuse me before you are
in a position to examine whether or not my action was right
or wrong?'

Moses answered: 'Two contrary thoughts invade my breast.
On the one hand I consider you a wise man, and therefore I
cannot believe that such a man could have given up the
religion that you held before, unless you genuinely recognised
that the one that you have now adopted, was the better. On the
other hand, because I adhere to the religion that I have, and
consider it to be superior, I must hold that your present step
is an error. I know not which view to adopt, and therefore I ask
you to dispel from my mind any doubt that exists there, and
then let us both go our separate ways and ponder it, until I can

arrive at a clear decision as to whether your action was right
or not.'

Peter said: 'Human nature has the peculiarity that in the
differentiation of true from false, the organ necessary for the
differentiation becomes useless, when the inside of man is, as it
were, troubled in some way by emotion. So now, if you do not
remove from your soul all those things that trouble you so that
we can act like intelligent men, and find out what is right
without disagreement, and without anticipating the result of our
undertaking in any way, all our words will be thrown upon thin
air.'

In this introduction the author has woven together a complete
doctrine of human dialogue and mutual understanding. It is not
based, as it is with the Scholastics, on logical laws for the management of thoughts, but on the socio-psychological conditions of
dialogue between men of differing opinions. The uneducated man,
that is a man who does not reflect, sets his own standard as a norm
to be unquestioningly followed, and condemns things ;fore he
gains knowledge of them. Petrus Alfonsi demonstrates this reaction,
based not on reason but on emotion. A proof of the points of view
of both sides, as well as a viable conversation and understanding
of the motives of the other party, might be possible after the
elimination of that emotion, and all prejudice silenced. A parallel
passage on silence in the *Disciplina Clericalis* should here be looked
at. To fill out this text one can utilise the theological-controversial
works. The primary idea is that one should learn from the man
who has at his disposal greater knowledge and experience. This rule
is however often broken, because man is inclined to speak through a
desire for respect, and through false pride is inclined to neglect
learning. In the third of the works of Petrus Alfonsi that had come
down to us, the *Letter on Study*, the problem is again dealt with.
It must have been of consuming interest to him. He there tells of the
reasons that were advanced by people for the study of Arabic
astronomy, a subject on which Petrus had given classes in both
France and England. There, most scientists were clerics, and the
argument was advanced that all science should help the Catholic
faith. The answer of the Spanish Jew reads:

If someone apologises for his inactivity by advancing this
excuse, in my opinion there are two reasons for it: some excuse

themselves because they are intellectually lazy, and others because they are too proud of their status as teachers to play the role of pupil.

Petrus Alfonsi here seeks also to discover the motives for denial of all discussion, investigation and proof, and considers them to be comprehensible only in the emotional sphere. It is very much in keeping with his profession of doctor, that he had had the experience which a modern colleague has formulated as follows:[11]

> To get inside the skin of the values of an alien group, and to really be on the same intellectual plane, is for most of humanity an insoluble task .... We are able to call up so many motives for no other reason than that of maintaining evaluations that are closely bound up with our own esteem, thereby rejecting any orientation to alien values.

Resistance to alien values, the closing of one's eyes to new developments in knowledge, the lack of comprehension of progress made by others, all can thus be seen as acts of self-defence. To be open to all is dangerous; safety is to be sought within walls.

The question of whether Petrus Alfonsi was a sincere and pure convert to Christianity or whether the prejudice shown by his former fellow-believers had some basis in truth, cannot really be answered clearly. It is, however, striking how much this convert was aware of the dangers of self-deception, to which a man is forced to succumb by virtue of the growth of his own self-confidence. He appears to possess that 'extremely disagreeable exercise in communion with himself', an exercise which is always occupied in 'admitting those dangers of self-deception into the sphere of knowledge and which can above all enable a man to enjoy a relative freedom of decision'.[12]

Striking also is the fact that the text of the *Disciplina Clericalis*, except for the prologue where the author characterises himself as 'a servant of Jesus Christ', bears no evidence of his conversion. He does not appear to have found it necessary to justify this work either to himself or to others. This is evidence of an intellectual independence, and quite clearly shows that Petrus was not at all unsure of himself.

The *Disciplina Clericalis* is not an exclusively Christian work. There is no demarcation or prejudice against 'false doctrine' contained in its secular wisdom; there is no trace of 'orthodoxy'. When Petrus Alfonsi speaks the language of the people—which he does to avoid literary exclusivity—he does not speak solely to the Aragonese Christians, but addresses his remarks to the whole of the East and West, in such a way that they can be understood by all. He is not interested in those factors which divide, but only in those which bind together. For this reason he uses in his little book a stock of stories, forms, attitudes and images that in the Middle Ages were the common property of East and West.

It was indeed a Buddhist story which was during the Middle Ages the edifying and widespread favourite reading of Christians, Muslims and Jews, the tale of 'Barlaam and Josaphat'.[13] From this work Exempla I and XXII of the *Disciplina Clericalis* are taken. Another common book was the Alexander legend, which is used in Exemplum XXXIII as a reminder of the ephemeral nature of human greatness. The Alexander legend is found not only in collections of Latin exempla,[14] but also in the Qur'an,[15] the *Arabian Nights*,[16] and the Talmud.[17] It is like a motto in that 'World of the three Rings', in which the followers of the three religions lived together, when we read in this story what the Indian sage said to the king: 'If we were all of one mind, the world would be lifeless.'[18] This spirit of tolerance is found also in the *Disciplina Clericalis*: 'It is better to have an intelligent man as one's enemy than a fool as one's friend.' This proverb is of Arabic origin,[19] but is found in a similar form in medieval Hebrew literature,[20] in Arabic books of proverbs, and in European florilegia.[21] Death is viewed not as ordered by official church teaching, but an attitude is adopted which could easily be approved of by religious men anywhere. The presentation of the last judgment in the Egyptian *Book of the Dead* had already contained a question as to where the great men of history remained, and we know from the tale of the brass city in the *Arabian Nights*[22] the proverb 'I am what you will be; what you are, I was once.' This became in the ninth century a much loved topos in Arabic proverb poetry,[23] and we can still read it on the grave of the Gonfaloniere Lenzi in the church of Santa Maria Novella in Florence.[24]

The enthusiastic reception that the *Disciplina Clericalis* found at the hands of Western Christianity shows that its author was at pains to avoid divisive factors and to express the common attitudes of both Western and oriental man, and how he actually expressed that appreciation of life in relation to which they were able to make themselves understood beyond the boundaries of religion. Petrus Alfonsi himself had proved the basic proportion, which he had adopted as the foundation of his own method of instruction, based on an interchange between two men of differing opinions; this was that an alien should not be condemned and set apart from others through self-defence, but should be accepted and peaceably received, inasmuch as it is possible to come to an understanding where divisive factors are concerned.

Of course to reach beyond denominational and traditional frontiers needs a mature intelligence which will not be at the call of every man. Whoever wishes to discover what various groups have in common, must be able to be criticised and compare in order to understand, and this is only possible if he has attained a critical consciousness of his own individual position. Besides there might happen to him what happened to the Jew from Majorca, about whom we are informed by a document dating from 1391; this man attended holy Mass, and by means of other actions and words, looked as if he wished to convert to Christianity, but nevertheless on the feast of the ninth of Aw, as is the Jewish custom, he went barefoot; after this, however, this Jew had again spurned the Mosaic law, by eating pork and dealing in money on the sabbath; finally he performed the prayers ordained by Islam together with his Moorish slave.[25] The fact that the king took it upon himself to deal with this case, was occasioned by one fact above all others, that this fellow had denounced other Jews. He was manifestly incapable both in character and intelligence of existing in a reasonable way in the 'World of the three Rings.' It was different with an Arabic professor teaching in Mosul in the twelfth century. He belonged to a particular school of Islamic law, but gave exact information even to the adherents of other schools , ccording to their tradition.[26] Both his Jewish and Christian pupils asked him to explain the law and the Gospel to them. He did not abandon his own position by simply knowing and understanding the alien.

In the *Conversations* Petrus Alfonsi had expressed his own standpoint both clearly and dispassionately. He had not fallen into any sectarian narrow-mindedness. In the *Disciplina Clericalis* he demonstrates that he knows no division between East and West, and that he comprehends both worlds.

8 THE JEWS IN CHRISTIAN SPAIN

Not only those Jews who knew him personally reproached Petrus Alfonsi, but also others who lived in the century after him held his conversion against him. Both the formulation of Steinschneider,[1] and the attitude and presentation in Zvi Rudy's *Sociology of the Jewish People*[2] betray the faulty understanding of these authors of that step taken by the Spanish physician. They are, of course, right to condemn his naïve statement that the only right course of action for a Jew consists in 'ceasing to be a Jew, turning one's back on one's religion and hiding oneself under the wing of Christianity'.[3] Juan I of Aragon busied himself in vain when he tried to dissuade the townsmen of Perpignan from this naïve view, that culminated in the words that all Jews should simply become Christians, and all the trouble would be at an end.[4] The Spanish kings have countless times, for the most part in vain, preferred, against the civil and ecclesiastical courts of the Christian obligation, to allow the Jews free will and not oblige them to be baptised. On the other hand, however, there was also a disregard of human freedom of decision, if Jews criticised their erstwhile brothers in belief for changing religion, and imputed to them possibly insincere motives.

In relations between Christians and Jews this has been largely the case, as can be read in the *Gesta Treverorum* in the report of the events of 1096 in Trier. Archbishop Egilbert reported at that time that he could guarantee the protection of any Jew who had been baptised, and Rabbi Micha declares: 'I call God to witness that I believe what you have stated and that I renounce Jewry. When times are calmer, I will investigate the matter thoroughly, but now baptise us quickly, so that we may escape from our pursuers.' This was the opinion of other Jews too. So the archbishop baptised him and gave him his name, and the priests who were there baptised the others. These however reverted to their old beliefs in the following year, but Rabbi Micha remained true to the archbishop and remained firm in his beliefs.[5]

There is also the case of the later Provost of Scheda, Hermann the Jew, who was won over to Christian beliefs through the personality and the calm arguments of Abbot Rupert of Denz (*c.* 1070–1130). In his *De conversione sua opusculum*[6] he tells of the talks he had with Rupert. He does not renounce Jewry in this, in fact he is rather proud of belonging to that people, and views his new-found brothers in religion, the Christians, with a critical eye:

> We are insulted and mocked by men, and we bear it with calm and good temper, as long as we persist in our allegiance to God's law and his ceremonial commandments; for it is better for us to fall into the hands of men than to stray from the law of God.
>
> You do the Jews a great injustice when you spurn them like dead dogs, and spit upon them and curse them, for you forget the fact that many years ago, God chose them from among all peoples to be his chosen people, and honoured them with this title, and taught them beyond the norm of their righteousness, in accordance with which they lived, to become holy as he himself is holy. This he did not only by his word, but by writing with his own hand on tablets of stone in order to inform them of these rules.

Unfortunately, exchanges in which the partner in the discussion is allowed freedom of expression are the exception.[7] The general lack of understanding that was shown, to take a random example, is demonstrated by this anecdote from Caesarius of Heisterbach:[8]

> Once in Paris a Christian disputed with a Jew. When they came to the point of the day's gospel (John 8: 59), the Jew said without enthusiasm: 'Of course; your God acted rightly, in that he fled and concealed himself. Otherwise he would have been stoned.' A student heard this and filled with religious zeal, and very indignant with the enemy of religion, he took off his wooden sandal from his foot and smote the Jew on the head with it, so that he cracked it, saying: 'And you, you stupid wretch, would never have been harmed by me, if you had hid yourself and kept silent!'

In such cases understanding is denied to the partner in the discussion, and he will never be recognised as a free man. A pure conversion is for a Jew only possible when he can remain a Jew in essence, and can accept his Jewish existence alongside his new beliefs. The usual insinuations, however, show that no one knows anything about the Jews. For example, how lacking in results is the indication given by intelligent people to the fact that the idea of stealing consecrated hosts could never be entertained by a Jew even when he does not believe in the Sacrament.[9] That stereotyped accusation was based on a primitive Christian piety, such as is demonstrated in the magical uses of the host, which are mentioned by Caesarius of Heisterbach, like the story of the woman, who, to cure her bees of a sickness, took the host home after communion secretly, and put it in her hive and discovered after a while that the bees had built a little chapel of wax fruit;[10] another story is that of the cleric who rids a woman of her bodily ills after touching the host and by laying his hands on her.[11]

Sometimes the rejection of the Jews intensifies itself and becomes a morbid worry. The Synod of Toledo of 694 had the point that the Jews wished to bring down the church, seize the throne, and kill all Catholics.[12] Particularly as regards Jewish physicians there existed the primitive awe of those ignorant of scientific matters: for example, in 1397, the queen of Barcelona issued the decree that the Christians should not deal with Jewish physicians: 'because the spiteful Jews thirst after Christian blood like enemies, and it is therefore particularly dangerous for Christians to entrust themselves to the care of Jewish doctors when they are sick.'[13]

Even in Luther, we read this trace of suspicion: 'The Jews, who pass themselves off as doctors, bring Christians who make use of their medical knowledge, to health and fitness.'[14]

The psychological reasons lying behind such disquiet are comparable to those once expressed by the elder Cato on the rejection of Greek physicians:[15]

> The Greeks will ruin everything with their science, particularly when they send their doctors here, for these men have sworn to kill all non-Greeks with their medicine; but they even pay money to gain people's trust and treat our slaughter as a joking matter, therefore I forbid you to have anything to do with physicians.

Man is afraid of that which he does not know, and he is even more afraid when he detects a superiority in the unknown, particularly if there is something uncanny about it. Instead of learning to understand the Jews, all too often the general attitude adopted has been one of fear and rejection. A particularly critical date in the history of this false education is the year 388, the year in which Bishop Ambrose of Milan held his important clash with Emperor Theodosius over the Jewish question. The emperor wished to rebuild at the cost of those guilty one of the synagogues burned by the Christians in a city on the Euphrates. Ambrose protested that the emperor was ordaining the reconstruction of 'a place of untruth, a house of Godlessness, a shelter of folly',[16] and so the emperor yielded and saddled the exchequer with the cost. The bishop demanded faithful obedience from the Christian Theodosius, by virtue of being his pastor, and thereby forced him to abandon his policy of moderation towards the Jews.[17] Here we have clearly before us the basic problem of allowing church influence to play a part in politics; the emperor is answerable to the entire field of state policy, the bishop only to those citizens who share his beliefs. When, therefore, the bishop pulls his influence on the emperor as a Christian to favour one religious group against another, he makes it impossible for him to exercise his obligations correctly. He cannot any longer discharge his task of protecting a minority of a different religious persuasion. Thus the administrators and denouncers of these minorities have a free rein.

In Spain, the adopted land of the Jews, which they called Sefarad,[18] because it was the most distant province of the Roman Empire, the Jews were particularly well off. But soon the effects of the change in policy towards the Jews, triggered off by Ambrose, made themselves felt. As they retired from the island at the approach of the Visigoths, they went from Minorca into the power of Bishop Severus, who tells us in a letter of the year 418 of their forced conversion, and thereby betrays his assessment of the Jews, who had meantime become Christians. He writes that his diocese would be a place where no wolf or other vermin, and by the same token no Jew, would be tolerated; for the Jews well deserve to be compared with those wild beasts in savagery and evil. Further he averred that there would be no poisonous snakes there, although there were many of them, and he said that suddenly through divine influence of the words of St Stephen even the 'serpent people' would be obliged to scorn the poison of unbelief.[19]

No questions were asked about Jewish beliefs in the course of his enforced conversion. No interest was shown as to how they would harmonise their previous religious experience with Christian teaching. To grasp Christianity as the fulfilment of their Judaism was beyond them, as they were unable to compare Jew and Christian. This was the way in which Disraeli (1805–81) gained self-understanding as a converted Jew:[20]

I believe that God spoke to Moses on Mount Horeb and you believe that he was crucified, in the person of Jesus, on Mount Calvary. Both were, at least carnally, children of Israel: they spoke Hebrew to the Hebrews. The prophets were only Hebrews; the apostles were only Hebrews. The churches of Asia, which have vanished, were founded by a native Hebrew; and the Church of Rome, which says it shall last for ever and which converted this island to the faith of Moses and of Christ, vanquishing the Druids, Jupiter, Olympius and Woden, who had successively invaded it, was also founded by a native Hebrew.

Today the church would like to demand and recommend knowledge and awareness, which are above all the fruit of biblical and theological studies as fraternal conversations, and she condemns very sharply any disparagement of the Jews.[21] Indeed the church advises her sons that through talk and interaction with followers of other religions, while preserving the integrity of Catholic belief, at the same time on they can preserve and strengthen spiritual and normal goodness that they find amongst disciples of other religions, together with any cultural and social factors of worth.[22]

The human propensity to purchase self-preservation by means of running down others and even persecuting them, is a fact that does not depend on worldly recommendation. A modern Catholic attitude cannot entirely suppress this when it states the following concerning the 'World of the three Rings':[23]

This tendency of the Christians in the kingdom of the caliph of Cordoba (where in the tenth century Arabs, Jews and Christians had already built a nation) to be close to the Muslims, was extremely doubtful in so far as some of them subordinated the knowledge of their religion to their own interest and fortune. There were many Christians who often forswore their religion in order to advance themselves. . . . The blame for provoking the repeated anger shown by the Muslims can be laid at the door of many Spanish Christians of that period. However, one cannot hold it blameworthy that even those small groups who were courageous in their beliefs were hindered by the fact that the Christians discontinued their opposition to Islam.

The basic contradiction contained in this characterisation is betrayed by reference to the latest period when Christian matters which had not been properly considered, were put on an equal footing with the politics of the Christian Spanish kings. For the rest, the text cited is completely correct:

> Frankness endangers individual existence. Individuality is better protected if one shuts oneself up and eliminates contemporary opinions and ways of life. The attitude of the church, when it now demands understanding and dialogue with opponents' views, apparently opens a third possibility, namely not forced conformity or doubtful plurality, but a spiritual existence that is self-sufficient and can exist together with different beliefs and different opinions.

This third possibility was granted a historic chance of coming into being in medieval Spain. However this chance was gambled away. In the year 711 the Arabs arrived in Spain and accorded Jews and Christians equal status as religious minorities, which did not assure them of civil rights equal to those of the Muslims, but at least assured them of religious liberty and made possible for them de facto opportunities of professional preferment in keeping with their abilities.[24] The Jews soon made themselves indispensable to the new masters as craftsmen, taverners, doctors, scientists and translators, so that Arab Spain became a refuge for the Jews, and the following three hundred years were the 'Age of Gold' of their post-biblical history.[25] The foundation of their social and economic position in Moorish Spain was the possession of land, and a century later when Spanish-born Jews found themselves in exile, and still felt themselves to be Spaniards, this is attributable to the fact that they viewed even at that time this possession of land as an ancestral right.[26] Thus they are not, as antisemitic propaganda would like to infer, 'the capitalist people par excellence' but are basically a people of farmers and labourers, as is clear from the Bible and the Talmud.[27]

Talented Jews soon made a place for themselves at court and in the administration of important departments. The first of these Jews who had 'climbed the social ladder' of whom we know anything in detail, was Yûsuf Hasdai ibn Shafmut, royal physician, translator of scientific works and diplomat at the court of 'Abd-ar-Raḥmân III (912–61). In 956 he received the ambassador of Otto I, negotiated a diplomatic treaty with the court in León, and in 958 one with Navarre. Through service of this type the forward-looking Jews gained that knowledge and potential that later made them indispensable to the Christian kings.[28]

As the Christians advanced in power in the south from c. 1060 onwards, they were fascinated by the superior culture of the conquered lands. At this juncture they needed the Jews who were at home with this culture and who spoke Arabic, to act as their interpreters of this culture and its favourable points. Conversely they seemed to these educated Jews men lacking in culture, these members of petty Christian principalities. Judah Ha-Leir advised the poet Moses ibn Ezra (ob. 1135) against service with the king of Navarre with the following words: 'Thou eloquent tongue! What dost thou want in the midst of these speechless men?'[29] The Jewish poets who wrote in Arabic had obviously adopted from the Muslims the high esteem in which the Arabic language was held, which considered Arabic to be the most perfect of all languages.[30]

Initially, the confrontation between Christians and Arabs, Spanish and Jewish adherents of the superior culture, existed in a spirit of reciprocal tolerance, as a particular story demonstrates— in Toledo which was captured in 1085, the same place of worship was used by Muslims on Friday, Jews on Saturday and Christians on Sunday, as their meeting place. The first archbishops of Toledo gave all their subjects, Muslims, Jews and Christians, equal rights just as did the kings in their spheres of influence. It was they who caused the Jews to translate the scientific and philosophical works of the Arabs into Latin.[31] In the royal documents that regulate the freedom to trade and court procedures for the adherents to these various religions, the Latin sentences show the names—Mauri, Iudaei and Christiani—all in the same grammatical case harmoniously together.[32]

In the same year as the capture of Toledo, the second famous Jewish convert after Petrus Alfonsi, the Rabbi Samuel, known as 'Samuel the Moroccan', became a Catholic. Even before this decisive step, he had written to his friend Rabbi Isaac an Arabic treatise in which he had, as is customary amongst Rabbis,[33] asked for a response—an answer on the master–pupil model—to important questions that were in doubt:[34]

God protect you, my brother, and remain with you until our

captivity be ended, our Diaspora lifted, our hopes fulfilled and our lives ruled by God's good will. Amen.

I know from experience that with you is the fullness of wisdom to be found in our time, and that you are our hope with your renowned interpretations, for with these will you maintain knowledge of the questions of doubt in the Law and Prophets. Therefore I would like to share in your knowledge and clear up as your instructor the difficulties that I have written on, passages from the Law and the Prophets, that fill me with fear and worry. Thus I take refuge in your unparalleled knowledge and wisdom, to which I commend this book, in the hopes that you will, deo volente, confirm me in wisdom, and make clear to me the questions that trouble me.

This book was translated into Latin in 1339 by a Spanish Dominican and given the title *Of the Coming of the Messiah who is Awaited in Vain by the Jews*, and it is under this title that it has been handed down in the writings of the fathers. Its argument is that of the Epistle to the Hebrews in the New Testament. The author puts questions in a disturbing way, as to the sense of the Jewish Diaspora and as to the inner agreement between Jewish and Christian teaching. Samuel is not affected by any social pressure, nor does he need to prove his relation to the ruling religion for conformist reasons. He is more impressed, just as the Christians were fascinated by the superior Moorish culture, by the religion of those men which was offered to him in a spirit of free competition. For a period of two years, this independent spiritual exchange was permitted in Toledo.

In the following period, we shall see a period where free discussion is possible without the answer being, as a matter of course and from the outset, settled by force, restricted to the court and its immediate circle.

This historic possibility, shown for a moment, whereby three religions could afford equal rights to the souls of men without political power being used to coerce them, was wasted. The records show a continuous struggle on the part of the kings against the representatives of religious communities and litigation over the rights guaranteed by the court to Jewish Muslims. The only development that runs purposefully on is the building of walls to guarantee the protection of minorities:[35]

Every Christian must, within one month, wall up doors,
windows or attics in his house that look into the Jewish quarter:
in the same way, only in reverse, must the Jews too act.

In the end Spain attempted to rid itself of the Arab and Jewish
elements. In 1492 Granada fell, and in the same year, the Jews had
to leave Spain. Ten years later it was the turn of the Muslims. It is
not without cause that the historian Friedrich Heer points to the
despairing efforts made by the already islamicised and semiticised
Spanish people to rid itself of its Moorish, Islamic and Jewish
heritage as 'the Spanish Tragedy'.[36] The recent past is a similar
case when the Germans denied or held for nought a great part of
their intellectual élite because it had some connection with the
Jews. The consequences can be seen in both these cases.

The fact that in Spain during that epoch the Jewish people was
granted an unique historical possibility of developing its particular
capabilities and potential without the distortion of persecution
making itself felt, is mirrored in Jewish literature in a manner that
is directly bound up with the *Disciplina Clericalis* of Petrus Alfonsi.

First, in their relations with Islam, the Jews opened themselves
up to impartial foreign, intellectual and spiritual influences. It is
clear that they were capable of being foremost in their activity in
the field of those sciences with which they had begun to occupy
themselves, by virtue of the highly individual organisation of
their spiritual life, which was not restricted to specialists, but rather
exercised, as theology, law and other sciences, by labourers and
workers.[37] Modern Jewish historians often point out with regret
that the Jews did not satisfy themselves with the Torah and its
exposition (at that time), but occupied themselves with philosophy,
grammar, medicine, mathematics and astronomy, and soon
became indispensable to both Moorish and Christian rulers[38]
because of the skills they had gained through these studies. However,
such an evaluation is the consequence of centuries-long persecution
and defamation, and it is also the result of a conditioned bias in the
criticism of that which is held to be 'the Jewish existence'.

In Spain the Jews applied a scientific system, as opposed to their
earlier method of collecting material, and in this system the
individual spheres of human life and nature were seen not merely
in their relationship to the Law, but rather as particular objects
of study, the treatment of which necessitated particular procedures.

Thus it was that there grew up for example in the sphere of education a completely new literary form; the 'Books of Ethics' ('sifre musar' = 'libri disciplinae').[39] The subject of such works was oriental wisdom for the conduct of life expressed in a pragmatic style: human relations, hygiene, financial management, etc. The material was drawn from the Bible, Greek philosophers, collectors of Arab proverbs and collections of old fables. The new factor that distinguishes these works from the earlier educational utterances of Jewish literature is the 'attitude to man' that they presuppose. Now it is not just a question of educating a pious Jew, but their ideal is the all-round education of all mankind in all possible respects, an education both complete and thorough.[40] This endeavour did not remain in the realms of pure theory, for at that period it was a fact that the level of Jewish education in Spain, Provence and Italy was higher than anywhere else in Europe.[41]

By means of a comparison of the *Disciplina Clericalis* with other works of this educational literature, to the tradition of which Petrus Alfonsi consciously adapted himself, as is seen by his choice of title, we can see the dominance over the centuries of a particular type of content and form. The continuity of human experience is also demonstrated. A thirteenth-century book of fables, composed by a Jew living in France,[42] shows us, for example, the statement from the chapter entitled 'True Nobility', where it is stated that the noble man has most to suffer in this world:[43]

The generality of mankind treats with scorn the man to whom more honour is due than them; they wish evil upon him and his goods and make up to him when they need him and his wealth. The deserving man must bow down before misery; he knows how to guide arms and command others.

Another source tells of a man from Toledo[44]

who was a distinguished leader of the Jews, very pious and gentle, and who held a post at the king's court. However he was slandered and was obliged by a royal order to submit complete proof of his possessions and outstanding claims.

When he had done this and the king had shown himself unwilling to express himself on the triviality of the inventory list drawn up for him, the Jew answered: 'you have desired to know what I possess; my riches which you at death can

remove in a second, I possess not, but what is set down in this
little book is really mine, and no man can take it from me.
These are the gifts and helpmates built up over a period of
years.'

This story is like Exemplum XXIX of the *Disciplina Clericalis*.
It is not the same story, but is based on a similar experience, and
shows the same approach to the formulation of an experience in
story form: it takes up the struggle against error, against adoption
of the unproven as proven, and gives no opportunity for their
correction, but rather by means of a process of apposite use of
similes clears the way.

All told, in this Musar literature we run up against that which
we know from the book of stories on Petrus Alfonsi, namely
proverbs,[45] and formulae,[46] scattered short exempla,[47] advice to
esteem good men, whatever their nationality or religion,[48] and
warnings against illusion and self-deception.[49] Even the emphasis
placed on the general sort of proverbs, in which the different
religions share, the 'supra-confessional' character of such teaching
of life, which is so amply demonstrated in the *Disciplina Clericalis*,
even this is everywhere established. Candour in the matter of
what is alien and clear-headed pride in individual existence is here
bound up with an intellectual equilibrium, never again to be found
amongst the Jews in the same way.

The success outside Spain and in a different intellectual climate,
of this type of 'education for life' documented in the Musar
literature, we know to have existed from texts coming from Northern
Europe, particularly Germany. The earliest belongs to the eleventh
century and, like the section on Silence in the *Disciplina Clericalis*,
contains rules for proportion in speaking:[50]

> My son, seek the company of wise men, never depend upon
> your own judgment, and do not force yourself on others. ...
> My son, in the school house pay no attention to every empty
> word, and only concentrate on the teacher's words. Do not
> ignore any remark, and despise no man. Often pearls of
> learning are found even in insignificant people ... be silent.

Here no thought is given to scientific explanation, as the Spanish
viewed it, but rather to the 'school house', namely the synagogue.
As against the broad horizon of our Latin book of stories, that

includes both East and West, we have found advice set out in the rather reduced milieu of the 'Jewish quarter'. The same is true of a comparison between the story of 'Abraham's Hospitality' with the wording of the Judaeo–German *Book of Eternal Life*,[51] or the discussion of the 'Choice between Wisdom and Riches' when compared with the exemplum from the Testament of Rabbi Judah ibn Ascher.[52] It is precisely because of the fact that the same themes are handled as in the *Disciplina Clericalis*, that one can consider their different treatment and see that those possibilities of life that were offered to the Jews in medieval Spain, never occurred afterwards or outside the 'World of the three Rings'. The sad lock-out which meant that the Jews had to succeed without those possibilities of a free, intellectually honest existence, has prompted one Jewish historian of literature to remark in a self-critical manner:[53]

> At that time the all-devouring Christian hierarchy absorbed
> the life of European man, with the exception of the Jews. Thus
> the power of resistance identifies the life of the Jewish 'church'
> with that of its adherents, and everything that was thought
> of or discovered was transformed by the Jews into a religious
> topic, i.e. an all-excluding topic. Only in the south of Europe
> did the Arabo-Judaic culture work in the opposite manner;
> in the north a form of life that was continually rejuvenating
> itself was able to assert itself in a united area. The Jews denied
> Christianity, and thus Judaism denied the rest of the world.

The 'denial' is no more than a further demonstration of that age-old tendency to exclusion, that had already appeared in that tract in the Talmud, the 'Awoda Sara', but the Jews subjected themselves in this way to that 'process of consolidation' which throughout the European Middle Ages caused the previously existing boundaries between the secular powers and spiritual powers (Western Christianity, Byzantium, Islam and Judaism) and the classes of society (noble, cleric, administrator, people) to become gradually an 'iron curtain'.[54] Thus one can regard the 'Jewish quarter' of the Spanish, French, Italian and German states not just as a body of oriental aliens, but rather one must view them as a consequence of that historical act by which the structure of Europe developed through the establishment of closed nations, religions and positions, to become a system of rival groups, which are at the roots of the contemporary settlement within Europe. The fact that this continuity still has meaning for the solution of man's historical problems after centuries of standing still, is shown by the absurd demand that the Jews should become Christians, and thereby all the trouble would cease,[55] which in recent times has been raised again under the guise of nationalism. This time it was suggested that the Jews should forswear their individuality and become Germans, thereby solving the Jewish problem.[56]

When, therefore, an enquiry is made into the relations of the Jews to Europe, reference should not be made to the merit they gained as stimulators of science by their spirit of enquiry, or as mediators in matters of literary form and content, but an attempt must rather be made to establish the extent and quality of their effect on the overall European fate, namely the isolation of groups. Because of the actual distribution of power, they were obliged to play a role between the rival groups. It was on this that the blame was put by Heinrich von Treitschke in 1879 in those words which were destined to become notorious, when he said: 'The Jews are our misfortune.' The paradox of this attribution of roles whereby a primitive social psychology, which is typical of all closed groups, seeks to establish a scapegoat for all unsolved problems,[57] lies in the fact that the only European group, the exclusion of which was always of a purely defensive nature, was made thereby into the ghost of some elemental danger. Theodore Mommsen was taken aback and asked how such a prominent advocate of history as a critical science could show such an unreasonable and intolerant attitude for[58]

good manners and an even higher sense of duty demand the discussion of the peculiarities of individual nations and races with forbearance and a sense of proportion.

9 SCIENCE AND SUPERSTITION

The text of the *Disciplina Clericalis* begins with the name of Enoch, one of the patriarchs.[1] In the book of Jesus Sirach, a work often cited by Petrus Alfonsi, the catalogue of the righteous philosophers[2] also begins with the name Enoch. In the apocryphal tradition of the East he is held to be the founder of human knowledge. We read in al-Qifṭî (ob. 1248):

The learned of different nations are at one in the question of who was the first man to discuss wisdom and its pillars, Propaedeutics, Logic and the physical and theological sciences. Each group desires of course to find this man among its own people; but in fact none of these was the first. Those people who have investigated this question carefully, have formed the opinion that prophetic knowledge formed the beginning of scientific enquiry, and this goes back to Idris.[3] All the pioneers who are to be found in various parts of the world, derive their knowledge from the teachings of his pupils, or from the pupils of his pupils.[4]

Amongst the Arabs Enoch is compared with Hermes Trismegistos,[5] that mythical philosopher, prophet, and king of Egypt, who, after the flood is held to have reinstated all arts and sciences the tradition of which had been destroyed by the catastrophe.[6] In the alchemical tracts that were written and read in both East and West—most of them masquerading under the name Hermes—Enoch is mentioned as one of the three persons united in Hermes. In one such work the following situation is related:

A scholar of Alexandria, by name Adfar, found the book of Hermes, studied it deeply, and was able through the knowledge that he gained therein, to help many men. Morienus, a young man from Rome, heard of these marvels and set out to become Adfar's pupil. Adfar taught him the secrets of knowledge, and after his death, Morienus became a hermit in the environs of Jerusalem. Now there was in Alexandria a sultan Khâlid.[7] This man was much given to the study of the sciences, and he gave orders that the man should be sought out who would be able to provide him with and explain the book of Hermes to him. When Morienus heard of this, he went to the court and greeted the sultan with these words: 'Good king, may God guide you to better things.' Khâlid gave him a laboratory where the sage made gold. As the other alchemists met with no success, their heads were cut off. At this Morienus went away without having betrayed his secret to Khâlid. After many years, he was once again sought out and found in a hermit's cell. He was brought back to court, where he disclosed his secret to Khâlid: in the philosopher's stone were contained the four elements, and that the stone was the 'All'. Morienus told

Khâlid in unintelligible alchemical terminology how he could
preserve the stone.[8]

Enoch frequently appears together with Elias as father and ruler
of mankind. In Caesarius of Heisterbach they are mentioned[9]
together as a pair, and it is said that they shall return at the last
day.[10] In *The Book of the Bee* of the Nestorian bishop Solomon of
Basra (c. 1222) they are the overseers of Paradise, Elias of the
unmarried, Enoch of the married, 'in order that the unmarried
may not lord it over the married, as would be the case if Paradise
were reserved only for the unmarried'.[11] In the apocryphal Book of
Enoch, the patriarch calls together his successors as he lies dying
to transmit to them the teaching that God had confided to him
during his translation to heaven. It is there that we find the first
instance of the advice that Petrus Alfonsi puts into the mouth of the
patriarch—'no man is greater than he who fears God; for this man
will be in his time the most mighty lord of all.'[12] In the same way the
theme of holy hypocrisy has its origins there—'Go not near to
righteousness with a heart full of discord.'[13]

It is from Enoch that derives not only knowledge of the secrets
of nature, but also the knowledge of the right way to conduct one's
life, and indeed that knowledge is most needed by the average man
who cannot withdraw from the world. The beginning of knowledge
that is set down under the name of Enoch, is, however, nothing
like 'experience', as Petrus Alfonsi claims in his *Letter on Study*,
but rather a prophetic knowledge which a man can obtain only if
he finds someone who has it already and can teach it. The system
used to reckon time has not been arrived at by the continuous
reporting and experience of men, but made manifest by Enoch.
According to this view it was seen by close interpretation of the
Bible that the 365 years of the patriarch's[14] life had formed the
basis for the 365 days of the solar year.[15]

Ibn Ḥazm (ob. 1064), the poet who wrote the famous 'Necklace of
the Dove', was statesman, poet and theologian, and he bears
witness to the fact that even medicine originates from that source:[16]

We know with absolute certainty that no man could have
arrived at the discovery of the arts and sciences without
help, nor could he have been guided by his own natural
ability without any form of instruction. This is true for
example of medicine, knowledge of temperaments, sicknesses

and their causes in all their multiplicity and variety. It is also true of the discovery of cures for all these things, and of medicaments that could never have all been tested. For how could a particular medicine have been discovered for a particular disease, where such an advance would necessitate a ten thousand year period of activity and medical advance into that particular sickness?

The fact that one cannot envisage what enormous masses of human experience mankind can gain over a few generations, has its cause in the fact that mankind just will not envisage it. Knowledge has to justify itself through its religious value. Any form of study that was concerned with purely physical and secular matters came under suspicion of heresy.[17]

By his reference to Enoch, Petrus Alfonsi the scientist expressed his attitude to the idea of knowledge, just as when, as relator of the traditional theory of the novella, he paid his tribute when setting out the didactic aims of his work. What were his real views on the matter of science are set out in his *Letter on Study*:

> I do not hold with the position of intelligent men who deliver judgments on matters of which they have no knowledge, and who reject something before it is proved. Knowledge must first be grasped through 'experience'. In the same way no man can consider someone to be a teacher of science without first having tested him.

As in the case of Enoch, Petrus Alfonsi repeats the general consensus of opinion, but he betrays his critical awareness to the knowing person who is used to reading between the lines.

In a particular passage in his works, he gives in veiled words a disclosure that shows him to belong to that group of people who conceive knowledge as something granted to them by God. Where he speaks of the seven basic types of knowledge, he mentions that he considers 'nigromancy' as the most important. One must understand this concept, which generally means a prophecy of the dead,[18] a science from which people expect exact information as regards the future. From the relevant passages in the *Disciplina Clericalis*, it can be seen that the author does not believe in such prophecies, by the veiled way in which he refers to them.[19] It can also be seen that he has landed himself with a ticklish problem.

In these passages the author shows how and in what way the religious opinions of mankind can err. The idea of knowledge characterised by the name Enoch, means basically that knowledge is to be comprehended as a stable system of truths, and that to pass beyond the boundaries, as Dante in his example of Odysseus' ghost illustrates,[20] must be viewed as a crime against God. But in the popular characterisation of Enoch, which is found among the alchemists, an Enoch who had given secret instructions for the making of gold, there is an audacity shown, that is much greater than that which is reproached in the researcher into specialized topics. People dream of a universal knowledge that makes man a godlike power. Lucinius in the Dolopathos story learnt astronomy from the secret books of Vergil, which opened the future to his eyes.[21] Sindbad in the *Mischle Sendabar* watched the stars closely and thereby gained exact knowledge of what was going to happen;[22] Dr John Faustus 'prophesied future events and happenings which showed themselves to be so'[23] by means of his 'praxis'. In all these cases the scientist is always treated as a magician who must possess supernatural powers.

Such powers are expected from a doctor above all men. A story from Teheran tells that Luqmân (who is also mentioned in the *Disciplina Clericalis*) had possession of a medicine that would restore the dead to life. Because the servant who was applying it to Luqmân's son, became sick himself and let the phial drop, the dead man had to return to the kingdom of the dead.[24] This characterisation that is found in some folk-tales, is met with even today by doctors. Abû Bakr ar-Râzî (ob. 925/935) the greatest of Arabic physicians after Ibn Sînâ (Avicenna), gives the following report on this subject:[25]

Amongst the things that estrange people from trained doctors and gain credence for quacks, is the illusion that the physician knows everything, and must never need to ask anything. When he examines some urine, or feels a pulse, he must know too what the sick man has just done or eaten. This is lying and deception, and is caused by tricks and all manner of artificial questions and answers by which people's minds are led astray. Many of these quack doctors hire men and women to keep them informed of every change in the state of the sick person, and to notify them of every story told by the servants, friends and neighbours of the sick man. The people who are hired, generally women, go to the gate of the physician's house on the pretext that something is wrong with their husband or brother, and they ask questions of those who are waiting. This way they help the quack doctor, who learns by means of his servants everything concerning the symptoms of his patients to be. Sometimes they accompany those whom they have been questioning, before the doctor, and tell him what is needful by means of signs, movements of their limbs, or words that constitute a code. The discovery and unmasking of such highly organised tricks often makes life difficult for the true physician. ...

I myself, when I first took up the art of healing, resolved never to ask a question when once a man had given me a sample of his urine, and I was much honoured because of this. Later on, however, if it was seen that I had posed some intricate question, my esteem sank quite noticeably in their eyes, and I was given to understand quite frankly—'We believe that you will be able to tell us all that needs to be done, immediately you see our urine, but we find that the opposite is so.' As soon as I gave them to understand that this was outside the scope of medical practice, they engaged the idle practice of charlatans. Further, if the physician is able to diagnose much from the symptoms of which the invalid had not informed him, he will never act like that man of whom the story is told—'Whoever left this urine, either slept yesterday with an old woman, or slept on his right side for so many hours of the night' and similar rubbish. ...

The public wants the physician to heal a sickness in a moment, like a magician; either that, or they want him quickly to prescribe some acceptable medicine, or some other thing that is special and not applicable in all cases and at all times. To oblige a doctor to make amends for nature is a great crime, but quacks and others of that ilk make their fortune by dealing with something disgraceful, and they are able to make a reasonable living from their base handiwork, whereas the true physician can scarcely obtain the necessities of life even with considerable labour and effort.

This masterly psychological study needs no additions. Particularly interesting is the fact that this idea of scientific knowledge and medicine as something magical, is still with us now. Even today a doctor can still always repeat the words written by ar-Râzî more than a thousand years ago. A doctor is viewed 'as a guardian of secret knowledge and the patient strives to hand himself over to him with heart and soul'.[26]

From the religious and psychological point of view, particularly informative is the unique conflict, whereby the very men who demand something supernatural from scientists engaged in the study of nature, and who pay not the slightest attention to the objections quite sensibly raised by the scientists, these same men do not hesitate to accuse scientists of pacts with the devil, and thus expel them from the community of orthodox believers. An example of this is what happened to a pious scholar of the tenth century, Gerbert of Aurillac (later Pope Silvester II), who was responsible for the introduction of arabic numerals and rules for calculations. The story told about his residence in Spain is a precursor of the Faust story, and is composed in its every detail from motifs in folk stories about magicians and those in league with the devil.[27] This naïve superstition is the reverse side of the orthodox conception of science.

Petrus Alfonsi uses one of the most widely circulated alchemical tracts, and takes from it the story of the sacrilegious king whose fall is prophesied by the philosopher Marianus[28] (Ex. XXV). He quotes as his source Plato's Book of Prophecies, a work also known under the title 'Book of the Cow'. This work is full of instructions to magicians, for example, how one can cause a man to appear, fill a house with serpents, seize fire with one's hands without burning oneself, and understand the speech of animals. As the title shows, the first experiment that is described in detail has to do with a cow.[29] The author was at one time held to be the great translator and physician Ḥunayn b. Isḥâq (ob. 873), but this is clearly a fiction, as people who lived after his death are mentioned.[30] The reason that it was held by Petrus to be a work by Plato has its origin in the fact that it went under the name of the *Laws*,[31] and Ḥunayn had translated Plato's other work.[32] The peculiar fact that Petrus Alfonsi used a work that was popular yet abstruse, stands strangely at odds with the fact that he does not utilise any of the magical stories that contributed to the long life of the book, but rather uses a story, the hero of which makes predictions only on the basis of his own experience of life and knowledge of mankind. He treats this highly popular and widely diffused literature impartially, and does not succumb to it uncritically. The opinion of Albertus Magnus on this type of literature is similar:[33]

> As far as concerns all mention of necromancy in these books, it appears to me, without a more detailed investigation (though that is necessary) that destruction of it serves merely to preserve it. The time is very near, when from a wide variety of reasons, about which I cannot now speak, it will be shown that to concern oneself with such matters will be useful. Obviously those people who busy themselves with such works must guard against any misuse of them.

The conflict that arises in such dealings with magical literature, and necessitates the stipulation of such a proviso, is characteristic of the 'peculiar twilight' in which modern medicine and physical sciences were born and perfected.

> In the twelfth century whoever was interested in the secrets of nature, and dared to make experimental investigations, exposed himself to a rather dangerous inclusion in the community of Magi, sorcerers, and alchemists. He was liable to inclusion in those secret conspiracies, which from lust for power and domination will even make pacts with the devil in order to uncover secrets that God has veiled.

Such a man is to be grouped amongst those who are always open to suspicion by officialdom, like 'Provençal Jews, the translators of Arabic tracts on alchemy, chemistry, medicine, and astrology'.[34] It was during this 'twilight', when true striving after knowledge, and magical practices, scientific experiment and fantasy—none of them in fact very different from each other[35]—all existed side by side, that the Jewish astronomer and physician who wrote the *Disciplina Clericalis* lived.

10 FURTHER INFORMATION ON THE LIFE OF THE AUTHOR

Judah ibn Tibbon, the man who translated into Hebrew one of the two great works of medieval Jewish literature, the *Kuzari* of Judah

Halevi, wrote a letter to his son Samuel, who later translated another great work, the *Guide for the Perplexed* of Moses Maimonides. In this letter he said: 'You know that the great ones of our people are now arrived at great and high rank through the writing of Arabic.'[1] As an example he mentioned the founder of the Scheschet family in Barcelona, who carved out an enviable niche for himself as translator, physician and administrator of the royal lands.[2] The thing that is here interesting is the knowledge of Arabic which is named as the first condition for success, other capabilities being put in second place. To be bilingual or polyglot is not simply to be valued as a 'technical' possession, but rather to be particularly prized, because skill in languages demonstrates intelligence in the general sphere. This compels a 'discussion with the middle man who acts as interpreter who must be acknowledged as a partner ... the tension that exists between the individual sphere and the foreign language must be endured and accepted in order that through the action of bilingualism, it may be resolved'.[3] This lies particularly in distinguishing 'the differing meanings of relationships, the aspects of both languages'.[4] 'The man who has the gift of tongues, must also have the ability to see things in their various aspects.' It is this faculty that makes polyglots suitable negotiators or diplomats. The fact that it was educated Jews in particular who because of their occupation with Arabic medicine and science, had learned Arabic, made the connection between service as interpreters and medical and diplomatic activity quite natural.[5] It was thus that well-to-do Jews gained a knowledge of the underlying practice of Arabic administration, in which Christian rulers had so strong an interest.

The above-mentioned precepts apply to Petrus Alfonsi. An indication of his activity as an administrator can be seen from the only document in which we find his name. It is a bill of sale dated 14 April 1121 with which one of the French knights who had served under Alfonso I had obtained an estate in Saragossa which previously had belonged to a Muslim.[6] Petrus appears as a witness, and it is to be supposed that he was acting on behalf of the king, who in 1118, three years previously, had captured Saragossa, and was then there arranging conditions in the valley of the Ebro, where the Muslims enjoyed particular protection. Clearly it was incumbent to use one of the Arab experts as a confidential agent in this matter.

With the Frankish knights who assisted the famous warrior king of Aragon[7] in the reconquest of these areas which had previously been under the rule of the Arabs, there were also some Cluniac monks who had come to the Spanish court. It is to their influence that the conversion of the royal physician is to be attributed.[8] The fact that it was a Jew who worked alongside Petrus Alfonsi as astronomer, mathematician, and Arabic correspondence secretary, a Jew who often showed signs of belief in Jewish messianism, shows how free of bias was the effect of the presence of these fervent Christians at the court of Aragon. This Jew was Abraham ibn Hijja, who in 1129 wrote a book prophesying the coming of the Messiah in the near future. He based his prophecy on astronomical calculations.[9] We need not go further than Toledo[10] to find a sceptical mention of the *Disciplina Clericalis* from those who believe in the possibility of 'scientific' prophecy. It must have been a 'topic of conversation' for people at court to be interested in it. The connection between Aragon and France does not consist solely in the exchange of military aid but also exists in the scientific sphere. Many threads came together to provide the example of Montpellier where French, Arabs and Jews studied medicine together, and where in the year 1180 the ruler, jealous of this scholastic freedom, defended it against any attempts at clerical influence.[11]

We do not know what the daily round of Petrus Alfonsi the Royal physician was like, but it cannot have been very different from that so clearly outlined by Moses Maimonides in Cairo:[12]

The king lives in Cairo, and I in Fustat. Each of these places lies two sabbath day journeys from the other. My position with the king is difficult, for every day I have to seek him out in the morning, and if he, or one of his children, or one of his harem is ill, I cannot leave Cairo, but must remain in the place for the greater part of the day. If, however, there is nothing special, even so, I cannot get back to Fustat before midday. When I arrive home, half-dead from hunger, I find my waiting room full of people, Jews and Muslims, high and low, friends and enemies, a ripe mixture, all of them waiting for my medical advice. I dismount, wash my hands and ask my patients to bear with me while I eat something—my first meal in twenty-four hours. Then I deal with my patients until evening, and

often deep into the night, and give prescriptions though I am
lying on a couch from fatigue. By evening, I am so exhausted
that I can scarcely speak, and because of this it is impossible
for any Jew to have private discussion with me except on the
sabbath. On that day, after morning service, the whole
community, or at least most of them, comes to me to seek
instruction. On this day, I take care to organize all community
business for the week, and to give a lecture. We study together
until midday, and then they all go away.

Because of some passages which he found difficult to translate
from Arabic into Hebrew, Samuel ibn Tibbon proposed to journey
from Provence to Cairo to ask the author himself, and it was with
this description that the great physician and philosopher
(1135–1204) who came originally from Cordoba, attempted to
dissuade him from his purpose. We must imagine the daily life of
Petrus Alfonsi to have been similar.

A doctor as important as Jibrîl b. Bukhtîshû', whose family
produced renowned physicians for three hundred years, became
personal surgeon to Hârûn-al-Rashîd in 805, and had a great
many therapeutic successes in court. However, a single piece of
slander was sufficient to condemn him to death. He was saved by a
wise minister. Under Hârûn's successor al-Ma'mûn (813–33) he
was also imprisoned twice more before his eventual rehabilitation.[13]
Whether the life of a Spanish royal physician was less fraught with
danger, as one might well think, is dubious when one sees in the
Disciplina Clericalis how much common sense and lack of illusion
is shown in the treatment of service in high places, and with what
perception the author recommends intelligence, vigilance and
silence.

Jewish physicians were much sought after in the European
Middle Ages and people were accustomed to 'lending them out',
as it were.[14] Thus it happens that we find Petrus one day as royal
physician to Henry I of England. This must have been in 1110.[15]
We can surmise that there must have been some diplomatic mission
bound up with the journey, but the really significant thing about
this journey to England is neither the presence of a royal physician
nor a supposed diplomatic mission but rather a cultural and
scientific exchange, so typical of that time, when the transmission
of knowledge was still a personal thing,[16] and not bound up with

institutions, but rather with the individual's desire for knowledge, which meant that people made journeys in search of those from whom they could learn something new. Petrus Alfonsi has addressed a treatise to those men of science with whom he had been in close contact during his journey in France, and this treatise gives both a very good insight into this personality exchange and into his programme for the revision of basic concepts in the sciences. It is called the *Letter on Study:*

Petrus Alfonsi, servant of Jesus Christ, wishes happiness and blessing from Him who alone can bring happiness and blessing. This he wishes, as a brother and fellow student, to all those children of holy mother church who concern themselves with the study of Aristotle, to all those whose education has been in philosophy, and to all those who in various parts of France are engaged in the study of one science or another. All those who have experience of the attraction exercised by any form of scientific learning, must love one another, and if one of them possesses some rare, precious and useful piece of knowledge that is still unknown to others, it is his duty to share this with the others in a friendly manner, so that in this way every man may wax greater in his own knowledge and become richer.[17] Because I myself should observe this rule, I have taken much trouble, because I have something special to impart, to find a way to bring you joy, and to offer something for your inspection.

I have discovered that every one of you is busy with the study of grammar, a subject that certainly cannot be grouped together with the seven basic sciences, for it is not a science open to argument, nor is it the same for all languages, but rather different in all of them. Nevertheless, it has its own particular worth, and is indispensable for the basic sciences, for it is by grammar that the words of one's mother tongue are governed,[18] as if by a plumb-line or rule, and without grammar the mind cannot comprehend what comes before it. Indeed, if there were no grammar, we would frequently put the singular for the plural, or vice versa; we would understand the future instead of the present with the result that we would in many cases run the risk of always being in doubt.

A number of you are also engaged on the study of logic, that science that is to be placed first in the rank of sciences. Indeed, it is a worthy and important science. You have gained the knowledge as I have, that it is in logic that all peoples of whatever origin, and speaking whatever language, excel in acumen, at least at the present time. I have called it a science of high and worthy rank, but it is not so much useful in itself as in its applications to other sciences, for which it is indispensable. It is like a balance in which gold and silver are assayed, for just as one can distinguish between gold and silver when they are placed in a balance, as to whether they are pure or alloyed, or just as one can use a file to establish whether, and to what extent, a material withstands use, in the same way logic can be used to distinguish right from false, true from untrue. And just as the balance and the file have their own real worth, even when there is no question of using them to test something, and no practical application, such is the precise case with logic. Logic has no practical application unless people attempt to study other sciences by using it; for with its help they can be learnt and mastered.

The fact that every science is both intrinsically useful and useful in respect of the contribution it makes to the study of other sciences, I can prove. I will take the example of arithmetic, which stands in canon to a second, and which has its own value and is indispensable for the other sciences. It has importance for geometry, in that it is used to calculate points, lines, angles, etc. Again it is useful in music for counting chords and their duration, intonation, intervals and harmonies. Medicine, too, uses arithmetic for the calculation of the elements and their bonds, types and phases, the quantities for medicines, sicknesses and the days, weeks and crises of fevers and many other important things. Astronomy, too, uses it for the calculation of constellations, signs of the Zodiac, degrees of angles, points and small differences of the planets and other stars, and indeed many other things, the enumeration of which would take too long. Even in itself arithmetic has a use, in so far as that those who have mastered it, even when ignorant of other sciences, can with its help accomplish much in everyday affairs and business. Similarly with regard to the other sciences, by thorough investigation, it can be established that each of them—except logic—has its own intrinsic worth, and is at the same time extrinsically useful.

Medicine, which is undeniably of the utmost importance and indeed completely indispensable for all life in this world, and which can be thought of as a science that guards people's health, and is occupied in estimating the length of people's lives in this world, can be most thoroughly mastered with the help of astronomy. The reason for this is that, through astronomy, the changes of the four seasons of the year can be known, even before their arrival, and by this one can foresee the ups and downs of the weather and the illnesses of man and beast. This foreknowledge makes possible a therapy by means of which sicknesses can be warded off, or rather cured more easily.[19] Astronomy can also be used to determine the correct juncture for cauterisation, the knife, the lancing of abscesses, bleeding, the placing of the cupping-glass, where that is needed, and the provision, or rather the taking, of medical advice, as also the time and day set for the development of fevers and for many other useful things that have to do with medicine.[20] That everything can be accomplished with the help of astronomy, is shown by the book translated from the Arabic by Constantine into Latin.[21] By the use of this science one can foretell good or bad weather, which is most useful, indeed absolutely necessary, for shipping and navigation, as well as many other things, not to mention the fact that the mind finds pure pleasure in heaven through simple knowledge of facts.

Therefore given the fact, as I have already stated, that astronomy is so indispensable for the proper study of medicine and other sciences, it follows that it is thereby more useful, more agreeable and more important than other sciences. Because I have found that all those with a Latin education know nothing of the science of astronomy, I decided, as I had studied it for a longer period than you, to share some part of my knowledge with you, if this is right for you, and I have therefore made thorough and careful preparations so that I might be able to set before you something that was rare, costly, beautiful and agreeable.

It has come to my ears that some of those who seek a deeper insight into the subject are making preparation—and this can be viewed entirely as a figure of speech—to journey to distant countries, to seek out neglected frontiers of knowledge, with the purpose in mind of attaining to a more complete knowledge of the science of astronomy. I answer them instantly that the thing which they wish to see is in fact here. They already have before them what they seek, and what they propose to gain by journeying afar is in fact near. If there is some doubt in your minds as to my ability in that science, I have in fact accomplished much already. As far as I am concerned, I have no interest in giving vent to my views to people who already know, nor am I concerned to dismiss anything before proof has been provided, for the concepts of science should first be grasped through experience. In the same way, no man can be recognised as a teacher of science without proof. It follows, therefore, that those who imagine that they have effected something in the sciences from reading Macrobius and others,[22] people who have already accomplished something, or so it appears, imagine that they need to go no further, and that they have attained to a thorough knowledge of science. If they therefore put to the test the teaching of those who maintain that they know the answer, question their reasoning, because you withdraw from them the whole content of their argument.

Such people who imagine that they have thus gained a complete understanding of our science are just like the goat in the vineyard. The same happens to both. Once a goat entered a vineyard, and after filling its belly with vine-leaves, it decided that there was no other food superior to that afforded by the vineyard. If a man who, day in, day out, busies himself with the stars, a youth in wisdom, requests from you some of your excellent fruit of this science, grudge him not this, but busy yourselves to defend your errors as if they agreed with the truth. Such people generally suffer the same fate as those who wished to sell pearls to onion-sellers. For once a man had a lovely, round, shining pearl, of great price, and he gave it to another man to sell it for him. This fellow came to market, and found himself among those who sell onions.[23] One of them asked him what he had to sell, and was shown the pearl. On being asked the price, the seller named a monstrously high figure. But the other considered that what was being offered him was an onion, and so estimated the cost of the pearl in terms of the price of an onion, and therefore he told the man

who was selling the pearl that he had at home many such that
were rounder and more shining, and thus because he could not
distinguish between pearls and onions, he despised the other
man as being a man who strove to sell so-called pearls at such
a high cost in comparison with the price of onions. ...

I believe that such people give up the study of this science,
because they have chosen a topic that is too difficult for them,
and beyond their understanding. I am also of the opinion that
those who are suited to study should not allow themselves to be
put off or frightened by the difficulty of the subject. Indeed they
should have no worries on that score, for the philosopher says:
'Sciences seek initially to create difficulties in order that those
who are basically unsuited to scientific study, or intellectually
lazy, may be frightened off by their lack of comprehension.'
But whoever has started off with the right potential for a
reasoned approach to study as soon as he is initiated into the
inner secrets of reading will rapidly be desirous to savour the
simple and agreeable taste of scientific study.

Further, there is another group whose opinion it is that no
profit is to be gained from this science. These people show
themselves even more than the others to be incapable dunces.
Again, there are those whose view it is that science is against
the rule of our Christian religion. How arrogant and incorrect
they are is shown by the fact that nature herself adequately
contains the argument to refute it. Whatever has to do with
science, has to do with truth: therefore because it has to do
with truth, it cannot be in opposition to truth. Therefore, it
follows that science cannot run counter to belief. If a man
excuses himself with such an argument, then he provides us
with two reasons for our opinion that some excuse themselves
because of intellectual laziness, and others because they are
proud of their position, as teachers, and are loth to play the
role of students. As regards such people the words of the
philosopher are true: 'Whoever does not try to cope with the
difficulties of learning, will never attain the glory of a
professorship.'[24] That reminds me of some words of Solomon
who said: 'He that refuseth instruction despiseth his own soul:
but he that heareth reproof getteth understanding.'[25] Further
to this, at the beginning of my translation, I placed a
foreword[26] which dealt with the truth of science and the

splendid advantages to be gained from it. I recommend this to
your notice, that you may see and realise how glorious is
science, and that I am at home in its joy and beauty.

The intention behind my lecture is however to forge a name
for myself that will outlast me and, further, to raise once more
to life the knowledge of that science which is in such a
deplorable state amongst those educated in the Latin manner.
I further intend to do away with all the excuses of those who
have promised to track this science [of astronomy] if they
could only find it. Every day messengers come to me from the
neighbouring confines to carry out, in the name of those who
send them, the promise that they had made of coming to me
to hear my lectures, as soon as I had begun my course. But no
man will begin his lecture as long as the audience is still lacking.
If I wanted to read my lecture to those whose education was
slight, and whose intelligence slow, I would be wasting my
time. I would like to have sharp, clever students in order that
I might have from the very beginning, those who could and
would continue my work in this science after me, and take my
place.[27]

In this letter a 'revision of basic principles' is advanced by which
science will be firmly placed on an empirical basis. No longer will
authority be claimed simply on the basis of the trustworthiness of
the source, without the information being subjected to a vigorous
proof based on the facts themselves. It is strange that Petrus Alfonsi
adopted this principle from a world which had begun to dissociate
itself from it, a world in which such a thought evoked none of the historical changes that would have resulted in the West. Indeed the most
exact formulation of the empirical method is to be found in Islamic
medicine at a time when scientific life was already paralysed there.
It is the well-known thesis of Ibn al-Khalib of Granada (ob. 1374)
who, speaking of the plague, says:[28]

The existence of infection is a positive fact known from
experience, study, and the testimony of intelligence. In addition
we have trustworthy reports as to its transmission by means of
clothes, dishes and ear-rings. It is further spread by people who
live together, by people who infect a healthy sea-port on arrival
from an area already infected, and through the immunity of
isolated individuals.

Whether or not the prophet expressly denied the possibility of infection,[29] the doctor follows without flinching his conviction that one of the traditions of Islam must be revised, when it is found to be in manifest conflict with the evidence of his own eyes.[30] The historical follow-up of this great thought was used by European students of Arabic medicine many centuries later, when they, by means of their middlemen, the travelling Jewish scholars, had learned the knowledge and experience gained in antiquity, handed down to them in an uninterrupted chain.

Petrus combines with his role of a middleman in scientific principles, an original thought, namely the psychological explanation of the opposition generally demonstrated by humanity to any new or unusual idea. After setting forth his conception of the interrelation of the individual sciences, as had already been done in the *Disciplina Clericalis*, where this sound scientific ideal had been used in opposition to the prevailing ideals of education, which were purely literary, he turns this point to psychological use: the people whose entire learning is gained from books embody for him a very deficient and restricted type of intellectual understanding. They are constantly delivering judgment on matters of which they are ignorant and dismissing ideas without proof. They are content with their intellectual ammunition, but basically they are eager to learn. It is precisely here that the narrator reminds himself of a word in order to illustrate this attitude through two examples: those who are self-contented, yet capable of experience, are like the contented goat or the unsuspecting onion-sellers. He further enquires into the excuses they offer for their psychological motives, particularly the reference to the incompatibility of scientific enquiry and the Catholic faith. Here too, we find that interest in matters of social psychology that Petrus Alfonsi had so variously demonstrated in the *Disciplina Clericalis*.

One of the 'pioneers of natural science in Christian Europe',[31] who had an intellectual candour and readiness to adopt an empirical attitude similar to that of the Spanish Jew, was a cleric from Lotharingia called Walcher. This country had already learned of Arabic scientific knowledge through Gerbert of Aurillac (Pope Silvester II) (ob. 1003), and the exertions of Petrus Alfonsi were viewed with great interest. Walcher, in a work that appeared between 1107 and 1112, entitled *Experientia*, had been able to show how exact astronomical calculations could be arrived at by the use of

Arab methods and instruments.[32] After the Spaniard had made his acquaintance, he studied under him and wrote down, as lecture notes, a work that has come down to us under the name of the *De Dracone*.[33] This work shows us what is uppermost in the mind of an educated man hungry for knowledge, when he sees that an unquestionable and valid system of basic concepts has been established in his conceptual world by rational and empirical means. Here is a paragraph that illustrates the information gained from his teacher:

> You will see that my realisation of the daily round of the sun, and the [false] gradations of the Zodiac,[34] are based on truth, when you can use them to forecast a future sunset. We must not allow ourselves to be confused by the fact that different peoples cause the year to begin on different days, and that days and months appear differently to different people. For example, the Egyptians held September to be the first month of the year, the Romans considered it the ninth, and the Jews the seventh. In fact, for all of them it is the same month, and the result of calculations does not show one month to one group of people and another to others. The observation is finally traced back to the man who located and established the beginnings and ends of periods of time by means of the signs of the Zodiac, and did this in a way different to that which we use, and so the sun never appears except where we see it.[35]

The opposition shown by a man who wants to learn is due to the fact that he suddenly realises that his hitherto existing orientation, which has had absolute validity in his eyes, has only a certain validity, and that now he must find the attestation of his newly gained re-orientation not in authority, as he had done previously, but in reason and experiment.[36] The problem, that here appears in its specialised scientific context as an example of disparate traditions concerning the computation of time, has a general importance, because the establishment of an absolute in a scientific system of orientation, or 'rules of grammar', is, in general, an expression of man's tendency to seek safety in models of prescribed behaviour, severe laws, and in the examination of non-closed propositions, in short in all sorts of restraints on thought. The experience of this socio-psychological situation, already dealt with in the *Disciplina Clericalis* in the chapter 'Hypocrisy' and in the introduction to the *Conversation*, played an important part in the scientific work of Petrus Alfonsi too.[37]

Another man who is to be found in the ranks of scientific activity together with Petrus Alfonsi, as a catalyst and middleman, was Adelard of Bath, one of the most prominent men of learning in Europe during the twelfth century. He spent a year journeying in Italy, Sicily and the Near East 'in order to seek out the learned of various countries'[38] and to learn from them. He is a different type from the thoughtful Walcher—self-sufficient, full of energy, and enthusiastic. In contrast to the cautious, critical formulations of Petrus Alfonsi, we find in Adelard a young man's zeal to learn the new science, and a thoughtless disregard of tradition. He drags into the open the Arab science of the Christian scholastics, because this science had been enslaved by tradition, and had surrendered to authority and followed where the latter led.[39] He feels himself to be at the high point of intellectual history, and considers himself a citizen of the world—'born and reared at the royal court of the whole world'.[40] The year 1120 sees Adelard in England again. In 1126 appears his famous translation of the comparative astronomical tables of the Arabic mathematician al-Khuwârizmî (eleventh century), from whom the medieval books of mathematical tables gained the name 'Algorithms'. This table is also found in some manuscripts attributed to Petrus Alfonsi, and shows evidence of many Hispano-Arabic words. Adelard of Bath, just like the Spaniard whose astronomical works had appeared five years previously in 1115, treats astronomy not as a 'subject-discipline', but as a scientific hypothesis plain and simple.[41] It is a sure fact that the two men made each other's acquaintance at the court of Henry I, and the Englishman must have gained much help and advice from the royal doctor and astronomer who was so well versed in Arabic.[42] The prologue that Petrus Alfonsi wrote to his own work based on the ground-work of al-Khuwârizmî's tables, reasserts the thesis already adduced in the *Letter on Study* that astronomy can be a scientific aid to medicine:

Petrus Alfonsi, servant of Jesus Christ, and translator of this book, has said: 'Thanks be to almighty God, our Lord, who has moulded the world from his wisdom, and ordered everything with his spirit. He has adorned the heavens with angels and stars, and has decked the earth with all kinds of creatures,

plants, trees and fruits. He has divided his heavenly creation
into two groups, spiritual and material beings, and has given
the spiritual beings power over all earthly creation subject
to guidance and instructions from the Creator, and the
fulfilment of his will.' As the psalmist says in the passage
where he distinguishes the two types: 'Bless the Lord, ye his
angels; that excel in strength, that do his commandments,
hearkening unto the voice of the Lord. Bless ye the Lord, all
ye his hosts; ye ministers of his, that do his pleasure' [ps.
103: 20, 21]. It is, I repeat, to these heavenly, spiritual beings
that power has been granted to arrange and organise earthly
creatures. But, in accordance with the text cited, it is to the
material, heavenly beings that power to carry out the rules of
nature has been granted.

In the same way, the qualities of the elements change by
reason of the movement of the sun through the four quarters of
the heavens, that is the directions of the winds whose fixed
points are the two solstices and the two equinoxes. Similarly the
sun's movement and the changing qualities of the elements
bring about the alternation of the four seasons, spring, summer,
autumn and winter. In addition, nature, because of the change
of season, alters all living things. That this is so, could not be
doubted by any reasonable man. Similarly, there is no living
thing in this world that does not experience in its turn renewal
and death, increase and loss. We can see this with our own eyes
by pointing to the winter solstice which we class as the
beginning of winter. We see then how the sun stands vertically
under the Pleiades, and how when it begins to climb again, the
days become longer, and the qualities of the elements begin to
alter in such a way that they become colder and moister. For
this we ascribe these qualities, which are actually peculiar to
water, to the winter season of the year. So too trees, by virtue
of this moisture in their roots and branches become fruitful
again because of the moisture in their subterranean roots and
seeds; all these things begin to live again and grow. With men
and beasts, however, increase is due to the slime that is the
peculiarity of this season, and this rises upwards, as if forced by
pressure.[43]

So during this period, from the aforementioned time until
the spring equinox, while the sun climbs ever higher in the sky,

everything is attracted by the damp, and gradually the cold is expelled as it becomes warmer. It is for this reason that we attribute dampness and warmth, which are the properties of air, to the spring at which time we find them in our own lives. In this season of the year, the warmth produces damp, the plants become green, the trees covered with leaves and every plant grows verdant and produces fruit, each in accordance with its kind.

It is for this reason that we have given the name 'season of bliss' to this season of the year. The blood rises in the bodies of men and beasts, and sickness that has its origins in the blood, departs. Natural sensuous desires creep unawares upon us, and all sorts of worms and insects take their being from decaying organic matter. Thus every manner of thing grows from this time right up to the summer solstice when the sun climbs higher and arrives at maturity.

From the summer solstice onward—generally called the beginning of summer—when the sun stands directly under Arcturus, and can rise no higher, the nature of the seasons changes from damp to dry. Therefore, we refer to this season as the hot and dry one, and we attribute its qualities to the element fire to which they correspond individually. During this period during which the temperature increases, and all damp is expelled, trees and plants become dry and fruits ripen. The red gall[44] waxes in men and beasts and increases to warmth. Bodies dry up and burn from an overpowering thirst. Those diseases that arise from this gall, appear, and from this point until the autumn equinox when the heat lets up, everything grows drier. From the autumn equinox to the autumn solstice, usually the beginning of autumn, warmth gives way to cold, and it is because of this, that we say that the autumn is cold and dry, the peculiar qualities of the element earth, and that it brings in a natural manner death to all. During this season, the earth, dried up and crippled by the cold, withdraws all roots, seeds and whatever else it nourishes, into itself, because it no longer has the power to nourish them. This is why plants dry up, trees lose their leaves, and birds die as do worms, beetles and other animals that stem from putrefaction. The black gall increases in both men and beasts, and every disease that has its origin there breaks out. So all beings that have their vital energy in this yearly cycle described here, gradually diminish from this time until the winter solstice.

Further, the sea changes its ebb and flow in accordance with the moon's movements through the four natural divisions of the day. As the moon passes through the four cardinal points, the tides change to spring tides and neap tides, that is to say, greater and smaller breakers. In summer—as the moon waxes or wanes in light, the weather too changes—winds, rainfall, clouds and sunshine. In accordance with this rhythm, in men and beasts the sap returns and rises, as does the blood, marrow, brain etc. ... Many other living organisms follow these rules of nature also, but to enumerate them would take too long, so now I will speak of the other stars, for not only do the movements of the sun and moon affect everything in the world, but other stars too, for example the planets, influence living organisms here below. To give an example: if the course of the world were to follow the laws of the sun only, there would not be so many changes in a year, but every year each of the four seasons would exert its influence in the same way. This is patently not so, for we can see from our own experience that in one year the winds blow more strongly than in another, that it rains more, is hotter, or colder, that there is more cloud or more sun, a better harvest, more sickness, or a higher mortality rate among animals and humans. We notice also many other disparities manifest in single events which cannot be explained singly by reference to the revolution of the sun, a combination of other causes being excluded. It would be the same if we attributed the tides to the influence of the moon alone, if the rise and fall of the corporal sap in all creatures were similarly attributed, and if the same things happened every month. We know, however, that this is not the case.

It is also an empirically knowable fact whose validity we are able to attest that the sun, moon and other planets exert an influence on the earth, and that much that happens here is due to their influence. The planets, for example, exert an influence on the four elements, as we have said, and in the same way the elements too work on the collective substance of all things made up from the elements. It follows therefore, that the planets influence terrestrial happenings. But, though they collectively influence secular beings, they must necessarily also manifest their particular working and influence on individual beings. All parts belong to a whole, and all individual happenings and events to a genus. Through empirical knowledge, we see also that all earthly creatures grow and bloom during that period from the time when the sun stands over the Pleiades until he comes into conjunction with Arcturus.[45] In the same way we see how when the sun returns from Arcturus to the Pleiades all creatures shrivel and withdraw into themselves. This is just as we find in the words of the Lord when he said to Job: 'Canst thou bind the sweet influences of Pleiades, or loose the bands of Orion?' [Job 38: 31]. It is the sun alone that causes everything to be opened and loosened, and brings all things to growth and fruition, when it is in conjunction with the Pleiades, when they are at the southern pole of heaven. It is thus the sun avails itself of the power of these astral groups. Contrariwise, when the sun is in conjunction with Arcturus, a star that shines at the north pole of heaven, everything becomes weak, and withdraws into itself, and into the innermost earth, as if into a fortress. In this the sun is aided by Arcturus. Everything, therefore, happens from the ascent and descent of the sun. This is what the Lord meant when he said: 'Canst thou bring ought to the day that is removed or locked up by the natural course of the stars?'[46] Countless other things also happen on the earth because of the course taken by the stars. Men of no education hold this to be false, but wise men who understand this science, are well aware of this secret, and know it to be true. When, therefore, something happens which is of such difficulty that an ordinary man's wisdom cannot deal with it or investigate it, this is not because the stars have no influence at all, but because human weakness of spirit, bothered by mundane worries, has meant that man is not ready to grasp and know everything. Solomon bears witness to this when he says in Ecclesiastes [3: 11]:

> He hath made every thing beautiful in his time: also
> he hath set the world in their heart, so that no man
> can find out the work that God maketh from the
> beginning to the end.

As long as Saturn remains conjoined with the signs of the warmest season of the year, it continues to be dry; and from this you will realise that through such a planet terrestrial happenings are subject to the influential working of heavenly bodies. God has divided terrestrial life into two types, rational and irrational. Man towers above all other forms of terrestrial life by reason of his acumen and his intellect, for the Creator has poured into him His wisdom, that man may know the Creator's work, and through the knowledge of the created attain to knowledge of the Creator.

Heavenly creatures, too, are, as I have said, divided into two types—spiritual and material beings. Man can only know the spiritual heavenly beings by revelation. The material beings, however, he can know by rational observation, description of phenomena, and controlled astronomy.[47] It can be divided into three sections: conception of idea, in which occurrences become noteworthy: description, in which they become knowable; and experiment, in which they become sensible. From these comes first the knowledge of the nature and extent of the heavenly sphere, together with everything that belongs there; this knowledge man's alert mind gains by means of geometric reckoning of number and mass. The second effect is the knowledge of the movements of heavenly groups and stars: this is grasped by means of arithmetic. The third effect is the knowledge of the rules obeyed by these constellations and stars, and their importance for terrestrial events which follow upon that obedience to laws, and the diversity of the movements [of heavenly bodies]. These consequences can be known by experiment.

It was my intention to write a book in which I would expound the usefulness of the science of astronomy, this science of the number and movements of stars and heavenly bodies, in the matter of the calculation of years, months, days, hours and astronomical dates. The next thing necessary is to establish the calendar-based beginning of both year and month. I have carried out this undertaking with great labour, and I have translated from Arabic, Persian and Egyptian books, in order to set the facts before those who know only Latin. And because I would wish that everything here broached would be considered to be of importance, I have divided every section up, and given it a title, and rendered everything I found in the original verbatim into Latin.[48]

Here the course of the year is described astronomically, and explained in the terms of the meteorological effects; and the doctrine of 'sap' which was the generally accepted theoretical basis of medicine, and these other factors are joined together in a most convincing manner. This is not a particularly original achievement, for the theory of 'sap' belongs to the basis of medical knowledge, which was part of the common inheritance, as can be seen from the story of the clever slave girl, Tawaddud in the *Arabian Nights*,[49] or in the sermon found in Caesarius of Heisterbach in which it is adduced as a simile for the harmony of creation.[50] It has been criticised as follows by a modern medical man:[51]

Medical science in both its practical and theoretical aspects found in the idea of the microcosm an excellent model for the morphological structure of mankind and the functional running of his organism, and also for pathogenetic possibilities as well as an adequate plan of treatment. Physiology was eukrasia of the four elemental saps, pathology their dyskrasia, and therapy, the restoration of the equilibrium of the elements. Indeed, in this far from primitive scheme, there are many happenings in the nervous system, the blood flow system and in therapeutic materials, which were misinterpreted. But this is not decisive; we, too, in our modern system still succumb to similar misinterpretations. We ourselves experience how, in medicine, orthodoxy changes, and how notions of humours, teaching about the regulation of the central nervous system, and thinking about the pathology of relations have once again won ground. Above all, we experience how a movement makes its breakthrough, which could not happen without some anthropological basic idea which is no longer believed in in medicine. Such a concept was already peculiar to the ancient doctrine of the microcosm; it was transmitted by the Arabs, but in a modified form; above all it was completely rationalised by them.

Today in a time of unsureness when orthodoxy is triumphant, the fundamental idea referred to is that which Virchow gave to medicine a hundred years ago, when he included it among the exact sciences. According to him, 'medicine has always been secure in the hypothesis of the cell-state, has intimated constant goals and important instructions to man, has believed in the power of its methodology to inform all forms of culture, and has been able to impress an attitude to the world on the science'.[52] Today our medical knowledge is 'overwhelmingly rich, but has become alarmingly confused', because 'the individual elements of research are perhaps still valid in their spheres of relation and similar aspects, but no longer have any true worth in the eyes of society'.[53] The question is, which is better: to have a scientist tied down by no traditional scheme of things, who is firmly convinced, despite all criticism, and in the face of all prejudice, that he has been granted a tremendous intellectual liberty for the furtherance of knowledge; or to have one who is deeply immersed in an old tradition, who corrects that tradition through his own knowledge and who must always assert his liberty against the demands of that tradition? The question is a psychological one: in which of these existences can a man gain greater awareness? In which can he better establish his own critical knowledge?

Although Petrus Alfonsi advocates 'sticking to the main road' in the prologue to this work too, his critical achievement is nevertheless considerable. He replaces the old role which astronomy had, in · its astrological form, played in Arabic medicine,[54] by means of an empirically based bioclimatology. Modern medical science based on climatic influences which 'is concerned with the influence of climate and weather on plants, beasts and men', finds itself in a similar position to Petrus Alfonsi, because as a 'relatively young science' it must make its way in the face of opposition from all sorts of orthodox misinterpretations.[55] In such circumstances the self-awareness of the researcher is decisive.

Once and for all, Petrus Alfonsi had effected an exact division between the spheres of competence of theology and scientific enquiry. He had characterised the stars as natural entities which obeyed natural laws. He succeeded in this achievement without coming into conflict with the church's view. In contrast to the contemporary misunderstanding of nature which surrounded him, he stands out and refutes astrology by pointing to the indirect natural influence of the movements of stars. He refutes also the claims of those 'who believe in the possibility of prophecies'[56] by pointing to the self-evident thesis that one can manufacture conditional prophecies by reason of long experience. The complexity of phenomena is stressed in contrast to those theoretical simplifiers, the weakness and limitations of human knowledge are held before the idealist, and the pious enemies of the exact sciences are shown that the exertions of the researcher, from which they shrink, inspire him with the pious demand of knowing God in his creation. The sage Skepsis of the Old Testament preacher (Ecclesiastes), also cited here, in the face of a closed system is very apparent in spite of the unified composition of the presentation. Criticism is also directed against those who are content with knowledge they have not put to the proof; if men are troubled by questions dealing with natural phenomena (this in the final section), they will be driven to realise that the problems with which the researcher concerns himself, really exist.

The intellectual awareness of the Spaniard is to be seen not only in his scientific attitude towards research, but also it is continually to be found in the multifarious forms of his activity in the world, and his daily conversations with his fellow men. In contrast to the youthful enthusiasm of an Adelard of Bath, we are faced with a cautious but ironical discretion, an attitude apparently due to the experience that it is more important to speak to men in a way that can be understood by all thus using the main road, than to go one's own solitary way doing one's own thing, regardless of others. Obviously such a complicated spiritual and intellectual attitude is often not completely understood. Pedro IV must have thought that when he pointed out to the governor of Mallorca in his instructions for dealing with the Jews, that he was dealing with a people 'who were subtle and complicated'.[57]

11 THE MEDICINE OF COMMON SENSE

It is our general habit to view medieval man's relationship to sickness and healing through the appropriate reports in the legends of the saints. For example, we read in a chronicle from the beginning of the eleventh century 'of a severe punishment for the disregard of the saints and the healing brought about by their continual worship'. A monk lay very ill with a migraine, and had already been operated on to no avail.[1] As he lay near to death he was seized by devils, 'who took particular books in their hands, and read in a loud voice all his acts that were there set down', but suddenly St Vitus appeared, drove away the demons, blessed the sick man and caused him to get up. This he did without difficulty.[2] St Germanus hurt his foot, but declined all medical attention. During the night angels came to him, lifted him from his bed and made him stand. When he woke there was no trace of the hurt to be seen.[3] St Blaise performed something that was not just simple art, when he had to remove a fish bone that was stuck in the throat of a child who was brought to him, by removing it by prayer and the laying on of his hands.[4] In an anonymous life dating from about 1100, a man sick with malaria was healed with sacramental oil.[5] The medical attitudes do not go further than what is offered in the New Testament, which acknowledges only the exceptional case of a miraculous healing[6] or else the action of a sacrament.[7]

In the Qur'an too, one can find evidence of a supernatural view of sickness and healing. The sick man is possessed by spirits.[8] The same understanding of sickness and healing existed in ancient popular medicine, where there are countless magical prescriptions given, like the following:[9]

> For pain in the Adam's apple ('uva') a man should hold a grape to the painful area and say: 'uva uvam emendat' (grape heals apple).

Even the medical school of Cnidos employed the old concept of sickness that originated in the East, but with the arrival of the Hippocratic school the 'concept of the individual sickness' became basic.[10] Likewise the idea of the demonic character of sickness is still with all of us consciously or unconsciously when we say: 'The 'flu has a hold of me, my cough is annoying me'[11] and so on.

Even at an early date we find already a presentiment of the 'medical' character of sickness. Thus the Qur'an acknowledges the existence of psychic causes of sickness.[12] In Jesus Sirach, therapy through drugs exists:

> God brings forth from the earth healing plants, and whoever is reasonable spurns them not. (38: 4)

But here there is Greek influence, whereas the opposition between natural and supernatural explanations of sickness is older. Primitive and 'enlightened' interpretations of reality are not to be attributed to epochs but rather flow, multifarious and mingled together side by side.[13] The question to be asked is where, and at what specific time did the 'element of common sense' gain more recognition than elsewhere. In the Middle Ages it is the East that has the edge on Western Christianity.[14]

Abû Ṭâlib of Mecca (ob. 996) tells the following story:[15]

Once Moses lay ill, and the Jews called him to demand the
services of this or that medicine. He however declined, and
said that God who heals without medicine, would restore him
to health. Finally however, God ordered him to adopt the
usual methods, and he was restored to health. Thereupon
God said to him: 'You wanted to set at nought my wisdom, for
you did not put your trust in Him who gave the drugs of
medicine their power.'

Here we have no natural explanation for sickness and healing,
but a religious instruction; what Moses considered to be trusting
in God, appears rather surprisingly as the contrary. The Jews
considered that lack of respect for natural methods of healing such
as is shown in this story about Moses, or in the legends of the
saints, was throwing doubt upon the divine order of creation, and
considered it an error as to the type of God's activity in this world:[16]

Rabbi Baruch was asked: 'Why is God called in the hymn
"Creator of medicines, Tremendous in praises, Lord of all
wonders"? Does it befit medicines to be mentioned alongside
His wonders and indeed before them?' He answered: 'God
does not wish to be praised as Lord of supernatural marvels.
Therefore here nature is introduced through these medicines,
and placed in front. But in truth everything is a marvel.'

In the same sense Rabbi Baruch, when his daughter was ill, delivered
the following reflection:[17]

It is God's will that my daughter Reisel recover, she needs
no medicines. But if God made plain his wonderful power
to all eyes, then no one would have any choice; for all would
know. So free choice is left to mankind, and God clothes his
acts in the mantle of nature. For this reason he has created
health-giving plants.

That type of trust in God that is demonstrated in the story of
Moses, has also something to do with human freedom. Whoever
mistrusts nature and longs for marvels, is not capable of loving
God in freedom:

Marvels are not enough to prove a truth! There was once a

debate in the schoolhouse between Rabbi Elieser and his colleagues concerning a question of the application of the Law of clean and unclean things. As all Elieser's reasons that he adduced to defend his opinion on this matter, were refuted, he became indignant and said: 'If I am right then this carob tree will bear witness for me.' The tree uprooted itself and betook itself to the other side of the courtyard. His colleagues asked: 'How can the tree help us in our question?' Then Elieser called the brook to witness and caused it to flow backwards. The men of learning still remained imperturbable, convinced Elieser was wrong. Finally the walls of the room came to the assistance of the Rabbi. They bent down and collapsed. At this Rabbi Jehoschua became angry and cried out: 'Walls! What have you to do with this?' At this they immediately grew still and remained bent and split, as if they had become erect. Then Elieser said: 'Only God's voice can give the right command!' Then there came a voice from heaven, and upheld Elieser. Rabbi Jehoschua riposted calmly: 'It is no longer in heaven, i.e. after God's word is entrusted to mankind there can be no other teaching authority.'[18]

The colleagues did not accept Rabbi Elieser's opinion. Rabbi Nathan was later told by the prophet Elias, when he asked what the Lord had said in answer to that discussion, that God had laughed and said these words: 'My sons have conquered. My sons have conquered!'[19]

This story shows in a humorous way and with a touch of self-irony the Jewish trust in human reason, and not that reason which is opposed to belief but that which puts man in the position to understand correctly the word of God. Intellectualism is at the same time a part of orthodoxy. The incident mentioned in this story concerning human belief in God's words reminds one of another story that again stresses the trust placed in the fullness of age of the reasonable man:[20]

When Moses appeared in heaven to receive the Law, the angels were shocked, and cried out: 'Lord, there is a woman's son amongst us! What sacrilege!' When the Lord told them of the reason for Moses' appearance, the angels were thoroughly incensed: 'The holy Law to go down to earth! Never! Keep this light, this jewel, in heaven!' So God went to Moses and

said to him: 'Moses, answer these opponents yourself.' At
first Moses was afraid of the fiery spirits, but the Lord gave
him strength and calmed him, so that he could begin his
riposte: 'In the Law which you have entrusted to me, Lord,
it is forbidden to worship false Gods. You angels, would you
be worshippers of false Gods? The Law orders the sabbath
day to be a day of rest. Do you work? Do you need rest? It
commands: "Honour thy father and thy mother." Do you
angels have parents? It forbids murder, stealing and adultery.
Are there then in heaven passions, appetites and impure
desires?' When Moses had thus spoken, the angels fell silent
and approved.

Judah Halevi in the *Kuzari* gives a medical example that demonstrates how pure intellectualism is demanded for knowledge of the
veiled word of God that is contained in the natural law. He
astonished the king of the Khazars by indicating that it was here
that the root of belief and that of unbelief lay. Whoever does not
put his trust in God and the natural order of things and attempts
to be influenced by astrology and all sorts of magical practices,
shows himself thereby to be an unbeliever. The believing man
orders his life in accordance with the knowledge of God's law that
he has gained from holy writ and the laws granted by nature. The
unbeliever however[21]

is like a fool who comes into the doctor's dispensary. Everyone
knows that the doctor's medicaments will be of use. He,
however, is not there, but people come and find the fool there
in his dispensary and ask him to help them. So the fool
dispenses material from the jars without any knowledge of
medicine, and without knowing how much medicine to give
for a particular disorder, with the result that he kills many of
the patients with the very medicines that could have been
helpful to them. Because it once, purely by chance, happened
that the stuff taken from a particular jar was of use, men turn
to it and believe in it, and it is a help to them until such time
as they, again purely by chance, find some other cure elsewhere
that has been effective, and so turn to that one. They do not
realise that the only thing that is of use to them is the advice of
the skilled physician, who has prepared the medicines and
measured out the correct proportions, and who has given the

sick man advice as to how he can bring himself back to full
health by proper attention to diet, rest, exercise, air, sexual
intercourse, etc.

A proper utilisation of natural matters through the knowledge
of when and how to employ them, and a self-critical estimate of
one's own existence are both necessary. God is the wise physician
who has given man the dietary rules that are necessary for him.
These rules, however, demand, as should every patient who wants
to be and stay fit, the exercise of restraint, reason and intelligence.

It is worth mentioning that amongst the Arabs too, the 'medicine
of common sense' defined the practice of medicine. In contrast to
the Jews who were, during the Hispano-Arabic period, the cultural
middlemen of many different types of intellectual influences, and
who had learnt to handle the tool of critical reason, Islam was
always mindful of its increasingly defined tradition, and took
refuge in it.[22] The fact that in the sphere of medicine an array of
new things had been opened up, and was being subjected to an
inductive treatment[23] could well be explained by the fact that the
physician, because of his daily encounter with the supernatural, had
a more positive appreciation of the value of experience than any
other man of learning. Thereby arose the situation that the profession of medicine in the East formed for the most part the material
basis of a life of learning, and because of this a type of intellectual
independence was made possible,[24] which was unknown in the
West, where, for the most part, clerics were doctors and savants,
and thereby obliged to be orthodox because of their calling. In the
East the physician was on the edges of society,[25] and often led a
nomadic life, settling down where a good living was to be found:[26]

Abu 'l Hakim Al Bahili [twelfth century] was born in Murcia
and went to Baghdad. As he met with no success there, he
decided to return to Spain, and set out on his journey. On
arrival at Damascus, he rested and sent his slave into the
city with a little money to buy food. This small amount of
money was sufficient for baked meats, fruit, cakes, wine and
other delicacies, and Abu 'l Hakim said: 'It would be idiotic to
leave a city where one can live so cheaply.' So he went into
the city, bought a house, established a dispensary and practised
as a physician.

Another professional piece of luck came to a doctor through the unrest shown by the caliphs in the transference of Greek science. They were fascinated by this, just as later were the Spanish kings by the Moorish culture in their newly conquered kingdom. It was due to the translations of Greek physicians made at the order of al-Muṭawakkil (847–61) by Ḥunayn b. Isḥâq, that a broad, theoretical foundation was laid, which during the Middle Ages gave rise to the first examples of a regular medical code, still completely unknown in Europe. Particularly famous were the clinics in Egypt, the first of which was already established in 875. Al-Maqrîzî (ob. 1442) has left us a description of the hospital, that in 1283 was founded in Cairo at great expense. Patients were received with no attention paid to money or social standing, and sent to the department that dealt with their particular disease. A great many physicians, nurses, cooks, housemaids, gardeners and so on, were employed. There were special diet kitchens, a dispensary, all sorts of store-rooms, consulting rooms, and a library.[27] Already in the tenth century clinical studies were conducted at the patient's bedside and the students were required to give constant reports on the sick and to this end their minds were exercised.[28]

This was all possible because Hellenistic culture had survived in the countries conquered by Islam, and traditions remained unbroken. A particular attitude, however, appears in the abilities of the semitic peoples in matters relating to practical, useful 'savoir vivre'.[29] The Greeks had insisted that a physician be a philosopher and live as such. Here the opposite is true. The philosopher is also a doctor. In the East we find no trace of the abstract thinker and his vast theoretical plans, so derided by the Thracian maid, because he fell in the well through his lack of knowledge of the world.[30] In the sphere of Eastern learning, the wise man is he who knows the psychology of man, and has a thorough understanding of it. He is a man rich in experience and in knowledge of the world, who knows what counsel to give when it is needed.[31] His type of abstraction is the comparison, the picture, the proverb. In the words of the Brockhaus *Dictionary* of 1817,[32] when defining the responsibility of a physician (as 'concrete philosophy') he was able 'to make the idea of living practicable'. It would be interesting to know how much the attitude to the medical profession owes to the oriental conception of the doctor as a 'knower of human life'.

The question why a doctor and scientist like Petrus Alfonsi

should have decided to write an unpretentious little book on how to live one's life full of experience, all lessons contained in age-old stories and proverbs, should now need no answering. He has only done exactly the same as his Eastern colleagues Ḥunayn, al-Mubashshir and many others. Such a literary operation belongs in their opinion to the diatetic duties of the physician:[33]

> I have also considered the infirmity of man's physical nature which makes it necessary to break up instructions into small sections, so that boredom does not set in. Also I have been mindful of the fact that in order to facilitate remembrance of what has been learnt, the pill must be softened and sweetened by various means, because man is by nature forgetful. ...

12　THE JEWISH EXPERIENCE

The psychological interest demonstrated and stressed by Petrus Alfonsi in all his literary output, whether scientific or narrative, whereby he showed the human reactions coming into play in every point he raised, is found in striking abundance and in a critical form in the whole of Jewish literature:[1]

> There lived in the neighbourhood of Mar Ukwa a poor man to whom he used to give, on the vigil of Yom Kippur, four hundred pieces of silver. One day he sent his son with the gift, who came back and said to him: 'He has no need of them.' The father asked him: 'What did you see?' The son replied: 'I saw that there gushed before him old wine.' Then Mar Ukwa said: 'Is he so pampered?' And he doubled his donation.

Here there is the question of the religious ordinance that requires alms-giving and at the same time the correction of usual practice. The father's question to the son already betrays the interest of a critical psychologist who does not simply accept the son's assertion, but asks how this came about. The father's reaction is the correction of the son's lack of understanding of the poor man's situation. Whereas the son thinks only of himself, the father succeeds in putting himself in the poor man's shoes.

This ability to put oneself in the position of another, led to a considerable loss of illusion in religious practice where the supernatural was concerned. In the Talmud there is a humorous catalogue of the seven sorts of false piety, the motives of which are to be found in social considerations, vanity, egoism or petty fears of divine retribution.[2] The passage reads like a commentary on this:[3]

> Johanan ben Zakkai lay dying and said to his disciples while blessing them: 'I pray for you that the attention you pay to God may always be as great as that which you pay mankind.' 'Is that your only advice?', said they, astonished. 'That should be enough', answered the Rabbi; 'man ever seeks, when he wishes to do something wrong, to hide it from his fellows. When, however, you are about to commit a sin, care a little about hiding it from God, from God who sees all (if you can).'

This analysis shows that men think more about their fellows than about God in their average, religious life, and it is mankind's approval they seek, and his rejection they fear. Two classical stories underline this point in a masterly demonstration of story-telling:[4]

> The story is told of Rabbi Bunam and one of those men that live in solitude. He said: 'Many withdraw into the wilderness and blink through bushes, if they see nothing in the distance to be admired.'

Here the Jewish rejection of the life of a hermit plays a role, but in the next story the topic is the doubtfulness of the approbation that many people seek from others because of their piety:[5]

> Rabbi Bunam was asked: 'What is the meaning of offerings to false gods? It is quite unthinkable that anyone would bring an idol an offering!' He answered: 'I will tell you a parable. If a pious and righteous man sits at table with another and wishes to eat something more, but forgoes this because of what people will say, that is an offering to an idol.'

The Rabbi had well experienced how quickly a man can lose true piety. This lesson has nothing at all to do with the superficial imitation of abstract models, but rather with the realisation of a man's own existence in the light of God's demands:[6]

> Just before death Rabbi Sussja said: 'In the next world no one will ask me, "Why were you not Moses?"; they will ask me, "Why were you not Sussja?"'

The psychological awareness is commonly found together with a self-critical element:[7]

> The Sasower once gave his last penny to a man who was notorious for his evil ways. His pupils reproached him but he said: 'Should I be more choosy than God who gave it me?'

It is not very often in other religious creeds that such an autocratic apology is found. Moses Maimonides once made a very pertinent remark to a proselyte who had learned the elements of the Jewish religion from him, when he said that the fathers had brought some heathen religious elements from Egypt, and that the Jews had never been free of them before the revolt.[8] In the same way Judah Halevi sees the Talmud and its limitations:[9]

> I confess to you, King of the Kusar, that there are things in the Talmud for which I cannot give a sufficiently clear explanation which will hang together properly. These the Rabbis adopted because of their scrupulous attention to everything written by the wise men, and their view that everything these had said should be studied. This is the reason for the care you must take in the compilation of whatever you take from their lessons. Their attention to detail is so far reaching that they retain the same words without even understanding them.

The unclear parts of the great Jewish book of instruction are here psychologically explained. The explanation can always be put to the proof: the learner is in the habit of adhering even to what he does not understand, because he thinks that the lack of clarity could lie with his teacher, and is to be understood not by thought, but by progressive insight.

> [Self-criticism] is a feature of Jewish writing from the very outset. The Jews could be classed as the founders of historical writing. From the very beginning they have never considered the fate of their own people, contrary to all other peoples, as the cause of their pride in themselves. Because of this they went even further than did the wonderfully objective Greeks later: they did not only leave themselves open to every influence, but also took the occasion to be responsible for their own faults and, in accordance with divine command, they

condemned and criticised themselves sharply.[10] Moses spoke
very hard words about his own people,[11] as did the prophets
later:[12] nor did criticism stop at rulers and crowned heads.[13]
This self-criticism belongs to the most worthy and sublime
parts of Jewish literature, and has impressed itself upon all later
Jewish expression.[14]

There is a marvellous example of this ability for self-criticism
in a Yiddish anecdote coloured by that self-ironical attitude so
typical of Jews in the Diaspora:

A merchant arrived in a small town, lodged in an inn, and as he
was staying over the Sabbath, he decided to deposit his money
with the Rabbi.[15] The Rabbi called the elders of the community
and informed them that the Jew had left ten thousand roubels
with him, and explained that he had put the money in an iron
strong-box. Early on the Sunday morning, the merchant came
to claim his money, but the Rabbi disclaimed all knowledge.
'What's this about money? I know nothing at all about it.'
'What do you mean, Rabbi, you know nothing?' said the
tradesman in a trembling voice, 'there were witnesses, the
elders of the community.' The Rabbi called these elders, but
they too gave the appearance of complete ignorance. 'What's
this about money? The man is in a fever.' 'Fellow Jews', sobbed
the man, 'this money was put in an iron box!' 'What's this
about a box? We have no strong-box!' laughed the elders, and
left the room. The Rabbi too disappeared for a while, but
afterwards counted out the foreign Jew's ten thousand roubels
deposited with him. 'Rabbi', said the merchant wondering,
'what has become of this whole game?' The Rabbi answered
him with a smile, 'I wished to show you what sort of a
community I have to deal with!'[16]

This is a variant of the Exemplum XV of the *Disciplina Clericalis*,
a type of story that is widespread in the storehouse of popular tales.[17]
The story is misunderstood sometimes, when it is thought that the
Rabbi was proud of his flock who were party to everything. But in
that case he would really have embezzled the money. This story
is no joke, but the expression, in an oriental fashion, where comparison is joined with humour, of harsh experience. This is what the
world is like! We Jews also are like that!

Empathy and self-criticism brought about a critical tolerance towards others. 'Go amongst people and see how they act' is the advice given in the Talmud to those who are obliged to live amongst foreigners.[18] In another passage it is phrased differently: 'Wherever you go, act as the customs or the place demand.'[19] The distinguished jurist Rudolf von Ihering, speaking of the Jewish law as relating to aliens, says in his *Purpose in Law* that 'This concept, not adopted by the Greeks or Romans in their legal corpus which generally considered the alien as lacking legal rights, is found expressed in the law of the Old Testament[20] with the utmost clarity and precision'.[21] The Talmud also draws no bounds, but demands that love be given and attention devoted to all men, whatever their religion:[22]

> Be reasonable in your devotions, give gentle answers, control
> your anger, be completely at peace with your brothers,
> neighbours and every man, even the heathen. This way you
> will be loved in heaven, admired on earth, acceptable to all.

Variety, multiplicity, 'otherness' are not considered as faults, but rather as things that aid self-knowledge: 'Pay attention to God's acts; for who can straighten what he bends?'[23]

The Jews have never been able to take it upon themselves to secure their self-preservation in the same way as other peoples have done, namely by closing themselves off with arms or walls, or by the deportation of aliens. They can only exist if they themselves can remain in an alien environment. 'Emancipation' did not solve their problems, for it merely underlined their individuality, and was unable to rid them of their 'otherness'. It is no resort to liberal thinking, but rather age-old Jewish lore, that makes the memorial set up in the entrance to the synagogue in Florence for those Florentine Jews murdered in 1943–4, bear the inscription:

> O that this foul sacrifice could bring the time of human
> brotherhood nearer, that brotherhood foretold for all peoples
> by the prophets of Israel.

The Jews have a longer experience of living in reasonable harmony with others, not only because of the hundreds of years of their life in the Diaspora, but also because of their own social structure. They acknowledge no differences in birth, no nobility, no clergy. They 'only recognised that nobility of disposition shown in condition, whereby a man can improve both his own lot and that of his children'.[24] This attitude knew no distinction between rich and poor, for everyone went to school from the age of five, and never really left it. Every child, every labourer, could by virtue of his education grasp the knowledge of any nation.[25] A particularly high standard of education amongst the Jews existed in the Spain of the Arabs, for there 'everywhere absolutely teemed with schools and teachers, and illiteracy was practically nil in the western caliphate'.[26] Spain was also the first country where a complete text of the Talmud was made available.[27] There existed there, too, a happy arrangement whereby the Jews did not relinquish a privileged religious position, but rather had their religion closely bound up with day-to-day life.[28] The whole Middle Ages were a period when the Rabbis lived in accordance with the age-old recommendations of the 'Sayings of the Fathers':[29]

> Beautiful is the study of the Torah when it is pursued in conjunction with worldly business; for if this is so, the labour expended on both leaves no room for sin. When the Torah is studied without any parallel involvement in worldly living, its ultimate value is nought, and sin is never far behind.

This close connection obliged the Jews to realise the demands of their religion at all times if they wished to have any claim to credibility. This fact was a further source of incessant psychological experience, and a further challenge to self-criticism. The organisation of their schools was not authoritarian but democratic. Free competition between different teachers was allowed:[30]

> The world breathes only through the breath of school children. . . .
> Therefore a community that has no school should be anathematised. . . . A master cannot keep his comrade in check, if he opens a school next to his.

These democratic principles of school organisation are well documented in the Talmud, where the Jews have handed down opposing views on education to be a topic of perpetual discussion to all succeeding generations:[31]

> It is a document which mirrors the soul, spirit, sorrows, errors, customs, hopes, advances, knowledge, pain and greatness of Israel over a period of eight centuries. It is not one of those

gigantic works all the product of one man's genius; no one man was the author, but a whole people, not one individual, but thirty generations. . . . The Scholar who came first left the memory of his thoughts, every generous passion found a response in him, every angry movement, every hope, sorrow and enthusiasm stored up in him its memorial.

The fact that in this book attention is always being paid to the particular awakening of psychological interest can be viewed as an important characteristic of Jewish life. For example, the following story:[32]

A labourer asked for his pay that he might provide for his family. The master said that he had neither money, fruits of the soil, nor anything else with which to pay him. And so the fellow went home sorrowful.

At the feast of the atonement the master loaded three mules with food and drink, added some money and went to the labourer. He counted out his wages, after they had eaten and drunk, and asked him what he had thought of his master's answer. The fellow answered that he had thought that his master had used the money for himself to effect some lucrative purchase, that the cattle had probably been claimed by some vow.

The master replied: 'I swear this was so. I had vowed to entrust all my property to the will of my son Hyrcan, who did not bother himself with advice. When, however, I arrived at my friends in the South, they absolved me from all my vows. As for you, however, as you have judged me for my kindness, may the omnipresent God judge you for your kindness!'

Here we have an idealised model of the yardstick which works for all psychological understanding: the man tried first to work out all the possibilities in order to reach a considered understanding of the position of his fellow man, before judging him. What happens, however, when a man yields to prejudice against his fellow man, can be further elucidated by reference to the Greek myth of Procrustes in the example of the unjust judge of Sodom:

They had a bed for foreigners to sleep on; if a man was too big, they cut off his feet, if too small, they stretched him.

A similar disregard of the rights of one's fellows was shown by this judge in his religious duties:[33]

> When a poor man came to him, he gave him a dinar, on which was written his name. But he did not give him bread. When the poor man died, the judge came and claimed that which was his.

Here we have the other side of the coin to Marukwa's finely developed empathy. He adapted his gifts to the needs of the poor man without any prejudice against his way of life.

The following story from Caesarius of Heisterbach can be compared with the social, ethical and psychological interest shown in the Talmud, even though it comes from a completely different spiritual background:[34]

> The Virgin Mary, who is greatly to be worshipped, obtained a particular favour from Christ, namely that, as often as people took communion in her presence, she could in some marvellous way distinguish by her spiritual power who was approaching the table of the Lord worthily or unworthily. Once at Easter when the people were coming to Holy Communion, she looked at the expressions on their faces, and realised that out of all that number only ten were worthy to share in the heavenly sacrament.

Thorlieff Boman in his comparison of Greek and Hebrew thought[35] has rightly characterised thought and understanding as two different but necessary types of knowledge, and shown the Greeks to be logicians and the Hebrews psychologists.[36] It is necessary for us to occupy ourselves with the latter 'because the psychological "thought type" is much further away from us than the logical' and 'because the peculiar greatness of Hebrew thought is misunderstood by most scholars and is confused with primitive thought as prelogical'.[37] We also find in Boman that psychological understanding 'is nearer to natural life'.[38] It is interesting that Boman also considers metaphorical expression as the correct form for this psychological 'thought type', and traces its use back to an important psychological experience:[39]

> Given the intention of winning over the listeners, it is expedient to evade the spiritual defence mechanism that everyone

instinctively constructs for himself in his inmost self. One of the best ways of doing this is by parables and similes the validity of which no listener can dispute. If the simile is pertinent, that is completely parallel to a particular instance in the hearer's life, then its powers of persuasion can be very great indeed.

This supposition that the Jews have generally been able to have those experiences that suggest themselves to them through indirect expression in proverbs and exempla, is called by Alfred Weber 'projection of development in intellectualisation' which is a characteristic of the Jews:[40]

> The Jew has been in the world much longer than those who surround him; he is already spiritually mature when the rest are still children. ... He divides ... the intellectual and emotional spheres into two quite separate and watertight compartments, and keeps the intellectual sphere free as much as possible from the entanglements of emotion, thereby distinguishing himself from more naïve types. In this as a thinking man. Therefore wherever a Jew is still, to all practical purposes, controlled by a gloomy mixture of undivided impulses of feeling and superiority, he recognises everywhere two series of motives for his relationships, expediency and blind impulse.

Behind this peculiarity of the Jews there lies not only a particular ability for psychological understanding and self-control, but also a peculiar and historical fate. In every new persecution, expulsion and oppression, the Jews have gained the 'experience of sorrow' which always seeks out their kind.[41] In the light of this, the lesson that they can still impart through their experience of present-day men, an experience which in the pluralistic 'rootless' society of today can still daily underline the division between reason and emotion, should demand particular credence.

The Jewish experience is a constituent part of Europe, an 'heirloom'. Jewish medicine has even in our time made great advances and produced many great scientists. One of the greatest of these created from the age-old Jewish gift of understanding, a new science. This was Sigmund Freud. To trace literary materials back to their source would take too long. The Jewish wisdom of life, as shown in the *Disciplina Clericalis*, has spread through all Europe. The concept of intelligence already found in the Proverbs[42] of Solomon in the image of the careful art, is used by Baltasar Gracian in his *Book of Oracles*[43] and Thomasius in 1688 in one of his first lectures in German to the college at Leipzig, 'On Gracian's basic rules for living a reasoned, intelligent and good life', made use of this same book.[44] Later Schopenhauer made a famous translation which was to become a favourite amongst books of aphorisms. There one can read of the importance of being able to keep silent,[45] of the dangers of illusions,[46] of the absolute necessity for self-control and self-criticism[47] and of the real nature of those things which a man needs in order to establish himself amongst men.[48] The basic proposition of Petrus Alfonsi, that a man does well if he stays on the high road, and adjusts himself to circumstances—this disowning of a world-improving idealism—is also the wisdom of Gracian.[49]

Without a doubt the 'Brethren of Righteousness' of Basra had this type of wisdom in mind when they desired that their ideal man should possess the experience of a Hebrew.[50] Since that time, the world has well seen at what price such experience is bought. What would the pious Muslim scholars say today?

Part Two

THE *DISCIPLINA CLERICALIS*

of
Petrus Alfonsi

Whoever wishes to translate from one language to another, and decides to observe a constant rendering for a particular word and attempt to preserve the order of words and paragraph construction of the original, will make for himself a great deal of trouble, and will eventually provide a translation that is ambiguous and muddled. This procedure is not correct. The translator should first of all grasp the tenor of the contents, then properly equip and instruct himself on the linguistic level so that he is completely at home in the foreign language. This cannot be attained without radical alteration of the order of sentences and statements (i.e. putting what comes first, second, etc.), nor can it be done without rendering one word by a multitude of words, or a group by one word, or omitting many phrases, and rearranging others until the tenor of the passage is quite clear, and the whole perfectly understandable in the language into which the translation is being made. This was the system followed by Ḥunayn b. Isḥâq when he translated Galen, and by his son Isḥâq in his translation of Aristotle. Their renderings were models of clarity. Therefore we intend to base our plan of action on that of these two men, and forget the others.

(Moses Maimonides to his translator, Samuel ibn Tibbon[1])

THE DISCIPLINA CLERICALIS[2]

PROLOGUE[3]

These are the words of Petrus Alfonsi, a servant of Jesus Christ, who has written this book:

I give thanks to God who is first without beginning, from whom all good things have their beginning, who is the end without end, and the fulfiller of all good, who is wise and brings wisdom and reason to mankind, who has breathed into us his wisdom and led us into the light with the marvellous clarity of his teaching and who, by the multiform grace of his holy spirit, has enriched us.[4] Therefore because God has designed to clothe me in his many-sided wisdom,[5] although I am a sinner, in order that the light given to me should not be hid under a bushel,[6] and at the prompting of that same holy spirit, I have been moved to write this book. And I beseech Him that He may adjoin to this the beginning of my little book a good conclusion, and that He may guard me, lest anything should be there said that might displease His will. Amen.

Therefore may God be my help in this undertaking. He, who has compelled me to write this book and translate it into Latin. For while I toiled to learn the causes of man's creation by every means and by frequent ponderings,[7] I have found that the human spirit has been set down for this very purpose by the precept of the creator, that so long as it is in the world it may study and busy itself with holy philosophy, to have thereby a better and greater knowledge of its creator, to live in moderation and continency and to learn to protect itself in the midst of the supporters of ungodliness, and to follow that path in the world which will lead it to the kingdom of heaven. When a man has lived according to the aforementioned rules of holy 'discipline', he has indeed fulfilled that for which he was created, and deserves to be called perfect.[8] I have also considered the infirmity of man's physical nature which makes it necessary to break up instruction into small sections so that boredom does not set in. Also I have been mindful of the fact that in order to facilitate remembrance of what has been learnt, the pill must be softened and sweetened by various means, because man is by nature forgetful and has need of many tricks which will remind him again of those things he has forgotten. For that reason, then, have I put together this book, partly from the sayings of wise men[9] and their advice,[10] partly from Arab proverbs, counsels, fables and poems, and partly from bird and animal similes.[11] So, I have thought out a way so that if perchance I should have to write more these writings should not be a labour to the reader but rather a help, so that both readers and hearers should have both the desire and opportunity for learning. The learned shall remember what they have forgotten through those things contained in this book, to which I have given a title, *Disciplina Clericalis*, a name that well describes the contents, for it renders the educated man well versed in knowledge. On the other hand, I decided that, within the capabilities of my senses, everything must be avoided in this book that might be found contrary to our beliefs or different from our faith. To do which may Almighty God to whom I dedicate myself, help me. Amen.

If, however, anyone should flick through this work with a human and therefore superficial eye, and see something in it where human nature has not been sufficiently on its guard, I advise him to re-read it again and again, and I propose that he, and all others who are perfect in the Catholic faith, correct what is wrong. For in anything invented by man, there is no perfection, as the philosopher says.[12]

Fear of God

The philosopher Enoch, called Edris in Arabic, said to his son: 'Let the fear of the Lord be your business, and you shall have wealth without toil.'[13] Another sage said: 'He who fears God, is feared by everything, but he who does not fear God, himself fears everything', and another philosopher said: 'Who fears God, loves him; who loves God, obeys him.' An Arab poet said: 'You do not obey God, yet you pretend to love him, and that is unbelievable, for if you really loved him, you would obey him. For he who loves, obeys.'

Hypocrisy

Socrates[14] said to his followers: 'Watch that you be not obedient and disobedient towards God at the same time.' And they said: 'Explain to us what you mean', and he said: 'Put aside hypocrisy. For it is hypocrisy to pretend in men's presence to obey God, but in secret really not to believe.' One of his pupils asked him: 'Is there any other type of hypocrisy[15] of which man must beware?' Socrates said to him: 'Imagine a man who both openly and secretly shows himself as obedient to God, that he may be considered holy by men, and thereby be more honoured by them. Another man more subtle than the first, disregards this type of hypocrisy in order that he may be aided in a greater, for when he fasts or gives alms, and is asked if he has done this, he answers: "God knows!", or rather: "No", in order that he may be viewed with greater reverence, and that it may be said of him that he is no hypocrite, because he does not wish to brag about what he has done before people.[16] Also I believe that there are few who do not share in this hypocrisy in some way. See to it, therefore, that you be not led astray by this and deprived of the reward for your exertions. To prevent this happening, do everything with a pure heart, lest you seek to gain glory.' Another sage said:[17] 'When you lean firmly on God, wherever you go everything shall be favourable.'

The Ant, the Cock and the Dog

Balaam, who in Arabic is called Lukaman,[18] said to his son: 'My son, let not the ant be wiser than you for it collects in summer what it will live on in winter.[19] My son, let not the cock be more watchful than you, for he is vigilant in the mornings when you sleep. My son, let not the cock be stronger than you, for he keeps his ten wives strictly in check, when you cannot even chastise one.[20] My son, let not the dog be nobler of heart than you, for he forgets not those who have done him kindnesses, whereas you forget your benefactors. My son, do not think that one friend is too few, and do not imagine that a thousand friends is too many; for I tell you the following.'

I THE HALF FRIEND[21]

An Arab who was about to die called his son to him and said: 'Tell me, my son, how many friends have you gained during my life?' The son answered: 'A hundred friends, I think, I have gained.' The father said: 'A philosopher says that a man should not count a man as a friend, until he has proved his friendship.[22] I am much older than you and I have with difficulty obtained only half of one man as a friend. How is it that you have gained one hundred?[23] Go, then, and put all of them to the test, that you may know who of all of them is a real, true friend.' The son asked: 'How do you advise me to put them to the test?' The father explained: 'Kill a calf, cut it into pieces and put it in a sack; but let the bag be smeared with blood on the outside. When you come to a friend, say to him: "My dear friend, I have, even as you see, killed a man. I entreat you bury him in secret, for no one will suspect you, and in this manner you can save me."'

The son did as the father ordered. But the first friend to whom he came answered him: 'Put the body on your back and go. If you have committed evil, you must suffer the consequences. You shall never from this day forth enter my house.'

One by one he went round all his friends, and received the same response from all. Then finally he returned to his father and told him what had happened to him. The father said: 'What the philosopher meant when he said: "Many are a man's friends, when he counts them, but few when he has need of them", has happened to you.[24] Now go to the half a friend that I have, and see what he says to you.'

The son went to this man and addressed him in exactly the same words as the others. He said: 'Come in. This is no secret that one should withhold from neighbours.' He sent his wife out and with all his servants he dug the grave. When the son saw everything ready, he told him the entire truth and thanked him. Then he told his father of what he had done. The father said: 'It is of such a friend that the sage speaks when he says: "He is in truth a friend who helps you when the world has deserted you."'

Then the son asked the father: 'Do you know a man who has found himself a perfect friend?' And the father answered: 'I know him not, but I have heard of him.' The son said: 'Tell me of him; perhaps I shall find myself such a man.' And the father began.

II THE PERFECT FRIEND[25]

I have been told of two merchants of whom one lived in Egypt, and
the other in Baghdad. They knew each other solely by hearsay,
and used messengers to inform each other of necessary business.
One day the one who lived in Baghdad went on a journey to Egypt
for business reasons. When the Egyptian heard of his coming,
he welcomed him joyfully into his house and served him in all
things for eight days, as is the custom amongst friends, and offered
him all sorts of music which were practised in his house. After
eight days the guest fell ill, and the master of the house was greatly
grieved for his friend, and called all the doctors of Egypt to see his
beloved guest. The doctors felt his pulse, inspected his urine again
and again, but could come to no diagnosis.[26] So as they were
unable to recognise any bodily sickness, they diagnosed love
sickness.[27] When the master of the house heard that, he went to
him and asked him if there was any woman in his house whom he
loved. To which the sick man said: 'Show me all the women of
your house, and if I by chance find the cause of my sorrow amongst
them, I will tell you.' When his friend heard this he showed him his
singing girls and his chamber maids, but none pleased him. Then
he brought all his daughters forth, but these too just like the others
he pushed away and paid no attention to.[28] Now the master of the
house had a girl of noble family in his house, whom he had brought
up for a long time in all manner of knowledge with a view to marry-
ing her later. He showed her to his friend, and scarcely had the
sick man looked at her when he said: 'She is the one who means
life and death to me.'[29] And when the master of the house heard
this, he gave him the noble maiden as wife, together with everything
that was with her as dowry. And further, he gave him all that which
he had planned to give to the girl should he have married her.
When these things were done, the friend took his wife and all the
goods that had been yielded to him, and when he had completed
his business, he returned to his own country.

Afterwards it happened that the Egyptian lost all his wealth
in various ways, and became a pauper. So he thought to himself
that he would go to Baghdad to his friend that he knew there and
ask him for help. Naked and hungry, he made his way there and
came to Baghdad at an inopportune hour in the middle of the
night. He was prevented by shame from going to the house of his

friend, because he was afraid that he would not be recognised on such a night, and be turned away. Therefore he went into an old mosque to spend the night there. But he was full of cares and while he turned over in his mind all sorts of thoughts, there came two men into the area of this mosque in the city, one of them killed the other and secretly fled. At the alarm, many citizens rushed out of their houses, found the dead man, and went into the mosque hoping to find the murderer. They found the Egyptian there, and asked him who had murdered the man. The answer came: 'I killed him.' For he had suddenly conceived a strong desire to make an end to his misery by death. So he was taken and put in prison. The following morning he was brought forth from the prison, was condemned to death and brought to the gallows. As is the custom, many people came there, amongst them his friend for to see whom he had come to Baghdad. When this man looked at him more clearly, he recognised the friend with whom he had been in Egypt, and he thought of all the favours that had been done for him in Egypt, reflecting also that after death he would be no longer able to reward him and so decided to suffer death himself in his place. Therefore, he called out in a loud voice: 'Why do you condemn an innocent man, and drag him to the gallows? He has not merited death: I am the murderer.' And so he was seized, bound and dragged to the scaffold. The other man they set free from pain of death. But now there came into the crowd of people the real murderer, who saw everything and said to himself: 'I am the killer, and that man is condemned. He is innocent and will be brought to the scaffold; I am guilty and walk freely about. What is the cause of this injustice? It can only be God's forbearance. But God is a just judge, and leaves no crime unpunished. Therefore lest He wreak vengeance and punish me later and more severely, I shall now give myself up as the guilty one. Thus can I both grant life to these men, and atone for my own sin.' So he gave himself up to the perils of death and said: 'I am he who did it! Let the innocent man free!' The judges, however, wondered not a little and they had him bound, and gave the other his freedom. But they had doubts about their judgment so they took this man before the king together with the other two, who had been set free, and they told the king everything that had occurred, and forced him too to have doubts. So they all took council together and the king pardoned them every crime of which they had accused themselves, on the condition that they explained to him how it came about that they had been accused. So they told him the truth and with one accord were all acquitted. The man of Baghdad who had wished to die for his friend, let him into his house, gave him every honour as a guest and said to him: 'If you desire to remain here, we will share everything that belongs to each other; if however you wish to go back to your own dear land, so will I share equally with you all that belongs to me.' But the friend had a great longing to return to his land, and so he took from his friend the half of all that he owned and went home.

At this story the son said to the father: 'It is scarcely likely that a man could find such a friend.'

Secrecy

Another philosopher has spoken of friends who have not been tried or proved with the following words: 'Be wary of enemies once, but of friends a thousand times;[30] for perhaps one day your friend will be your enemy, and he will thus be able to do you wrong more easily.'[31] Another wise man said the same: 'When you ask someone for advice, be wary of the counsel he gives you unless you have already proved his reliability.' Again another philosopher has said: 'Give advice to your friend and be on his side even if he will not believe you, for it is just that you give him good advice, even if he rejects it and does not follow it.'[32] Another has said: 'Do not dissipate your advice on everyone, for whoever retains his advice in his heart, has the possibility of making an even better decision.'[33] Another has said: 'Advice that is kept in secret is imprisoned, as it were, and you are its keeper, but advice that has been made plain holds you in its thrall.'[34] Again another philosopher has said: 'Do not associate with enemies, when you can find other companions, for if you do evil, they will notice it, but if you do good, they will ignore it.' A poet says: 'It is one of the most objectionable facts of this age that a free man is obliged to ask help from an enemy.' In the same way an Arab was once asked: 'What was the worst experience you ever had?' The answer: 'The worst thing that happened to me was that I was once forced to seek out an enemy and ask him to do something for me.'

Evil Company

Someone has said: 'Never associate with a wanton, immoral

person,[35] for association with such people does not become your dignity.' Another has said: 'Do not glory in the praise of a lecher, for his praise of you is vituperation, and his vituperation praise.'

A philosopher was going along the road and he met another philosopher who was joking with an idle gossip. He said to him: 'It is the property of a magnet that like attracts like.'[36] The other man replied: 'I have never really been in this man's company.' The one who was passing on his way replied to him: 'Why then were you applauding him?' The other answered: 'I have not done so, but even an honourable man is forced by necessity to seek the latrine.'[37] Another philosopher has said: 'My son, it is difficult to climb up to lofty houses, but easy to fall from them.'[38]

Intelligence

The words of another philosopher are: 'It is better to have a wise man as an enemy than a fool for a friend.'[39] Another has said: 'Do not attach any great weight to the friendship of a foolish man, because it is not permanent.' Another philosopher has said: 'The society of a simple man educated amongst wise men is infinitely preferable to that of a wise man brought up amongst the morally loose.' Yet again has another philosopher said: 'For a wise man a hard life amongst wise men is preferable to a soft life amongst fools.' These are the words of another philosopher: 'There are two sorts of wisdom, one a man is born with, the other he gains through learning and experience. Neither of these, however, can exist without the other.' Yet another philosopher has this to say: 'Do not expect wisdom from stupid men, for this would be unfair to them; but at the same time do not deny wise men their intelligence, because you would be depriving them of what is theirs.'[40] Another said: 'The gifts of this world are of many types, for to some men is given wisdom, and to others possessions and wealth.'

A man once asked his son in the course of a conversation: 'Which would you prefer to be given, money or wisdom?' The son answered: 'Each of them has need of the other.'[41] There was once a famous poet, who was, however, penniless, and who was for ever bewailing his poverty to his friends. He even wrote a poem on the subject in which he expressed approximately the following: 'You who apportions out life's roles, tell me why mine is totally abandoned. You are not to blame, but tell me whom should I blame? If the stars have decreed my life to be a hard one, then this too is without a doubt your work. But you are both judge and council between me and my life's role.[42] You have given me wisdom without wealth; therefore tell me what can wisdom do without substance? Keep your wise man's role and give me the role of a rich man. Do not allow me to lack that the loss of which will be to my shame.' A philosopher has said: 'There are three ways to understand men's dependence on each other. When a person does another a good turn, by that very fact he is superior to the other; when a man needs nothing from another, then both are on exactly the same footing; but when a man has need of something from somebody, then is he inferior to him.'[43] Another has said: 'Wisdom makes the soul shine forth, whereas money merely creates fame for the material body.' Yet another said: 'Wisdom can with its light bring dead bodies back to life just as the wetness of rain makes green again an arid land.'[44]

Silence

A pupil asked his instructor: 'How should I conduct myself that I too may be counted amongst the wise disciples?' The teacher answered him: 'Remain silent until such time as it be necessary for you to speak! For the philosopher has said: "Silence is a token of wisdom; loquacity a sign of foolishness."'[45] Another advised: 'Do not rush to answer until the question be finished, and if a problem arises in the course of a discussion, do not rush to solve it, when you see amongst those present one who is wiser than you. Do not answer a question that has been directed at someone else, and be not eager to enter upon a matter of which you know nothing.[46] For a philosopher says: "He who seeks glory in a field of which he is ignorant, will be proved quite clearly a liar."' Another philosopher says: 'Agree with what is true and do not enquire whether you discovered it or some other person.'[47] Yet again it is said by another: 'Do not glory in your own wise words lest the statement of the sage be fulfilled in your case: "Whoever boasts of his own wise words, is proved an idiot."[48] If you follow all these maxims, then you will be counted amongst the wise and prudent disciples.'

A philosopher says: 'Whoever determines to conduct an investigation on reasonable lines, will also reach the right solution on reasonable lines.'[49] Another says: 'Whoever is ashamed to seek enlightenment from others, will be even more ashamed if others ask him for enlightenment,'[50] Another says: 'He who is ashamed to spend a period at school learning, will be ashamed for all time because of his lack of education.' Another points out: 'Not everyone who is termed wise is wise, but only he who learns and retains his wisdom.' Another states: 'Whoever is deficient in education will scarcely be helped by noble origins. Nobility has need of education, and intelligence needs experience.' Yet another has said: 'Whoever lacks nobility in himself, is in no way benefited by the nobility of his ancestors.' Another has stated: 'Nobility that comes from my own personal worth, is to me more worthy than that which I derive from my forebears.'[51]

III   THE THREE POETS[52]

There was once an Arab poet, very intelligent and amusing, but of lowly birth. He brought some verses to a king, and the king noted how clever they were and honoured him with all manner of honours. At this the other poets, who were of noble lineage, envied him and went to the king and said: 'Lord King, why do you so honour this fellow who is of such lowly birth?' The king answered: 'You thought that you were maligning him, but in fact you have paid him even greater honour.'[53] The man who had been maligned added the following words: 'No one blames the rose because it springs from amongst thorny thickets.' The king honoured him with rich gifts and sent him away kindly.

Now it happened that a poet born of noble parentage, but of slight capabilities, brought to a certain king some of his verses. When the king had heard them, he condemned them as being badly composed, and did not give the poet the usual present. At this the poet said to the king: 'If you will not give me anything for my verses, at least give me some reward for being noble.' The king then said: 'Who is your father?' The poet told him, and the king then replied: 'His seed has degenerated in you.' The poet riposted: 'It often happens, my lord, that weeds spring up in a field of corn.' In reply to this adage the king said: 'You have indeed shown yourself to be of much less virtue than your father'; and he dismissed him without any reward.

Yet again there came another poet to a king, whose father was of lowly birth, but whose mother was noble in her origins. His education was not widely based, and the verses he brought forward were badly put together. Now his mother had a brother, who was a master of literary form and very witty. The king received him without any great show of honour, and asked him whose son he was. The poet answered pretending that it was his maternal uncle at which the king roared with laughter. His courtiers enquired why he laughed so much and he explained.

IV THE MULE AND THE FOX[54]

Said the king: 'I read something once in a book of fables, and I can see it firmly fixed in front of my eyes.' The courtiers asked: 'What is the fable?' So the king told them.

'A fox found himself with a newly born mule in the pasture, and admiring it greatly asked: "Who are you then?" The mule answered that it was one of God's creatures, at which the fox asked: "Do you have a father and mother?" The mule answered: "My mother's brother is a noble steed."'

Now just as the mule did not want to acknowledge its father, the ass, because it is such a deformed and obstinate animal, so this wretch, too, is ashamed to name his father who is unknown because of his incompetence. Then the king turned to the poet and said: 'I would like you to show me your father.' The poet pointed him out to the king. The king recognised that his father was an insignificant and uneducated man, and he said to his servants: 'Give him something from our treasury, for the seed has not degenerated in him.'

True Nobility

An Arab said to his father: 'I am astonished that in times gone by men who were noble, or witty, or intelligent were viewed very highly, but now the only people to be respected are men of no morals.'[55] The father answered: 'You must not be surprised at this, for those who are educated respect the educated, those who are honoured the honourable, the witty their peers, and idlers idlers.' The son went on: 'Something else too have I noticed, namely that men of learning are not revered for their learning, and are become idlers[56] and thus obtain honour for themselves.' Then his father said: 'This is all part of the moral decline of the world.' Then the son asked: 'Please, dear father, give me a true definition of that which is called nobility.' The father explained: 'It is exactly as Aristotle describes it in his letter to Alexander.[57] The latter had asked him whom he should make his counsellor, and Aristotle answered him: "Choose a man who is instructed in the seven liberal arts, and well versed in the seven rules for good conduct, and well practised in the seven knightly skills; such a man I would consider to be representative of true nobility."' The son then said: 'But this nobility cannot be found amongst my contemporaries. The only nobility that I know depends entirely on gold and silver, as the poet says:

> He who is deprived of high birth, will become rich and
> famous,[58]
> But poverty oppresses even the noble family.

A poet has written some verses on the subject of the adversities of the world which befall those who are of noble birth: he puts them into the mouth of a nobleman, who speaks as follows: "Answer those who despise us for the misfortunes that befall us, and tell them that this world makes life difficult for the man who is noble. Can you not see that the sea brings up mist and spray from its surface, whereas the precious jewels sink to the bottom?[59] And can you not see that there is in the sky a huge number of stars, the exact number of which we do not know, and that not one of them except the sun and moon undergoes an eclipse?"'[60] The father answered: 'It is due to the unpleasantness of the world that men think that glory is only found in riches.'

The Seven Liberal Arts,[61] the Seven Knightly Skills and the Seven Rules of Good Conduct

A pupil asked his instructor the following question: 'There are seven subjects of study, seven skills that one must know, and seven precepts for good conduct. Please tell me what they are. and describe them in "order".' The master answered: 'I will do this. These are the subjects: Dialectic, Arithmetic, Geometry, Medicine, Music and Astronomy. Over the seventh, there is some dispute for the men of learning who admit the possibility of prophecies, say that Necromancy[62] is the seventh. Some however, who do not believe in prophecies, hold that Philosophy is the seventh subject, and others who do not bother themselves with philosophy, signify Grammar as the seventh subject. The skills that one must be acquainted with are as follows: Riding, swimming, archery, boxing, hawking, chess[63] and verse writing. The precepts for good conduct are: one should not eat too much, or drink too much, or be loose; nor should one harm anyone, lie to anyone, be envious of anyone, or keep bad company and conversation.'[64] The pupil said: 'In my opinion, no such man is alive today.'

Lying

A philosopher once corrected his son: 'Stay well clear of lying although it smell sweeter to you than the flesh of fowls.'[65] Another said: 'Although it is easy to tell a lie, why does it appear so difficult to tell the truth?' And yet another philosopher has said: 'If you are afraid to say something that you might rue, it is better to say "No" rather than "Yes".' Another has said: 'Walk on, lest the shame of saying "No" cause you to lie; for it is more honourable to deny something than to procrastinate forever over one's acceptance of it.'[66] Yet another has said: 'In this world the art of saying "No" is to always put off the questioner.' Another philosopher said: 'If someone does himself good by telling a lie, how much more good would he do himself by telling the truth.'

A plaintiff was once brought before the king as judge and though he denied the crime of which he stood accused, yet eventually he was convicted. The king said to him: 'You will be punished twice over; first for your crime, and second for not confessing to it.' There was another who was similarly on trial, but he did not deny that he had committed a crime. The judicial advisers of the king said: 'He will be punished for the offence he has committed.' 'No,' said the king, 'for the philosopher says, "who confesses to his crime, should be judged more mildly."' So he gave the man his freedom and let him go.

Socrates has said: 'Just as there is no room for a liar in the entourage of a prince, so too will he be shut out from the king of heaven's court.' A sage once said to his son: 'If a man says that evil can only be conquered by evil, they call him a liar; for even as fire cannot quench fire, so one evil cannot overcome another.[67] But just as water can be used to quench fire, so can one overcome evil by the use of good.' Another has said: 'Do not give evil in return for evil, lest you be placed on a par with evil men, but give good in return for evil, that you may be better than an evil man.' Another philosopher has said: 'Do not put your trust in an evil man, if you have escaped some danger, or you will find yourself once again in danger, and this time it is not certain that you will get out of it in the same way.' An Arab spoke to his son: 'If you see someone doing wrong, do not get mixed up with it! Whoever looses the weight from off its bearings, will find it falling on him.'[68]

V THE MAN AND THE SERPENT[69]

A man was once going through a wood and found a snake which had been stretched out by some shepherds and tied to stakes. He freed it, and tried to warm it in order to bring it back to life. As soon as the snake became alive again it began to wind itself around the man who was tending it and when the man was completely tied up in its coils, it started to choke him. The man then said: 'What are you doing? Why do you return evil for good done to you?' The serpent answered: 'I am only doing what my nature orders!' The man answered: 'I did you a good turn and you are now repaying me with evil?' They argued with each other to such an extent that a fox was called to judge the matter. The fox was told everything that had happened from the beginning, and then said: 'I cannot make a judgment in this matter on hearsay alone. I must see with my own eyes what originally happened between you.' So the snake was once again tied up as it had been before. 'Now, snake,' said the fox, 'if you can escape from that, do so. As for you, Man, do not bother yourself to free a snake. Have you never read that the weight falls on him who has removed the bearings from it?'

An Arab once said to his son: 'If you find yourself in difficulty and you have the possibility of escaping from it with ease, do not dally, for if you wait for a better opportunity, you will find yourself in even greater straits. Never let what happened to the hunchback and the poet, happen to you.' 'What happened there?' asked the son.[70] Then the father began.

VI   THE HUNCHBACK AND THE POET[71]

Once upon a time a poet wrote a poem and presented it to the king. The king praised his skill and ordered him to ask for something. The poet asked if he could be gate-keeper of his city for a month, and ask for a dinar from each hunchback,[72] a dinar from each scabby man, a dinar from each one-eyed man, a dinar from each leper, and a dinar from everyone with a rupture. The king granted this and confirmed it with a signed certificate. When the poet had obtained his request, he took up his place at the town gate and exercised his authority.

One day a hunchback arrived at the gates who was wearing a hooded cloak, and carrying a staff. The poet went up to him and demanded a dinar, but the hunchback refused. The poet seized him and wrenched off his hood, thereby discovering that the fellow was one-eyed too, so he asked him for two dinars, as previously he had demanded one. Again, the fellow refused to pay, so the poet held on to him. When the fellow saw that there was no way out, he tried to escape, but he was dragged back by his hood, which came off, thereby showing him to have a rash. At this the poet demanded three dinars. When the hunchback saw that he could neither escape nor find help to get him out of this awkward situation, he began to resist with force. His arms were thereby exposed, and it became clear that he had impetigo, so he was asked for a fourth dinar. As the man struggled the poet tore the lower half of his cloak, with the result that he was shown to be a hernia case too. At this the poet asked him for a fifth dinar. So it happened that the man who refused to give one dinar freely, was obliged to part with five against his will.

A wise man spoke to his son: 'My son, take care not to take your way through the abodes of evil men.[73] For passing through such places causes one to stop; stopping there makes one stay and by staying you get mixed up in evil doing.'

VII   THE TWO CLERKS WHO ENTERED A TAVERN[74]

The story is told that once two men of learning left their town one evening and went for a walk. Soon they came to a place where all the drinkers gathered. One of them said to the other: 'Let us change our route and take another way, for the sage says: "One must not make one's route through the habitations of evil men."' His companion answered: 'To pass through will not harm us, as long as nothing further happens.' As they were passing through the place they heard a song. And the second of the two men stopped and stood, held back by the sweetness of the song. His companion urged him to pass on, but he refused, and so after his friend had left, he remained alone, and led on by the song, entered the house. There, he received invitations from every side, and so he sat down and as soon as he had sat down, began to drink with all the others. But all of a sudden, there entered the drinking shop the prefect of the city, who was on the track of a spy who was fleeing the city. The spy had entered the drinking shop and the prefect had followed him. 'Here', said he, 'is where the spy is staying; from here he started out, and here will he return. You have all been his accomplices and fellows in crime.' And so all of them were led to execution, and the clerk amongst them. He exclaimed in a loud voice and preached to them all: 'Whoever enjoys the company of immoral men, must suffer the pains of death without doubt, even when he does not deserve it.'[75]

VIII   THE VOICE OF THE SCREECH-OWL[76]

The story is told that two students once had left a town and came to a place where they could hear the beautifully modulated voice of a woman. The words she sang were well arranged, and the musical form of the song fell on their ears most pleasingly and bewitchingly. One of them stood still, held by the song, but his companion said to him: 'Let us get away from here!' And they went away, whereupon the man said: 'Whoever hears the song of the bird and allows himself to be bewitched thereby, must surely die.' At this the man said: 'This voice is very much more beautiful than the one I heard once before with my teacher.' His companion asked: 'What was this voice? How came you to hear it?' The other told him: 'It happened that we were leaving the city, when we heard a voice that was very harsh; the song was completely lacking in any sort of musical order and the words too were without sense. Whoever was singing, often repeated the same thing. We lingered there in spite of the rough music as if we found pleasure in it. At this my master said to me: "If it is true that, as men say, the voice of the owl signifies a man's death, then that voice which is undoubtedly that of an owl, portends some death."[77] Thereupon I said to him: "I was marvelling why such a horrid song should provide such pleasure for that man." My teacher answered me: "Do you not remember the words of the philosopher who says: 'Mankind finds joy in three things, even if they are not well done, his own voice, his own poetry and his own dear son'?"[78]

As soon as this man had spoken of himself and his teacher, the two of them went away from there.

An Evil Wife

A philosopher said to his son: 'Follow a scorpion, a lion or a snake, but never follow an evil woman.'[79] Another philosopher has said: 'Pray God that he keep you free from the tricks of good-for-nothing women, and take care never to be led astray.'

It is said of a particular man of learning that he once came to a place where a bird-catcher had laid his net to catch birds, and he saw a woman flirting with this bird-catcher. The philosopher said to him: 'You who try to catch birds take care lest you too become a bird and be limed by this woman.'[80]

A pupil said once to his teacher: 'I have read in the books of the philosophers where the warning is given that a man must beware of the tricks of an evil woman. Solomon too warns against this in his book of Proverbs.[81] If you therefore know of any story or proverb concerning the guile of such a woman, please tell it to me, so that I can learn from it.' The teacher answered: 'This I will do as best I can, but I am afraid if naïve people read my story about the wiles and tricks[82] of women, a story I have written to admonish them and instruct you and others, where you can read how these women have without the knowledge of their husbands called their lovers to them and embraced them and kissed them and fulfilled all their lusts with them, I repeat, I am afraid, if all this be so, that they will naïvely believe that I too am as immoral as those women.' At this the pupil said: 'Do not be afraid on that count, Master, for Solomon in his book of Proverbs and many other sages also have written similar stories to hold up as blameworthy the depravity of women, and they have not gained blame themselves through this, but rather fame. If you for our useful instruction write in the same way of women, so will you too not receive blame but rather a crown of glory. Therefore, do not delay, but tell me now what I ask.' And so the teacher began.

IX   THE VINTNER[83]

A man went forth to harvest his vineyard. When his wife saw this, she thought to herself that he would be occupied for some time in the vineyard, and so she sent a messenger to her lover, and made ready a slight feast. But it happened that her husband was injured in his eye by a vine branch and went home quickly, as he could not see anything with his damaged eye. He came to the door of his house and knocked. When his wife realised who was there, she was very worried, and she hid her lover in her bedroom. Then she went to open the door for her husband. He came in, and being in great pain and trouble because of his eye, ordered his bed to be prepared in the bedroom, so that he might lie down. His wife was afraid lest he should go into the bedroom and see in front of him her lover who was hiding there, so she said to him: 'Why are you so eager to get to bed? Tell me first, beloved, what is grieving you?' So he then told her everything that had happened. She then said: 'Allow me, my most dear Lord, to attend your good eye with medicaments and charms, so that the good eye too, may not suffer the same as the other eye which has already been damaged. For your pain is mine also.' And with this she laid her mouth on his sound eye and kissed it until her lover removed himself from the place where he was hidden, without her husband noticing. Finally she stood up with these words: 'Dear husband, now I am sure that the same will not happen to this eye as happened to the other. You can now go to bed if you wish.'

At this the pupil said to his master: 'You have given me good instruction, master, and what you have told me of women's tricks, I have taken to my heart that is thirsty and desirous for knowledge. All this that I know from your story, I would not change for all the riches of Arabia. But if you wish to continue please do so and tell me of those things that I can utilise in my profession, when I too by virtue of my age will be asked for advice and guidance.' The master said he would do this.

X THE LINEN SHEET[84]

The story is told of a man who had a desire to journey overland, and who entrusted his wife to the safekeeping of his mother-in-law. His wife, however, loved another and told her mother of this. She took the daughter's part and favoured the relationship. She called the lover to her and sat down to eat with him and her daughter. While they were still eating, the lord of the house came back unexpectedly and banged on the door. The wife arose, hid her lover and then opened the doors for the master. He came in and ordered his bed to be made ready, because he wished to rest as he was exhausted. His wife was completely at a loss what to do, and this was noted by her mother who said: 'Do not rush to make up the bed, daughter. First we must show your husband the linen that we have woven.' With these words the old woman dragged out the linen from the chest, picked it up by getting hold of a corner and holding it as high as she could and gave the other corner to her daughter to hold. With the linen stretched out in this way, the husband was deceived, and in the meantime the lover managed to creep out whence he was hiding. Then the mother said to her daughter: 'Stretch the sheet over your husband's bed, for it has been woven by your hands and mine.' The husband remarked: 'And you, noble lady, do you know how to make such linen?' She answered: 'My son, I have made many such.'

At this the pupil said: 'What I have just heard is marvellous. But I pray you, instruct me further so that I may be better informed of the deception practised by women, and may therefore be more on my guard to keep myself protected.' The master answered him: 'Good; so I will tell you a third story, but you must be content with my stories that I give you to educate you.' The pupil said: 'Please, I will be content as you wish.' And so the master began.

XI THE SWORD[85]

Again the story is told, that a man desired to make a journey, and left his wife in the custody of his mother-in-law. But she was secretly in love with a young man, and she immediately told her mother about him, who favoured the liaison, and prepared a banquet to which she invited the young man. As they sat at table, the husband came home and banged on the door. The wife got up and let her husband into the house. Her mother stayed with the lover of her daughter, and as there was nowhere to hide him, she did not know what to do. But while her daughter was opening the door for her husband, the old woman seized a sword that was unsheathed, pushed it into the lover's hand, and ordered him to stand by the door with the unsheathed sword in his hand when the husband came in, and to give no answer if the husband addressed him. He did as he had been told.

When the door was opened, and the husband saw the young man there, he stopped short and asked: 'Who are you, then?' The lover made no answer, while the husband at first astonished, grew afraid. Then the old woman said: 'Dear son-in-law, keep silent, lest anyone hear you.' He, full of astonishment, asked: 'What does this mean, dear lady?' She then explained: 'My dear son, three people were pursuing this man and they chased him here and we opened the door and let him in with sword until they who wished to kill him should go away. But the young man in his anxiety took you for one of the pursuers and this is why he did not answer you.' Then the master of the household said: 'You have done well, noble lady, to save this young man from death in such a way.' And he came in and called his wife's lover to him and made him sit down and eat with him. He calmed him with sweet words, and when it was late evening let him go.

The pupil said: 'What you have just told me was quite remarkable. Now I wonder even more at the unheard-of audacity of women. But I would still wish you would tell me something more about their tricks, if it is no trouble to you, for the more you tell me, the more will I become dedicated to your service.' The master replied: 'What? Are you still not satisfied? I have told you three stories, and you still won't stop asking for more!' The pupil answered: 'By telling your three stories you have indeed increased the number of things related but there were but few words to hear. Tell me also a story that fills my ears with a richness of words. That should suffice me.' So the master answered: 'Take care that what happened between the king and his story-teller may not happen to us!' The pupil asked: 'What happened to these two then?' Then the master began the story.

XII THE KING AND HIS STORY-TELLER[86]

Once a king had a story-teller who every night used to relate five stories. It happened that the king still worried by the day's business could not sleep, and wished to hear more stories than usual. So the story-teller told him three extra stories, but kept them short. The king desired to hear more, but the story-teller had no desire whatsoever to continue because, as we have already seen, he had already told the king many tales. The king protested: 'You have told me a great number of stories already, true, but they were all short. I would like now to hear a story which needs many words to make its point, and then you may sleep.' The story-teller agreed and began:

'There was once a countryman who possessed a thousand solidi. He went to the market and bought himself 2,000 sheep, each one costing six dinar. When he was returning home, it happened that the brook became swollen with flood water and he was unable to cross it either by the bridge or the ford. Therefore he continued further up the brook and anxiously searched for a place at which he could put his sheep across. At last he found a small boat which would, however, only carry two sheep together with the farmer at a time. As there was no other way across, he put two sheep on board, and crossed over.'

After relating this, the story-teller fell asleep but the king woke him, and ordered him to finish the story he had begun. The story-teller replied: 'The river is broad, the skiff is very small and the flock of sheep is a big one. Allow the aforementioned farmer to transport his sheep across the river, and then I will finish the story I have begun?'

This was the method by which the story-teller pacified the king who wanted to hear longer stories. You have obliged me to follow up the stories already related with more, but I shall myself deliver from story-telling by quoting this example as a help to me.' The pupil protested: 'The old proverbs say that the man who is sorrowful because of money reasons, has not the same sorrow as the man who is troubled by his own body. The story-teller did not love his king as much as you love me, because he wanted to take advantage of the king with his story-telling, but you have no desire to do that to me, who am your pupil! Therefore I beseech you not to cut short the stories that you have already started, but rather tell me more of the guiles of womankind against which you have started to warn me!' Then the master continued.

XIII   THE WEEPING PUPPY DOG[87]

The tale is told of a certain man of noble birth who had a wife who was very beautiful and very chaste. It happened by chance that he desired to go to Rome to study oratory, but did not wish to leave his wife in any custody other than her own, for such was his trust in her honour and upright habits. And so he made ready his train of followers, and set out. His wife remained at home living chastely and prudently.

Now it happened that she found it necessary to leave her own house and go to visit a neighbour, which act she accomplished and returned home. But she had been seen by a young man who fell violently in love with her, and sent countless messages to her desiring that he might be loved by her for whom he himself burned with love. But she dismissed them and did not bother to answer them. The young man realised that he was disregarded and became so sorrowful that finally he became very ill. Time and again he went back to the place where he had first seen his lady when she had left her house, desiring to meet her, but he met with no success.

As he wept for love, he met an old woman dressed like a nun, who asked him what was the cause of his sorrow. But the youth did not wish to betray what troubled his soul. The old woman said to him: 'The more a sick man neglects to inform a doctor of what troubles him the worse becomes the sickness with which he is troubled.' When he heard this, the youth told her in order what had happened to him, and so betrayed his secret. The old woman said: 'With the help of God, I shall find a cure for these things you have told me of', and leaving him returned to her own house.

Now she had in her house a bitch puppy, and this she forced to fast for two days. On the third day she gave it bread that had been cooked with mustard. When the dog tasted this, its eyes began to weep due to the bitterness of the mustard.

After this the old woman went to the house of the chaste lady whom the young man loved so violently. The old woman was received by the lady with the greatest honours because of the impression of great holiness that she gave. She had the puppy with her. When the woman saw that the dog was weeping, she asked what was wrong with it and why it was weeping. The old woman replied: 'My dear friend, do not ask what causes it to be so, for the sorrow is so great that I cannot speak of it.' At this, however, the woman laboured all the more to be told the story, and the old woman said to her: 'This puppy which you see here, was once my daughter, a very chaste and beauteous girl. A certain youth loved her dearly but she was so chaste that she spurned him utterly, and rejected his love. He was struck by such sorrow that he became very sick, and for this sin is my daughter of whom I spoke most wretchedly changed into a dog.'

At these words the old woman broke down with grief and wept. The lady said to her: 'Dear lady, what shall I do, I who am guilty of a like sin? What, I say, shall I do? There is a young man who loves me too, but I have spurned him for love of chastity, and he, too, is affected in the same way.' The old woman answered: 'Dear friend, I advise you to act as quickly as you can and show mercy to this young man, and do as he asks, lest you, too, be changed into a puppy. For if I had known anything of the love of that young man for my daughter, she would never have been so changed.' The chaste lady answered her: 'I beseech you to give me some useful counsel that I may not lose my own form and be changed into a dog.' Said the old woman: 'Gladly, for love of God, and for the salvation of my soul will I seek out this young man for whom I too am as sorrowful as you are, and if I find him I will bring him to you.'

The young woman thanked her heartily, and in such a way did the crafty old woman give credibility to her words, and brought the young man whom she had promised to the lady's house, and so joined them together.

The pupil said to his teacher: 'I have never heard such a wondrous story: this, I believe, is the work of the devil.' And the master answered: 'There can be no doubt.' Said the pupil: 'I hope that a man who is clever enough to be always afraid of deception by a woman's guile, will perhaps be able to guard himself against the tricks of a woman.' The master answered: 'I have heard of a man who laboured much to guard his wife, but met with no success.' The pupil asked: 'Master, tell me what he did, so that, should I marry, I shall know how to guard my wife better.' Then the master began.

XIV   THE WELL[88]

There was once a young man who devoted all his energies, senses and time to learning every feminine trick, and having completed this study, he wished to marry. But first of all, he set about acquiring advice, and to this end he went to the wisest man of the region, and asked him how he could guard the wife whom he thought he would marry. The wise man listened and gave him the advice that he should build a house with high stone walls and place his wife within, give her enough to eat, and a not too luxurious supply of clothes. The house, said the wise man, should be so built that there was only one door, and only one window through which she might see, and this window should be placed at such a height, and constructed in such a way that no one could either enter or leave through it.

When the young man heard the advice of the wise man, he did as he was instructed. When he left the house in the morning, he locked the door and similarly when he came in, and when he was sleeping, he put the house keys under his pillow.

He acted thus for a long time, but one day, when the young man was at the market, his wife, as was her custom, went up to the window and intently watched the comings and goings. On this particular day, while she was standing at the window, she saw a young man who was handsome in both face and form. When she saw him, she was immediately set on fire with love for him.

As the woman loved the youth, and as she was guarded in the manner already outlined, she began to think of ways and means of arranging a rendezvous with the beloved youth. As she was a clever woman and full of guile, she thought that she would steal the keys while her husband slept. And so she did.

She developed the habit of filling her husband full of wine every evening and getting him drunk, so that she could more safely get out to see her friend and fulfil her desires. The husband who had learned from the advice of the wise man that none of a woman's actions are without some trick, began to wonder why his spouse was plying him with drink every day, and what she could be cooking up. Therefore, he pretended to be drunk so that he could keep her under his eye. But the wife did not know this, and one night she got out of bed, went to the door, opened it and went out to her friend. The husband got up slowly in the quiet of the night, went to the door of the house which he found open, and closed it with the bolt. Then he went up to the window and stood there until he saw his wife coming back clothed only in a night shirt.

When she approached the house, she found the door locked, and she was very worried and began to knock on the door. The husband heard and saw his wife, but pretended not to know her and asked who she was. The wife begged pardon for her sin, and promised never to do it again; but all to no avail, for the husband was angry, and said he would not let her in, but would show her parents what she was really like. The wife cried out more and more, and said that, unless he opened the door of the house, she would jump into the well that was near the house, and so put an end to her life, and that he would then have to account to her friends and relations for her death. The husband disregarded these threats, and continued not to allow his wife to enter. So the wife, full of craftiness and guile, picked up a stone and threw it into the well with the intention of making her husband think, when he heard the stone fall into the well, that she had fallen in. When she had done this, the wife hid herself behind the well.

The husband being simple-hearted and foolish and unknowing, when he heard the stone falling into the well, immediately rushed out of the house, and ran to the well, being really convinced that he had heard his wife fall in. When the wife saw that the door was now open, she forgot not her tricks but went in and locked the door. She then went up to the window.

When the husband saw that he had been deceived, he said: 'You false wife! You schemer of the devil! Let me enter, and believe me that whatever you have done will be forgiven you.' But she insulted him and prevented him from coming into the house in every way, and cursed him with oaths: 'You lecher, I shall show to your family what you are really like, and what you have done; how you go out secretly every night away from me and go to the brothel.'

And she did this. The parents thinking that what they heard was true, cursed him. Thus did the woman through her guile deliver herself from her crime, and piled the disgrace that was nightly hers on the head of her husband. It did him little good keeping close check on his wife, but rather a great deal of harm, for the worst thing about his misery was that he was held by the majority to have suffered what he deserved. So he was robbed of goods and dignity, his name fouled in the mud, and he suffered the punishment of an accusation of incontinence all because of his wife's evil tongue.

The Good Wife

The pupil said: 'There is no one who can protect himself against the trickery of women unless he be protected by God. This story which I have just heard is a warning to me not to marry.' The master said: 'You must not think that all women are like that. In many women one finds great goodness and chastity, and you must know that in a good woman one finds good company, and that such a woman is both a good home and a faithful guard. At the end of the Proverbs Solomon has written twenty-two verses on the honour and virtue of a good woman.'[89] To this the pupil said: 'You have once more given me courage! But have you ever heard of any woman who has used her intelligence to do some good?' The master answered: 'I have heard of such a woman.' So the pupil asked: 'Please tell me about her, because to me it seems something new.' The teacher told this story.

XV   THE TEN CHESTS[90]

I was once told of how a Spaniard journeyed to Mecca, and while on his journey went through Egypt. As he had a desire to go into the desert and cross it, he thought that he would leave his money in Egypt. So before he actually decided to leave his money, he asked if there was a trustworthy man in that region to whom he might entrust his money. The local people pointed out an old man whose trustworthiness and uprighteousness were famous. So he gave this man more than a thousand talents of his money. Then he started out and after the completion of his journey returned to the man to whom he had entrusted his money and asked for the return of what had been deposited with him. But this man showed himself to be full of wickedness, and said that he had never seen him before in his life.

When the Spaniard saw that he had been deceived, he went to the local worthies, and explained to them how the man to whom he had entrusted his money had dealt with him. But, as they were neighbours of the fellow, they did not wish to believe what they heard, and so said that it was nothing. But the man who had lost the money went one day to the house of the man who was wrongly holding back his money and with honeyed words asked him to return the money. When the deceiver heard this, he abused him and told him not to come to his house again, nor to make any more such accusations: he added that should he do this, he would be suitably punished.

When he heard these threats from this deceiver, the Spaniard sadly went away, but as he was going along the street he met an old woman dressed in the trappings of a holy hermit. She was walking along propping her feeble limbs on a stick, and moving the stones of the road lest passers-by should strike their feet,[91] praising God the while. When she saw the man weeping, she recognised him as a foreigner, she was moved by pity for him and called him and asked him what had happened. He told her everything in order. When the woman had heard what he said she spoke: 'My friend, if what you report is true, I shall help you.' He said: 'How can you do that, handmaiden of God?' She answered: 'Bring me a man from your country, whom you trust in both actions and words.' So the Spaniard brought such a man.

The old woman told this fellow countryman to buy ten chests picked out in precious colours on the outside, with silver plated clasps and good locks, and the inside full of pebbles, and to take these to the house of his host. When the woman saw that everything had been prepared in accordance with her instructions, she said: 'Now look for ten men who will together with me and your compatriot carry the chests to the house of the man who deceived your friend in a long file one after the other. As soon as the first arrives at your deceiver's house and stays there, you must come and claim your money. And I am sure, for such is my trust in God, that your money will be returned to you.'

So everything that the old woman said was carried out, and she did not forget, but went her way, and came together with the Spaniard's friend to the house of the defrauder. She said, 'I have a Spaniard who wishes to go to Mecca staying as a guest with me, but before he goes he wants to find a trustworthy person with whom to leave his money which is in ten cases, until he comes back. Therefore, I ask you to do me a favour and keep and protect them in your house. I have heard it on good authority that you are an upright and trustworthy man, and I do not wish anyone, except you to have the safe-keeping of this money.' While she was speaking, the first bearer came with his chest, while the others could be seen in the distance.

Meanwhile the man who had been defrauded of his money did not forget what the old woman had told him, and came after the first chest had arrived, as he had been ordered to do. Now he who had hidden the money, was afraid in his wickedness and cunning when he saw the Spaniard arrive, for he thought that if the Spaniard asked for his money, the other who was bringing would not entrust it to his care. So he went out to meet the Spaniard, saying: 'My dear friend, where have you been all this time? Come in and take your money that has been entrusted to me for so long, for I have found it and I no longer wish to be burdened in guarding it.'

At this the Spaniard was overjoyed, and thankfully took his money. When the old woman saw that the man now had his money again, she got up and said: 'Now will I and my guest go for our chests and hasten their delivery to you. Wait for our return, and look after what we have already brought.' And he was delighted, and guarded well what he had already received, and awaited their return—which he may still be doing to this day. So it was that the Spaniard regained his money through the crafty idea of the old woman.

The pupil said: 'That was a wonderfully useful idea; in my opinion, no philosopher could have thought of a more subtle trick by which the injured party might more easily regain his money.'

The master answered: 'A philosopher could easily do this by means of his own innate intelligence and additional training which he has gained by investigation of the secrets of nature. The old woman, however, was successful solely because of her native wit.' The pupil said: 'Indeed, I believe that to be so. But if you have laid up anything of this type gained from the sages in the library[92] of your spirit, I beg you tell me your pupil, and I will commend it to my faithful memory so that sometime I may be able to set before my fellow students who here in school are nurtured on the milk of wisdom,[93] a tasty dish.'

XVI   TEN OIL VATS[94]

It happened that a man had a son to whom at his death he left nothing except a house. This son by dint of great personal exertion was scarcely able to provide even the necessities of life for himself, but he did not wish to sell his house, no matter how hard necessity pinched him. Now this son had a very rich neighbour who strongly wanted to buy his house to make his own bigger. The young man, however, would not sell either for money or when beseeched. When the rich man saw this he fell to thinking what tricks and means he could use to wrest the house from the young man, who, however, inasmuch as he was able, refused to have anything to do with him.

Eventually, the rich man was very much vexed on account of the house and because he was unable to deceive the lad, and so he came to him one day and said: 'Young man, grant me a small part of your yard at a price, as I have ten oil vats that I wish to store underground. This will harm you in no way, but rather will you gain from this some help for your household costs.' The young man gave in to necessity and gave him the keys to his house.

Meanwhile he went after profit, as was his custom, by serving free men freely. The rich man after receiving the keys dug up the yard of the young man and placed there five tuns full of oil and five half-full. After this he called the young man and gave him back the keys of the house and said: 'My friend, I entrust my oil to you, and place it in your custody.' The young man, ingenuous as he was, believed that all the tuns were full of oil and took them into his keeping.

After some long lapse of time, it happened that oil became expensive in that country, and the rich man seeing this said to the young man: 'My friend, come and help me dig up my oil which I left in your custody some time ago. You will receive payment for your work and guardianship.' When the young man heard this request he determined to help the rich man as much as he could.

The rich man, however, was mindful of his own craft and brought up buyers for the oil. In the presence of these folk they dug up the earth and found five barrels full and five half-full. When this fact was observed, he called the young man and said: 'Friend, I have lost my oil through your guarding it, for you have fraudulently abstracted some it. Therefore I desire that you restore what is mine to me.'

When he had said this he seized him and took him against his will before the justice, and when the judge saw him he opened the prosecution, but the young man knew nothing of what sort of reply he should make to this accusation. However, he asked for the case to be put off one day. This was granted by the judge, as indeed was only right and just.

Now in that city there lived a sage who was named 'Helper of the Needy'. He was a good religious man. The young man, who had heard the fame of this man's goodness, went to him and begged his advice saying: 'If those things I have heard of you on the authority of many are true, please come and help me, for I am unjustly accused.'

When the philosopher heard the young man's plea, he asked him straight out if they accused him justly or unjustly. The young man swore on his oath that he had been unjustly accused. At this the philosopher saw that he was dealing with an honourable matter, and was moved by brotherly charity and said: 'With God's aid I shall help you, but as you have received from the judge postponement until tomorrow, you must on no account miss the appointed time, and I will be there ready to help your true statements and damage their lies.'

So the young man did as instructed, and the morning after, the philosopher came to the court. When the judge saw him, he called him to sit beside him,[95] as he was another learned and wise man. Then the judge called the accused and the prosecutor and ordered them to explain their cases. This they did, and as the two parties were on the spot the judge said to the philosopher that he should listen to their pleas and make a judgment. At this the philosopher said: 'Sir judge, order the oil to be measured out of the five full barrels, and you shall know how much liquid oil is there. Do exactly the same with those five that are half-full, that again you may know how much liquid oil was there. Then may the oil that has thickness be measured in the five full barrels,[96] and from that you shall know how much thick oil was there. Do exactly the same with the five half-full barrels, and again you shall know how much thick oil was in them. If you find as much thick oil in the half-full barrels as in the full, you know that oil has been stolen. If, however, you find in the half-full barrels a percentage of thick oil corresponding to that of the liquid oil that was in them, which you can also find in the full barrels, then you know that no oil has been stolen.'

When he heard this, the judge confirmed the judgment and so it was enacted. Thus the young man escaped through the cleverness of the philosopher. Then the philosopher said to him: 'Have you never heard that philosophers' saying: "Do not buy a house before you know your neighbour?"' The young man answered: 'We had this house before ever this fellow moved in next door.' The wise man answered him: 'Sell your house rather than remain next to a bad neighbour.'

The pupil said after this tale: 'That is really the opinion of a wise man. Thanks be to the grace of God, he was rightly called "Helper of the Needy",' and he went on: 'Even though what I have heard fills my spirit, one is still driven on by the desire to hear more.' The master said: 'Gladly I will tell you more', and he began as follows:

XVII THE GOLDEN SERPENT[97]

The story is told that a rich man was on the way to his city with a sack of a thousand talents on the top of which there lay a golden brooch in the shape of a serpent, with eyes of amethyst.[98] The man lost the whole thing. Now a poor man came along the road, found the treasure, gave it to his wife and told her how he had come upon it. His wife listened to him and said: 'Let us keep what God has granted us.'

The next day a herald came along the road and he cried out: 'Whosoever has found such and such a treasure, let him return it, and he will receive a hundred talents' reward if all is correct. At this the man who had found the treasure said to his wife: 'We will give back the treasure, and thus we will gain a hundred talents without committing a sin.' To which the wife answered: 'If God had not willed that we should have his treasure, he would never have lost it.[99] What God has granted us, let us keep.' The man, however, who had found the treasure, wished strongly to return it but his wife resisted in every way. But the husband, disregarding what his wife wished or did not wish, returned the treasure and asked for the reward of which the herald had spoken. The rich man, however, full of evil, answered: 'I know that a second serpent is missing.' He said this with the disgusting intention of depriving the poor man of the promised talents. The poor man answered that he had found nothing else.

Now the people of that city came and they were on the side of the rich man, and so they blamed the poor man, and whipping up an inexorable hatred against the poor man for finding the treasure, dragged him before the judge.

The poor man cried out and swore that he had found nothing else, as has already been told. As this case of the poor and rich man passed from mouth to mouth, at length the news reached the ears of the king through the medium of his courtiers. As soon as he heard, he ordered both the rich man and the poor to present themselves before him with the money.

When they were all there, the king called for the philosopher called the 'Helper of the Needy' to come before him together with other wise men, and ordered them to listen to the depositions of both parties and clarify the matter. When the philosopher heard this order, he was moved by pity for the poor man, and he called him to him and secretly said to him: 'Tell me, brother, if you have in fact kept anything of this man's money. If you have not, with the help of God, I shall try to free you.' The poor man answered: 'God knows that I have returned what I found.'

At this the philosopher said to the king: 'If it pleases you to hear the right judgment on this matter, I shall speak it.' At this the king asked him to speak, and so the wise man said to the king: 'This rich man is a very good and eminently credible person and has ample warrant for his love of truth, and therefore it is unbelievable that he should ask for something that he has not lost. On the other hand it seems equally credible to me that this poor man who is accused found no more than he gave back, because if he were a cheat he would not have given back what he did, but would have retained everything.' The king asked the philosopher what his judgment was in the matter. He answered: 'Your majesty, call for the treasure and give the poor man a hundred talents, and keep what remains until someone comes who shall ask for this treasure, for the man to whom it belongs is not here. And let this rich man go to the herald and ask him to enquire after a sack with two serpents.'

This judgment was to the liking of the king, as it was to all the others who were present. But the rich man who had lost the sack when he heard it, said: 'Good king, I tell you that this treasure is really my property, but because I did not wish to give the reward to this poor man who was made known to me by the crier, I asserted that there was another serpent which belonged to me, and was missing. Only show me mercy, my king, and I will give the poor man what the crier spoke of.' So the king gave the wealthy man his treasure and he the poor man his reward. In such a manner did the philosopher by his sense and inspiration free the poor man.

The pupil remarked: 'This really shows the spirit of wisdom. People would wonder at this illustration no more than at the judgment delivered by Solomon in the case of the two women.'[100]

The Society of Aliens

A philosopher said: 'Do not undertake a journey with anyone unless you know him already![101] If someone that you do not know joins you *en route*, and enquires after your proposed journey, tell him that you wish to go further than you have decided. If he draws a lance on you, turn to the right and if a sword, turn to the left.'

The Utilisation of High Roads[102]

An Arab admonished his son with these words: 'Follow the main roads even if they are a longer way round than the footpaths.' And the same: 'Take a young girl to wife even if she is a little bit old.' And again: 'Take your goods to great cities even if you believe that you will sell there more cheaply.' The son answered: 'What you have said about high roads is true.'

XVIII   THE FOOTPATH[103]

One day I and some friends were on a way to a town. It was nearly sunset and we were still some way from the city, when we saw a path which, as far as we could ascertain, offered us a short cut to the city. We came upon an old man, from whom we asked advice concerning the route via this path. He said: 'The path is nearer to the city than the high road, but you will arrive quicker at the city by taking the high road rather than the path.' When we heard this, we took him for a fool, so we left the main road and took to the path. We followed it first to left then to right, and when night fell, we had gone very much astray, and had not reached the city. Had we stuck to the main road, however, we would have indubitably been already within the city gates.

The Ford

Following upon this story the father told this tale: 'This happened once to us when we were on the main road to some city or other.

It happened like this. In front of us was a river which we had to cross somehow or other before we could arrive at the city. We were marching along, when the road forked, one fork leading to the town via a ford, the other via a bridge. We saw an old man and asked him which of the two routes would bring us more quickly to the town. He answered: 'The road through the ford is nearer by two miles to the town than via the bridge. But you will come more quickly to the town if you take the bridge route.'

Some of our people laughed at the old man, just as did some of yours in the earlier story, and set out through the ford. Some of them lost their companions through drowning, others their horses and baggage, many bemoaned their sodden clothes, and others the fact that they had lost their clothes. We, however, went with our old man over the bridge, and arrived on the other side with no trouble or misfortune and found them on the further bank of the river terribly upset at their loss. The old man said to them as they stood weeping and searching the depths of the river with sickles and nets: 'If you had come via the bridge, you would not have this trouble.' They answered him: 'We did this because we did not wish to delay our journey.' The old man answered: 'Now you have an even greater delay.'

We left them and went happily through the gates of the city.

Such is a proverb that I heard once: 'The long way to heaven is better than the short one to hell.'[104]

An Arab admonished his son: 'My son, if on a journey with a fellow traveller, love him as yourself, and think not to deceive a person, lest you too be deceived[105] as happened to the two townsmen and the countryman.' The son said: 'Tell me, father, that posterity may gain something useful.' And so the father began.

XIX   THE TWO TOWNSFOLK AND THE COUNTRYMAN[106]

The story is told of two city men and a countryman who were making the pilgrimage to Mecca. They had common arrangements for food, but when they were approaching Mecca, their food ran out, so that they did not even have enough flour to make even one small loaf. The two townsmen said to each other when they noticed this: 'We have only a little bread, and our companion is a big eater. We must find some way of cheating him of his portion of bread and eating it ourselves.' So they arranged together that they would make a loaf and bake it and sleep while it was baking, and whichever of them had the most marvellous dream would have the bread all to himself. They said all this with the idea that the countryman was too stupid for such a trick. So they made a loaf, put it to bake in the fire, lay down and slept. But the countryman who had seen through their plan, took the half-cooked loaf out of the fire, ate it and went back to sleep.

One of the townsmen however was terrified by a dream and woke up. He said to his companion: 'What have you to tell?' The other related that he had had a wonderful dream, and that in his dream two angels had opened the gates of heaven, taken him up and placed him before the face of God. The other said when he heard this, that what his companion had dreamed was indeed marvellous, but that he had dreamed that two angels had led him from earth down into hell. The countryman heard all of this, but pretended to be still asleep. The two townsmen were deceived by this even as they themselves wished to deceive the other and called the countryman to wake up. He craftily acted as if terrified and answered: 'Who calls me?' They answered: 'We, your companions on the journey.'

The countryman said: 'Are you back now?' They answered: 'Where have we been, that we are due to return?' The countryman then related how he had dreamed of two angels who had taken one of them and opening the gates of heaven had led him before God, and how two others had taken the other and opening the earth had led him into hell. 'When I saw this', he said, 'I thought that neither of you would come back, so I got up and ate the bread.'

The father decreed: 'My son, this is what happened to those who wished to deceive their fellow traveller, and who were themselves deceived by his sharpness of wit.' The son said: 'They met with the same fate as is mentioned in the proverb: "Whoever wants everything, loses everything."[107] This is the nature of the dog, and on this they modelled themselves. For one dog will steal food of another. If, however, they had imitated the nature of the camel, then they would have had as a model a milder nature, for the nature of the camel is such that if food is offered to many of them at the same time, none will eat until all can at one and the same time. And if one of them is so sick as to be unable to eat, then all the others fast until that one is removed from amongst them.[108] Those two townsmen, if they wanted to take on the nature of an animal, should have taken to themselves the nature of the mildest animal. They deserved to lose their food. Indeed I would have wished that the same had happened to them as happened in the old story I heard from my teacher. In that story the king's tailor, because of his pupil Nedui, received a beating with staves.'

Hearing this the father said: 'Tell me, my son, what you have heard? What happened to the pupil? Such a story will be a joy and delight to heart and soul.' And so the son began.

XX NEDUI THE PUPIL OF THE ROYAL TAILOR[109]

My teacher told me how once a king had a tailor who attended to the cutting of different garments for different occasions for the king. This tailor had many apprentices each of whom laboured with great skill to sew up what the master tailor of the king had with the greatest skill cut out. Amongst the lads was one called Nedui, who could sew better than all his fellows.

Now as a feast day drew near, the king called his tailor to him and ordered him to prepare costly garments for himself and his court for the festal occasion. To facilitate and expediate this he ordered a eunuch who was one of his chamberlains, whose job it was to look after such matters, to guard the tailors and asked him to provide them with all things necessary for their task, and watch their fingers. One day the servants gave the tailor and his companions some warm bread with honey[110] with other dishes. Those who were there began to eat. The eunuch said to them as they feasted: 'Master, why have you started to eat when Nedui is not here, rather than waiting for him?' The master tailor answered: 'He wouldn't eat honey even if he were here.' And they all set to their food.

At length Nedui appeared and asked why they had eaten in his absence, and had not even saved his share. The eunuch answered that the master had told them that he would not have eaten honey even if he had been there. So Nedui kept silent and thought of ways that he could repay his master for this.

After the meal was ended, the master went out, and Nedui whispered to the eunuch: 'Sir, my master sometimes suffers from a madness, loses his wits and sets upon those who are present completely madly, and is extremely dangerous.' The eunuch said: 'If I knew the moment that this would happen, I could tie him up with thongs and chastise him to prevent him from doing something untoward.' Nedui said to him: 'If you see him looking here and there, striking the floor with his hands, rising from his seat and moving the stool he was sitting on, then you know he is having an attack, and if you do not do something for yourself and your fellows, you will all have sore heads.' The eunuch answered: 'May God bless you for telling me how to take care of myself and my companions.'

After telling the eunuch all this, Nedui on the following day hid his master's scissors. The cutter searched for his scissors, and on not finding them began to feel around on the floor with his hands, looking here and there, and standing up moved the stool he had been sitting on to one side. When the eunuch saw this he immediately called his men and ordered them to bind the tailor and beat him hard lest he should strike everyone else. The tailor however cried out: 'What have I done? Why do you beat me thus?' But he received no answer, but was rather beaten the harder. When they became tired of beating him, and he of the beating, they left him half-alive. He breathed again and after some while enquired of the eunuch what he had done. The eunuch answered him: 'Your pupil Nedui told me that sometimes you became insane and could only be calmed if bound and beaten, and for that reason I caused you to be bound and beaten.'

When the tailor heard this he called Nedui and asked him: 'My friend, how long have you known that I was insane?' His pupil answered him: 'Since the time that you knew that I didn't eat honey.' At this the eunuch and the others laughed and adjudged that both had received suitable punishment.

The father remarked of the story that what had happened, had happened justly and that if the precept of Moses had been obeyed, that a man must love his brother as himself,[111] none of this would have come about.

A wise man was advising his son in the following theme: 'Take care never to impute any crime to your companion whether it be in jest or earnest, lest what occurred in the case of the two jugglers before the king should happen to you.' The son said: 'Tell me this story, please, father,' and the father answered: 'Good, it shall be done.'

XXI   THE TWO MINSTRELS[112]

Once a minstrel came to a king. The king called him to him and made him sit down and eat with another minstrel. The first of these minstrels, however, began to be envious of the newcomer whom the king and all his courtiers preferred to him. And so to prevent this state of affairs from continuing, he began to think of ways of shaming the other so that he would of his own accord go away. So while all were eating, this minstrel secretly collected all the bones and laid them in front of his colleague. When the meal was finished he pointed out the stacked up heaps of bones, and said sarcastically: 'My lord, my colleague has eaten up everything that was on these bones.' The king gave him a grim look, but the accused said: 'My lord, I have done what my nature, which is human, demanded. I have eaten the meat and left the bones. My colleague has done what his nature, which is that of a dog, demanded. He has eaten both flesh and bones.'

The Generous Man, the Miser and the Spendthrift

A wise man has said: 'Honour him who has less than you and give him of your goods as much as you wish, that the man over you may honour you more, and give you some of his property.' Another has said: 'For a rich man to be a miser is a great disgrace; for a man of moderate means it is a fine thing to be generous.' The pupil said: 'Please define for me what is a generous man, a miser and a spendthrift.' The father answered: 'The man is generous who gives to those who are in need, and refuses to give to those who have no need. The miser refuses to give both to those to whom giving is forbidden, and to those to whom it is not forbidden. He who gives to both those in need and those not in need is a spendthrift.'[113]

Riches

Another philosopher has said: 'Do not associate yourself with a failing concern and do not hesitate to take part in a growing matter.'[114] Another said: 'A little happiness is better than a house full of gold and silver', and yet another said: 'What is useful pursue with greatest attention, but not with great speed.' Another has said: 'Look not with jealousy upon the man who is richer than you, lest you sin against God, but rather look upon him who is poorer than you, that you may thank God for your well being.' Another has said: 'If you are poor, do not deny God, and if rich do not be proud.' Another says: 'He who desires much, is always ill in his hunger for more.'[115] Another says: 'If you desire to have in this world only so much as is demanded by nature, then it will not be suitable for you to collect riches. But if you wish to satisfy a greedy mind, you may collect together all the wealth of the world and yet still burn with a thirst for possession.' Yet another philosopher has said: 'He who spends his wealth sparingly, will have his possessions a long time.' Another says: 'The root of peace lies in not wishing for another's goods, and the fruit of peace is to have tranquillity.' Another again says: 'The man who wished to leave the world sees to it that he keeps nothing by him that belongs to the world; for not to do so would be tantamount to trying to extinguish a fire with sticks.' Yet another said: 'The man who hoards money works much, and worries himself into insomnia for fear of losing it. But at the last he has the sorrow of losing what he has gained.'

The pupil asked the master: 'Do you advise me to acquire money?' The master answered: 'Yes, make money, but fairly and spend it right and for good purposes, and do not hoard it as a treasure.' Another says: 'Do not covet another's goods and be not sorrowful about things you have lost, for you can recover nothing by weeping.' The story is told, based on this, of:

XXII THE COUNTRYMAN AND THE LITTLE BIRD[116]

Now a certain man had a garden in which flowed streamlets, and fresh green grass grew. Because of the beauty of the place the birds found it most agreeable, and used to come there and with delightful voices sing their many different songs. One day, when the master of this little garden was tired and was taking his ease, a bird sat on one of the branches and sang most delightfully. As soon as the man saw it and heard its song, he lassoed it with a sling. The bird said to him: 'Why have you expended so much toil to catch me? What need of me have you that you have captured me?' The man answered: 'I am desirous to hear your song.' The bird replied to this: 'On no account! So long as I am in captivity, I will never sing either for reward or in answer to entreaties.' The man answered: 'If you do not sing, I shall eat you.' And the bird answered this: 'How will you eat me? If you boil me to eat me, what use will such a little bird be? Even the flesh will be tough. If you roast me, I shall be even smaller. If, however, you let me go free, I shall be most useful to you.'

The man hearing this asked the bird: 'What sort of use would you be to me?' The bird replied: 'I shall tell you the three rules of life, which will do you more good than the flesh of three bullocks.' The man was confident in the promise and freed the bird. Now the bird said to him: 'The first of the promised rules is this: do not believe everything that is said. The second: what is yours you will always possess. The third: be not sorrowful if you lose something.'

When the bird had said this it flew up into a tree and began to sing sweetly: 'Praised be God who has closed the light of your eyes and taken your wisdom from you! For had you searched the coils of my intestines you would have found a jewel weighing a pound.' At this the man began to weep and bemoan and strike his breast with his hand that he had trusted the words of the little bird. But the bird said to him: 'You have very quickly forgotten the sentence I told you. Did I not say to you: "Do not believe everything that is said!" How can you take a jewel from me which is a pound in weight when I do not as a whole weigh so much. And did I not also say: what is yours you will always possess? How then can you take a jewel from me when I am flying in the sky? And did I not say too: be not sorrowful if you lose something? Why then are you so sorrowful because of that precious stone which is inside me?'

When the bird had mocked the countryman with these words, it flew off into the broad wood.

Books That Are Not To Be Believed

A philosopher was teaching his son with the following words: 'Read whatever you find, but do not believe all that you read!' The pupil said: 'I believe that this is so. What is found in the books is not true, for I read something similar in the sayings of the philosophers, namely, there are many trees, but not all bear fruit; many bear fruit, but it is not all edible fruit.'[117] An Arab was teaching his son, and he said to him: 'My son, do not abandon the present for the future, in case you lose both, as happened to the wolf when the two oxen had been promised to him by the countryman.'

XXIII THE OXEN WHICH THE COUNTRYMAN HAD PROMISED TO THE WOLF, AND THE JUDGMENT OF THE FOX[118]

The story is told that the oxen of a countryman would not stay on the right path. He said to them: 'The wolf will eat you up.'[119] Now the wolf heard this and was very pleased and so as the day drew near to evening, when the countryman had loosed the oxen from the plough the wolf came to him and said: 'Give me the oxen which you promised me.' The peasant answered: 'If I ever said such a thing, I never confirmed it by oath.' The wolf replied: 'I must have the oxen that you granted to me.' So the two agreed to go before a judge.[120] On the way they met a fox and this crafty beast asked them: 'Where are you going?' So they told the fox what had happened, and the fox answered them: 'You have no need to look any further for a judge, for I shall deliver a right judgment on the case between you. But first allow me to speak first with one of you and then with the other. If I can succeed in reconciling both of you without a court case, there will be no need of a public judgment. If not, then it must be dealt with in public.' Both of them agreed with this.

The fox first took the countryman to one side and spoke to him: 'Give me a hen, and my wife one too, and you shall have your oxen.' The ploughman agreed. Then the fox spoke as follows with the wolf: 'Listen, my friend, because of the services you have already rendered, I am bound to employ all my eloquence on your behalf. I have arranged things with the countryman so that he will give you a cheese as big as a great round shield if you leave his oxen in peace.' The wolf agreed to this, and the fox added: 'Let the peasant lead away his oxen and I will bring you to a place where this man's cheeses are made, so that you can choose from many the one you want.'

So the wolf, deceived by the words of the crafty fox, allowed the the countryman to go away undisturbed. The fox, however, led the wolf here and there and, inasmuch as he was able, confused the wolf, eventually leading him as night fell, to a deep well. The wolf stood on the edge of the well and the fox pointed out to the wolf the form of a half moon that was mirrored in the depths of the well, and said: 'There is the cheese I promised you. Go down if you wish, and eat it up.'[121] The wolf answered: 'You go down first, and if you cannot bring it up unaided, when I will help you and do as you advise.' When the wolf had said this, they saw a rope hanging down into the well and on the end of this was fastened a bucket and on the other end another bucket. These buckets were so arranged that when one went up the other went down.

Scarcely had the fox realised this, than he acted to carry out the wolf's request, and sat in one bucket and went off to the bottom of the well. The wolf was very glad at this, and said: 'Why do you not bring my cheese up?' The fox answered: 'I cannot, it is too big. Get into the other bucket and come down as you promised.' So the wolf sat in the bucket, and because of his great weight, rushed rapidly down to the bottom of the well. The other bucket, however, that contained the fox, who was much lighter, shot up to the top of the well. As soon as the little fox saw the edge of the well, it leapt out of the bucket, and let the wolf fall back to the bottom.

Thus the wolf that spurned what was before it for what was in the future, lost both oxen and cheese.

The Taking and Approving of Advice

An Arab taught his son as follows: 'Take advice from a man who has experience of the subject of which you are enquiring. This way you will have cheaper advice than if you yourself ran the risk of acquiring this experience.' Another gave his son the following counsel: 'Do not believe every piece of advice that you hear until its utility somehow has been proved to you, lest there should happen to you what befell the thief who believed the advice of a householder.' At this the son asked: 'What happened to him then, father?' And the father began:

XXIV THE THIEF AND THE RAY OF MOONLIGHT[122]

The story is told that a thief came to the house of a rich man with intent to steal. He climbed on to the roof, reached a window from which smoke was coming, and listened to see if anyone was awake. The master of the house heard this and quietly said to his wife: 'Ask me in a loud voice how it happens that I have such a great treasure. Really put yourself to some trouble to get the information from me.' So she said in a loud voice: 'My lord, how is it that you have such a great treasure, when you have never been a tradesman?' He answered: 'What God has given, keep. Satisfy your desire, but do not ask me how I got so much money.' But she, as she had been instructed, pressed more and more to know. At length as if forced by his wife's entreaties the man said: 'Take care never to disclose our secret to anyone. I was once a thief.' At this the wife said: 'It seems marvellous to me that you were able to acquire such a vast treasure by theft, for we have neither experienced any idle gossip nor any slander because of this.' He answered: 'My master had taught me a magic formula, that I used to repeat when I was climbing a roof. When I came to a window, I would grasp at a moonbeam with my hand, and repeat my magic word seven times, namely "Saulem". This way I was able to climb down without danger, and whatever I found in the house I snatched up and took. On the completion of this I would return to my moonbeam, repeat the same magic word seven times, and climb up together with everything I had taken. Finally I brought all my loot to my house. This is the trick I used to obtain the treasure that I now possess.'

The wife said: 'It is a good thing that you have told me all this. When I have a son I shall teach him this charm so that he shall never be in want.' The man answered her and said: 'Let me sleep, for I am tired and need rest', and in order to deceive the thief even more, he began to snore as if in a deep sleep.

Now the thief was very pleased by all he had heard. He repeated the magic word seven times, grasped at the moonbeam, and fell through the window with a great noise, as neither his hands nor feet found a grip. He lay there with a broken leg and arm. The master of the house as if ignorant asked: 'Who are you, who have so fallen?' The robber replied: 'I am that unhappy thief that believed your false words.'

The son said: 'Praised be you, for you have taught me to avoid deceitful counsel.'

A philosopher has said: 'Beware of advice that is unproven. Be on your guard until it has been put to proof.'

Good Works

Another philosopher has said: 'Do not listen to this man, who advises you to deny someone's good acts, for whoever denies good deeds accuses himself in the eyes of Him who sees all.' Another has said: 'If everything goes well with you, take care not to sin, for very often the greatest property is thereby either lessened or lost.'[123]

The pupil asked his teacher: 'The philosopher forbade denial of a good work, but he made no distinction between the good act of the Creator, and that of a creature.' The master answered: 'I'll tell you that he who denies a good act, denies God; and he who is disobedient to king or ruler is disobedient to God.'[124] The pupil then asked: 'Explain to me the reason for that.' The master answered: 'No good act proceeds from creature to creature unless it proceeds first from God. Those who deny good deeds, deny those who effect good deeds, and thus they deny God.'

The Good and Evil King

It is said: 'A king who is a true ruler is the staff of God on earth; he who obeys the staff obeys the ruler; he who does not obey the staff, does not obey God.' Another philosopher has said: 'Guard yourself against the king who is wild like a lion, and also against him who has a mind like that of a child.'[125] Another has said: 'Who speaks ill of a king, shall die before his time'; yet another states: 'God allows that king to reign longer who is an abject sinner in his own personal life but mild and good to his subjects, rather than the king whose personal life is blameless, but who treats his subjects cruelly and badly.' Aristotle in his letter to King Alexander gives the following counsel: 'It is better to rule your subjects in peace with the aid of a few soldiers than to have a great army.'[126] And again he wrote: 'Observe right and justice in your dealings with men, and they will love you. Do not be eager to exact reprisal for good or evil, for a friend will wait longer for you, and an enemy will fear you longer.'

XXV THE PHILOSOPHER MARIANUS

Plato tells us in his Book of Prophecies of a Greek king, an old man, who showed himself most cruel in the treatment of his subjects.

Against this king there arose from all sides a great war, and he, in order to know the outcome of this war summoned all the wise men of his kingdom and of the neighbouring lands. When they were all come together he said to them: 'See what a great war grows up against you and me! I believe that this is happening to you because of my sins. If then there is anything in me that is reprehensible, tell me, and I, in accordance with your judgment, will try to correct the fault.' The wise men answered: 'We know of no sins in your person, nor do we know what the future will bring to you and us. But three days' journey from here, there lives a philosopher called Marianus who speaks inspired by the Holy Ghost. Send some delegates from your wise men to him, therefore, so that he may clarify for you everything that will happen to you in your whole life.'

At these words the king sent seven of his learned men to this man. As soon as they reached the town where he had previously lived, they found it largely deserted. When they enquired as to the whereabouts of Marianus, they were told that he and many of his fellow townsmen had taken themselves off to the desert. On hearing this the philosophers went off to see him. As soon as the sage saw them he said: 'Come, come, you delegates of the disobedient king! Indeed has God given him many different peoples to rule over, but he has shown himself to be a cruel tyrant, and not their true ruler. But God has created him and his subjects from the same stuff, not different. He has long suffered this extreme evil, and has warned him in many ways to improve his ways. But at last he has stirred up barbarous and merciless peoples against him to wage war on him and slay him, as this king has shown himself to persist in his evil ways.'[127] When he had said this the philosopher fell silent, but the wise men sent by the king and all others present there wondered at these words.

Three days later, the philosophers asked if they could go home, to which the awesome man replied with prophetic spirit: 'Return, for your lord is dead. God has installed a new king there, who will be a just ruler, and kind to his subjects.' At these words, four of the seven philosophers returned to their own land, but three remained in the desert with the wise Marianus. The four found everything had happened exactly as it had been prophesied to them.

An Arab said to his son: 'Do not stay long in the country of a king whose outgoings exceed his income.'

XXVI   THE TWO BROTHERS AND THE BUDGET OF THE KING[128]

The story is told that a king, with the entire agreement of his nobles, handed over the reins of his kingdom to one of his household whom he had already realised was well versed in the ways of the world. It would be his duty to collect the revenue of every province, to deal with legal decisions and to organise the court, its personnel and its expenses.

The brother of this man was a rich merchant of a different country and lived in a very remote town. When he heard of his brother's good fortune, he prepared a suitable caravan, and went off to visit him. Lest he should arrive suddenly or quite unexpectedly, he sent a messenger on ahead to tell his brother of his arrival.

And so he drew near the city where his brother lived. When the brother heard of his arrival, he rushed out and welcomed him joyfully with great solicitude.[129] After a few days had gone by, at a well chosen time and place, he informed the king that amongst other things which he knew, he would be pleased to know also of the arrival of his brother. The king answered him: 'If your brother agrees to stay here in my country with you, then I grant that all your offices—even your custody of my property—shall be held in common by you and him. If, however, he finds the burden of office too much, I will grant him great lands here in my city, and I will free him from all duties and requirements that are incumbent upon him. If he develops nostalgia and wishes to return to his own country, then I will grant him many fine suits of clothes, and whatever is necessary for him, I will grant him in abundance!'

When the man heard these words he went to his brother and related to him everything that the king had promised. The visitor said: 'If you want me to stay here with you, tell me what is the incoming revenue of the king.' His brother told him all the details. Then the other brother asked what were the outgoings and these too were shown him. Then the two brothers together worked out that the incoming revenue was exactly the same as the expenditure. At this the visitor said to his brother: 'My friend, I see that the king spends as much as he has. Supposing some other king were to make war on him, or something similar, how will he obtain soldiers and find the money to pay them?' The brother who was minister answered: 'We would find some way or other of doing this', but his brother said: 'I am afraid that my wealth may be part of this plan; therefore farewell. I do not wish to remain here longer.'

Familiarity with Kings[130]

A philosopher has said: 'A king is like fire: when one is too near, one is burnt, and when one is totally removed, one freezes.'[131] An Arab asked his father: 'If I am to believe the words of the philosophers, I should never become the confidant of a king.'[132] The father answered him: 'My son, it requires great intelligence to be on good terms with a king.'[133] The son then asked: 'Father, instruct me how I can best obtain the goodwill of a king; what intelligence and knowledge must I show, should I ever have to serve a king?' The father answered: 'Many things would be necessary for me to give such advice, and these I cannot recall to mind; perhaps as you are still young, you would even lose interest in the whole matter. But I will mention a few points, taken at random, which will be most useful to you if you observe them.' Then the son said to him: 'Even though my ears burn to hear many things, I ask you to tell me at least what you promised. I am so eager to hear something.'

Then the father began: 'The man who wishes to be on good terms with a king must take the greatest care that he can stand for a long period without sitting when at court, until ordered to do so by the king; nor speak except when necessary, nor remain with the king unless ordered to remain;[134] he must keep a faithful silence on all matters of counsel, and be ever intent on what the king says so that the king need never give an order a second time. Whatever the king ordains, he must do. He must beware of lying to the king, and he must further make it his business to love the king and be obedient to him; nor must he associate with any man whom the king might view with displeasure. When he has done all this and more, then perhaps even then he will still not have any great advantage from his familiarity with the king.' The son said: 'Nothing worse can befall a man than to serve a king for a long time, and reap no benefit from it.' The father answered: 'That has already happened to many men, and it is for this reason that the philosopher gave the opinion that no one should stay too long in a king's service. And further, another sage has said: "Who serves a king without, so to speak, gaining any good fortune, loses both this life and the other."'[135]

Eating Customs[136]

The son asked: 'Father, why have you forgotten to tell me how a man must behave at the royal table?' The father answered: 'I have not forgotten to tell you because there is no difference whether one eats with a king or with anyone else.' Then the son said: 'Then tell me how I must everywhere conduct myself at table.' The father began:

'After first having washed your hands before eating, you must not, so long as the meal lasts, touch anything other than the food. You should not eat bread before the other dishes are on the table, lest you be termed lacking in self-restraint. Never take such a large mouthful in your mouth that pieces fall out on either side, lest you be seen to be a glutton. Never swallow a mouthful until it has been well chewed, lest you choke! Do not drink until your mouth is empty, lest people call you a wine-bibber! Do not talk with a full mouth, lest something catch in your gullet and find its way into your windpipe, and be the cause of your death. And when you see a tasty morsel that you would like on that part of the dish[137] in front of your neighbour, do not take it, lest people reproach you as being a boorish churl. After eating, wash your hands, because it is both hygienic and good manners. Many people have contracted a disease of the eyes on account of the fact that they have not washed their hands after eating, and they have wiped their eyes with their hands.'

The son pursued his questioning and asked: 'If someone asks me to dinner, how should I reply? Should I reply immediately or not?' The father answered: 'Act as the Holy Scripture instructs the Jews to do. For it is said: "If someone invites you, suit your reply to the rank of the host. If someone of high rank sends you an invitation, reply at once. But if this is not so, then adapt yourself to the circumstances, and reply after the second or third invitation." This was ordained by Abraham, who one day as he stood in front of his door, saw passing three angels in human form. He asked them with great respect and dignity to come into his house, wash their feet, take some refreshment with him, and refresh their weary limbs in sleep. As he was a person of high rank, they accepted his invitation. When they however came to Lot's house, and were repeatedly invited to enter his house, they accepted as if forced, because he was a person of no standing.'[138]

A young man asked an old man: 'If I am invited to a meal, what should I do? Should I eat a lot or a little?' The old man answered: 'Eat a great deal, because if the man who has invited you is your friend, he will be very pleased by this. If, however, he is an enemy, he will be grieved.'[139] When the young man heard this, he laughed, and the old man asked him: 'Why are you laughing?' The youth answered: 'Your words make me remember what I heard about the negro Maimundus. An old man once asked him how much he could eat, in reply to which he got the question: "At whose table? At my own or at someone else's?" The old man then answered: "At your own", to which Maimundus responded: "As little as possible."[140] When the old man asked how much he would eat at someone else's table, Maimundus answered: "As much as possible."' The old man then said: 'Your words remind me of a glutton, a sloth, a fool, a chatterbox and a buffoon. There are many more stories about Maimundus on these same lines.' The young man replied: 'I would very much like to hear more about him, because every story about him is an amusing one. Tell me then whatever you know about any of his quick-witted answers and quips, and I will thank you.' And so the old man began.

XXVII THE SERVANT MAIMUNDUS[141]

Now his master had ordered him to shut the gate of the house at evening, but he, Maimundus, could not rise because of his laziness and said that the gate was locked. The following morning, the master said to his servant: 'Maimundus, open the gate!' He answered: 'Master, I knew beforehand that you would want the door opened this morning and so last night I decided not to shut it.' Then his master realised that he had shirked his duty through laziness, and said: 'Get up, and get about work! It is now day and the sun is already high in the heavens!' At this the serf said: 'Master, if the sun is high, give me something to eat!' His master answered him: 'You good-for-nothing wretch, do you want to eat in the middle of the night?' To which Maimundus replied: 'If it is night, then let me sleep.'

Another time during the night, the master said to his slave: 'Maimundus, get up and see if it is raining or not.' Maimundus called the dog who lay in front of the gate, and when he came to him felt his paws. When he felt them to be wet, he called to his master: 'Master, it is raining.'

Another time during the night the master asked his servant whether there was a fire burning in the house. The servant called the cat from the store and felt to see if it was warm. When he discovered it was cold, he said: 'Master, the fire is out!'

At this point the young man interrupted: 'I have now heard of his laziness, but I would like to hear something of his talkativeness too.' Then the old man began to tell another story.

The story is told that his master returned from market very pleased at his success in a business transaction, as he had made a great deal of money. At this the servant Maimundus went against his master. When the master saw him, he was afraid that he would gossip as he generally did, and so he said to him: 'Take care, not to spread any evil rumours about me.' Maimundus replied that he would not spread any evil gossip about, but that their little dog Bispella, was dead. At this the master asked him how she had died, and the slave told him that their mule had been terrified and broken its halter and had trampled the dog to death with its hooves as it escaped. The master then asked him what had happened to the mule and was told that it had fallen into a well and was dead. The master then asked how the mule came to be so terrified, and the slave told him that his [the master's] son had fallen off the balcony and had also met his death: this was the cause of the mule's terror. The master then asked what the boy's mother's reaction was, and was told by his slave that the mother too was dead by reason of her overwhelming grief at her son's demise. 'Who, then', said the master, 'is looking after the house?' The slave answered: 'No one. It is completely burned down together with everything in it.' The master asked how it had been set alight, and the slave told him that on the night when the mistress of the house had died, the maidservant who was looking after the house on behalf of her mistress, had forgotten the lamp in the room and thus the whole house had been burned. The master then asked where the maidservant was, and the slave told him that she had tried to put out the fire, but in so doing, a beam had fallen on her head, and she too had perished. Said the master: 'How did you, you idle wretch, manage to escape?' The slave answered: 'When I saw the maidservant dead, I fled.'

The master was very grieved by all this, and went to his neighbours to ask one of them to put him up and give him hospitality. On the way there, he met one of his friends. When this man saw how sad he was, he asked him the reason for his grief, and the master told him everything that the slave Maimundus had told him. The other man then attempted to comfort his grief-stricken friend with the following words:

The Instability of All Worldly Things

My friend, do not be sad! It often happens that a man is so over-whelmed by such tremendous ill-luck that he would even wish to bring his life to an end, by a dishonourable death,[142] but then he immediately has such good luck that it thenceforth becomes pleasant for him to remember his previous misfortunes. This immense fluctuation in human circumstances is brought about by the will of Him who controls everything. As a corroboration of this, the example of the prophet Job can be adduced, who did not despair in his heart although he lost everything that was his.[143] Have you not heard the words of the philosopher: 'Who can find in this unstable world anything that is stable, or who can find anything in this life that is lasting, when everything is transitory?'

An Arab said to his son: 'My son, when ill luck befalls you, do not grieve or be sorrowful, because this is God's way of refusing, but rather always praise God both for any ill fortune that he sends you, as well as any good fortune. Many things that are unpleasant befall mankind, in order that what is even worse may be kept from them, and many things that are unpleasant eventually turn out for the good of mankind. Therefore you should always praise God and trust in him, as the poet says: "When you are sad, do not worry about it, but resign everything to the keeping of God. Keep all future good before you, and you will thereby forget all evils, for many things come to pass that are evil, but end for the best."[144] A wise man has said: "The good fortunes of this world are mixed; one cannot eat honey without poison."[145] Another has said: "Everything that is of this world is suitable. What the future holds for you in respect of good fortune will come to you even if you are weak; on the other hand, even though you be strong, you will not avoid bad fortune."[146] Yet another philosopher has said: "A lazy man often obtains what he wants without any work on his part, whereas many who are active are denied the fulfilment of their desires." Another poet has said:

Whoever bedecks himself, is always denied splendour by the world. Whoever thinks only of himself, is swallowed up entirely by the earth.

And here are the words of another on the same:

> The glory of the world passes in a moment.
> It is fleeting: therefore expect no happiness in it.[3]

XXVIII   THE STORY OF SOCRATES AND THE KING[147]

The proverb is that Socrates shunned the tumults of the world, and wishing to lead a rustic life, set up home in the woods, and instead of a house lived in a half-barrel, the bottom of which faced the wind and rain, and the opening the sun. The huntsmen of the king came across the place, saw him and mocked him because he was killing the lice from off his body, and stood in front of him in such a way that they kept the warm sunshine from him. He said calmly to them: 'Do not presume to take away from me what you do not grant me.' At these words they became angry, and wished to throw him out of his barrel and lead him off into the wilderness, so that their king's eyes should not be offended by the sight of such a vile person. As they were unable to do this, they threatened him and said: 'Go, lest something nasty happens to you, because of your impudence; our lord and king will pass this way with his entourage and nobles.' While they were thus insulting him, the philosopher looked at them and said: 'Your master is not my master but rather the servant of my servant.' When they heard this, they looked at him with evil in their hearts, and some suggested killing him, but others less base suggested sparing him until their king should deliver his judgment.

While they were thus quibbling with each other, the king arrived and enquired the cause of their strife, and his people told him what had happened and what words had been exchanged. The king desired to know whether the vile things that he had heard were true or false, and so he rushed up to the philosopher and asked him what he had to say in respect of the matter. He answered him, just as he had answered his courtiers, telling him that he was the servant of his servant. The king received this in a friendly manner, and asked him to clarify his statement somewhat. The philosopher kept his dignified mien, and said: 'My will is subdued and serves me, not I it. You, however, are subject to your will and serve it, instead of it serving you. Therefore you are a slave of him who is my slave.' At these words the king lowered his face a little and said: 'Your words show me that you do not fear my power and might.' The philosopher sank deep into thought and said: 'You yourself know that your ambition for worldly fame has entirely seized control of you, and that you have sought opportunities to gain glory through martial deeds so that your valour might not grow old unsung, as you yourself confess. But in truth you have acted entirely for reasons of the lust for fame. How paltry such fame is, and how little meaning it has, can be seen from the following; your earlier glory has no more potency, so that it need no longer be feared, nor need your future glory be respected, for its outcome is doubtful and uncertain. As for your present fame, it is so slight, that it can be crushed in the twinkling of an eye. Therefore on no account is your power to be feared.' When the king had listened to these words from the philosopher, he said to his companions: 'He is a servant of God. See to it that you do not harm or trouble him in any way.'

Life's End

In the same way the pupil asked the teachers: 'If worldly things are so vile, why do we take so much trouble over them as if they were durable?' The master answered: 'Because the end of our life lies in uncertainty. A philosopher has said on this point: "Strive for the world to come as if you were even now about to die, and for the present as if you were to live for ever.[148] For it is better that your enemies should obtain from you what they desire after your death, rather than that you should lack during your life that with which your friends could help you." Another has said: "The world is, as it were, a period of transition;[149] therefore take care to provide yourself with everything, but honourably, for the course of life is short." Yet another has stated: "The world is like a bridge; therefore cross it, and do not stay." Yet again is it said by a philosopher: "The world is like a shaky bridge; its entry is the womb of one's mother, and its exit is death."[150] The poet says:

Death is an ever open door through which all that is of this world takes its way. But I ask myself whether there be some house on the far side of the door.

There is indeed a house full of joy, in which God's servants will live, and another quite different for those who deserve its punishments.' An Arab asked his father: 'How can I earn entry into this house full of joy and glory?' The father answered: 'Whatever you have that is costly and of good quality, bring there to be guarded, and when you come there, you will find everything ready for you.' The son asked: 'How can I store up gold in that house, when I do not even know how to find its door?' The father answered: 'Listen, and hear what the son of the royal wazir did after his father's death.' The son said: 'Speak, father, and I will not neglect to follow this advice.' So the father began:

XXIX   THE PRUDENT SON OF THE ROYAL WAZIR[151]

Once upon a time there was a king who had a very wise counsellor who was very close to him. This man followed the route of all mortals, and left behind an heir who although young was well educated and well versed in court manners. The father had bequeathed, before his death, all his property which was substantial and all his monetary wealth to his son. After the father's death, the king called the boy to him, and advised him to be sad no longer at his father's death. He also confirmed whatever matters had been entrusted by the father to the son in his will, and further he promised him that he would take the place of his father when he grew to full manhood. The boy took his leave, glad at heart and returned to his own home.

The king soon forgot him, and the young man did not hasten to return to the king. However, after many years had gone by, it happened in that region where lived the youth, that the necessities of life began to fail and there was great danger of a famine. When the young man, who had a good heart, saw what need there was, he was moved by compassion, and he emptied his barns and distributed the corn amongst the needy. In the same way he distributed his stocks of wine and meat also amongst the needy. As the famine grew worse, his money dwindled and was no longer sufficient for those in need. After he had given all his wealth for corn, he had laboured to the full extent of his powers to keep alive people who were suffering from hunger and thirst. But his stores were not enough. He did the same with his clothes and jewellery, and so a whole circle of the year went by in which he redeemed not a few from death, who would surely have died without him.

Now there lived in that region a lawyer of the aforementioned king, and this man was jealous of the young man, and in his heart fostered bitter enmity against him. He made mischief against the young man with the king, with the following words: 'My lord, your majesty's lenience in the matter of the son of your late counsellor who was left such vast sums by his late father, has been too great, if I may say so and avoid saying something stupid. For now neither you nor he has the money, which he has spent in such a foolish and extravagant manner.' At this the king became very angry and summoned the young man. Then he spoke to him as follows: 'You are the foolish son of a wise father, the spendthrift heir of a generous man, the bungling offspring of an able councillor. How did you manage to consign to ruin the riches so wisely collected together and entrusted to your safe keeping?' At this the young man fixed his eyes to the ground, for he was afraid of the face of the king and his dark looks. Then he said: 'My lord, if I may speak, I am not, as some people suggest, the foolish son of my wise father. My father bequeathed me a treasure, and as he bequeathed it to me he left it in a place from which thieves could steal it, and he left it to me, and you could take this treasure from me, or it could be set ablaze or it could be lost to me through some other chance happening. I, however, have placed it where it will be faithfully kept both for my father and for me.' The king asked him what he had done with it, and so the young man told him everything he had done and how he had disposed of the treasure.

When the king realised how astute the young man was, he rewarded him, praised him in the presence of all those there, and having sung his praises offered him anew the post of his father. The young man from that time forth acquired new and much greater riches from his post. Thus did the son of the royal minister lay up for himself a treasure in the house of joy.

When he had had this story from his father, the son said: 'That young man acted wisely, and showed that he would be a great paragon of charity. He acted just like the advice given by a philosopher to his son: "My son, sell this world for the next, and you will be rich in both." And this happened to that young man.'

The World to Come

Another man gave the following advice to his son: 'My son, work for the world to come before death snatches you from work.' Another said: 'Take care that the joys of this world do not deceive you, and that you be not ensnared by the falsities of the world, lest you forget that death is to come, and lest there happen to you what happened to the thief who entered the house of a rich man.' The son then asked: 'Tell me, father, what happened.' And the father began the story.

XXX   THE THIEF WHO WANTED TO TAKE TOO MUCH[152]

A thief entered the house of a rich man and found it full of treasures. He was so beside himself, that he took from all the different piles more and more and something from the piles of precious things that was yet more precious. Anything of lesser value he left, but he spent so much time in choosing that day broke, and found him still deciding what to do. The guards who had wakened without his noticing, found the thief still choosing. They seized him, beat him with staves and thongs, and threw him into a deep dungeon. Eventually sentence was given on him, as for anyone who has made a confession, and he had to listen and face the sentence of death. Now if this man had thought at the right moment of how near dawn was, he would never have been beaten with thongs and sticks, nor, what is worse, would he have been made a head shorter.

Another philosopher has said: 'The treasures of this world are as transitory as the dreams of a sleeping man who, when he wakes, loses without trace in one minute everything he has dreamed of.'[153] Of this the following popular tale is told:

XXXI   THE SHEPHERD AND THE CATTLE DEALER[154]

A shepherd dreamed he had a thousand sheep. Now a cattle dealer[155] wanted to buy them to resell them at a profit, and it seemed to the dreamer that he was ready to pay two solidi for each sheep. But when he sold them, he was asking a dinar over the two solidi for each sheep. While the two of them were haggling over the price, the dream suddenly disappeared. When the seller realised that it was a dream, with his eyes still shut, he began to shout loudly: 'Offer me for each beast twenty dinars and you can take away all that are here.'

In the same way those who pursue the fleeting joys of the world, and strive in many ways to retain them, are all suddenly faced by the arrival of that day, that is the end of life, and that day takes them from the world, and snatches from them everything they desire whether they wish it or no.[156]

Death

In the same way the son remarked: 'Is there no way we can escape the toils of death?' The father replied: 'No! His bite is without heal, and no physician's[157] art can help us flee his miserly hands.' The son asked again: 'How shall we then arrange things so that he cannot harm us too much?' The father answered: 'Do as the poet advises:

What you cannot avoid, suffer steadfastly,[158]
Thus death that was terrible will not harm you overmuch.'

XXXII   THE LEARNED MAN PASSING THROUGH THE GRAVEYARD[159]

The story is told that a certain wise man was passing through an old cemetery. There he saw a marble plaque placed over the urn that contained the ashes of a dead man. On this plaque were written verses which spoke of the man there buried to the passers-by in the following words:

You that pass by afar off and give no greeting, stop and stand and receive my words with heart and ear—I am what you will be, and I was what you are now,[160] a mocker of bitter death, for as long as I lived in peace in the world. But when death came, I was snatched from my friends and loved ones. My family robbed of its father; sorrowfully it laid me in the earth, bemoaned the fact that I lay there, and gave my ashes the last honours.

There did the earth rot the beauty of face, and the beautiful, fine form that once was mine lies now down under. You would not know that I was a man, if I were now to be uncovered and bared of earth. Therefore pray God for me with pure heart, that he may grant me eternal peace! And all of you that pray for me, may you all become one and live also with me in heaven!

The wise man read these words once and then over again. Then he forgot this world and became a hermit.[161]

XXXIII   THE GOLDEN GRAVE OF ALEXANDER[162]

The same story is told of Alexander, namely, that his grave would be of gold and that it would stand in a hall to which all would have access. Many wise men came there and one of them said: 'Alexander has guarded a treasure for himself from gold, but now conversely gold is become his guardian.' Another said: 'Yesterday the whole world was not enough for him: today four ells of cloth suffice him.' And another: 'Yesterday peoples feared him; today they hardly respect him.' And another said: 'Yesterday he had friends and enemies; today both are equal in his sight.' But it would be too lengthy an undertaking to retell what all the thirty-two philosophers who were there said about the mightiest king of all.

XXXIV   THE HERMIT WHO PREPARED HIS SOUL FOR DEATH[163]

There was also once a wise hermit who chastised his soul with the following words: 'My soul, know and learn, as long as there is power in your hand, what you have to do before you betake yourself from your abode to that place where the judge awaits you, to the gate of judgment, where you will read in the book what your hand has committed in this world! Angels from heaven will be on the left and the right, and they will open up your innermost thoughts and announce everything in a loud voice to the assembled company whatever you have thought in your heart. Then will your trial be before God, and when all the good you have done is laid in one half of the scale, and in the other all the evil, then at one weighing will judgment be made clear in your case. And all your brothers and friends will not gain your redemption, and they will therefore desert you, and leave you utterly. Therefore do you, today, occupy yourself earnestly with your redemption, namely do good without stopping, and turn back to God before the day of the last exhortation comes, and do not say: "Tomorrow I will return to Him; I shall not tarry", because if you procrastinate thus, some new desire will hinder you, and perhaps you will even be prevented from repentance by the last day. Therefore think of the days of this world and on the peoples of earlier times who have all now passed away, and let them be a warning to you! Where are the kings, the princes, the rich men who amassed treasure and were vain of the fact? They are now as if they had never been; their being is past as if they had never lived; they are like a leaf that falls from a tree, which will never return there. Fear not, my soul, be not greatly afraid! Let your fear have no basis in the adversities of this world, but rather fear the day of your judgment and tremble at the multitude of your sins. Be mindful of your maker, for he is your judge and your witness.'

The Sayings of Other Hermits

A hermit once asked a teacher: 'What should I do in this world that might prepare me for the next?' The teacher answered: 'Do what is good in your power.'[164] Another hermit went crying through the streets of a town: 'Do not forget that which will last for ever, out of desire for things that have an end!' Another cried: 'Love your souls as your bodies, and you will reap much gain.' Another philosopher gave the following advice: 'Do not forget Him who does not forget you; and serve the ruler of the world.'

The Fear of God

Another philosopher has said: 'Fear God, for Fear of the Lord is the key to every good, and the sole tenure for the attainment of glory.' In Ecclesiastes, Solomon has said: 'Let us hear the conclusion of the whole matter: Fear God, and keep his commandments: for this is the whole duty of man. For God shall bring every work into judgment, with every secret thing, whether it be good, or whether it be evil.'[165]

EPILOGUE

Therefore do we humbly beseech the boundless mercy of almighty God, that we may, on the day of the great judgment, when our good works have gone before us, take our place on the right of His son, and be honoured together with all the faithful with the enjoyment of eternal peace in the heavenly palace, where for us our Lord Jesus Christ is a stronghold; to whom be honour and glory together with the Father and the Holy Ghost for ever and ever. Amen.

ABBREVIATIONS

ATh	Antti Aarne, Stith Thompson, *The Types of the Folktale*, Helsinki, 1961³ (FFC 184)
DC	*Disciplina Clericalis*
EI	*Encyclopedia of Islam*,² 1960 ff.
GR	*Gesta Romanorum*, edited by H. Oesterley, Berlin, 1872
KHM	*Grimms' Fairy Tales*
MGH SS	*Monumenta Germaniae Historica*, 1826 ff., *Scriptores*
NT	New Testament
OT	Old Testament
PG	J. P. Migne, *Patrologiae Cursus Completus*, Series Graeca
PL	J. P. Migne, *Patrologiae Cursus Completus*, Series Latina
RE	Pauly's *Realencyclopädie der classischen Altertumswissenschaft*, revised edition by G. Wissowa, W. Kroll *et al.*, 1894 ff.

NOTES

PART I

1 'To Have the Experience of a Jew'

1 Further on the Ikhwan ṣ-ṣafa see von Grunebaum, pp. 40, 42, 198, 215–19, 226, 317, 331; Goldziher, p. 301, n. 22 (a secret shiʻite society accused in 983). [See further Reuben Levy, *The Sociology of Islam* (Cambridge, 1969), pp. 471–96.]
2 von Grunebaum, p. 331.
3 Ibid., p. 226.
4 H. H. Schaeder, *Der Mensch in Orient und Okzident*, Sammlung Piper, Munich, 1960, p. 158.
5 A. Mitscherlich, *Auf dem Wege zur vaterlosen Gesellschaft, Ideen zur Sozialpsychologie*, Sammlung Piper, Munich, 1963, p. 78.
6 The relationship between Jewish experience and the function of an intellectually independent existence in modern society has been dealt with by Thomas Mann in a letter dating from 1921, published by the *Frankfurter Allgemeine Zeitung*, 15 January 1966 (no. 12).
7 The problem of a Jewish identity is found first among assimilated Jews in modern society, who have given up their Jewish individuality without completely being able to abandon their 'otherness'; P. L. Berger, *Invitation to Sociology*, W. H. Allen, London, 1964.

2 An Outsider in European Literature

1 The same is shown of another period by E. Staiger, *Stilwandel zur Vorgeschichte der Goethezeit*, Zürich, 1963, pp. 19 ff.
2 Vossler, pp. 188 ff.
3 Cf. Misch, vol. III, 2, 2, p. 746.
4 van Caenegem, p. 12, n. 1 and pp. 114 ff.
5 In the stories taken from the *DC*, the merchants become knights.
6 W. Delius, *Geschichte der Marienverehrung*, Munich and Basle, 1963, pp. 160 ff.
7 Landau, p. 80.

8 As attested by Juan Manuel, the author of the oldest book of novelle in Spanish.

9 Fitzmaurice-Kelly, p. 32.

10 It is noteworthy that in the manuscript the word 'saber' (to know) is found in place of 'profecia' (prophecy) which has been erased (cf. chap. 9)!

11 This first aphorism of Hippocrates came into Spanish through Ḥunayn's book of proverbs (*Libro de buenos proverbios*) and became common property (Knust, pp. 64 ff. and 124 ff.).

12 *Libro de los Engannos*, ed. Bonilla, p. 10.

13 Chauvin, vol. IX, p. 2.

14 Knust, pp. 587 ff. (There was already a further Old English translation by 'Sir John Fostalf' = Falstaff?)

3 A Much Travelled Story

1 *Fastnachtspielregister*, no. 61.

2 ATh, 1515. Ljungman, p. 301, takes the view that the diffusion followed principally in the literary path.

3 Gerhardt, p. 318.

4 ATh, 1352 A.

5 ATh, 875 D.

6 Littmann IV, 259–371.

7 Gunter, p. 129, n. 87.

8 A. Hilka, *Neue Beiträge zur Erzählungsliteratur des Mittelalters*, 90 *Jahresbericht d. schles. Ges. für vaterländische Cultur*, Breslau, 1913, pp. 18 ff. Cf. the reversal of the motif in Boccaccio, *Decameron*, III, 6!

9 Littmann IV, 294 ff.

10 Littmann IV, 340 ff.

11 Littmann IV, 274 ff.

12 Littmann IV, 281 ff.

13 *Hist. Septem Sap.*, I, no. 6, pp. 11 ff.

14 Comparetti, pp. 46 ff.

15 Loretz, p. 115.

16 Cf. Wulff, pp. 3 ff.

17 *Arabian Nights*: Littmann IV, 280 (Qur'an 12, 28 and 4, 78); Hermes, pp. 118 ff. and 149 n. 27.

18 (Vincent of Beauvais) *Speculum Morale*, liber III, pars 9, dist. 5. In the Gospel of Egypt it is said that Christ came down to earth 'to put an end to the work of women' (Clement of Alexandria, *Stromata* III 9 63, 2).

19 Schnürer, p. 492.

20 Goethe, *Italian Journey*, part III, entry for October 1787.

21 Knust, p. 560. It can obviously be considered that this variant of the Xanthippe topos adapts well by reason of the fact reported, because al-Mubashshir had written the sayings of Socrates.

22 Knust, pp. 589 ff.

4 The Answer of the Physician and the Theory of the Novella

1 *DC* XIII = *GR*, 28 (only the introduction is adapted, as always, to the fiction that Roman History was being related).

2 No. 171 = *DC* II (about half the stories of the Spaniard are found in the *GR*).
3 No. 166.
4 OT, Genesis 34: 1–5.
5 Hermes, pp. 83 ff.
6 Pabst, pp. 16, 73.
7 Hermes, pp. 50 ff.
8 D. B. Macdonald, *EI*, II, pp. 321–4 S. V. ḥikāja.
9 W. Jens, *Deutsche Literatur der Gegenwart*, Munich, 1964, pp. 57 ff.
10 Schnürer, pp. 165 ff.
11 Pabst, p. 2.
12 'Valerius Rufino ne ducat uxorem': *PL* 30, 262–9; Wulff, p. 14 [on the authorship of the tract see Ph. Goldschmidt, *Medieval Texts and their First Appearance in Print*, p. 45].
13 In the Talmud a teacher acted thus (Sabbath 30B): 'At the beginning of the lesson he said something cheerful, and the pupils were pleased. Then he sat down respectfully, and began the lesson.'
14 *DC*, Prologue.
15 E.g. Horace, *Ars Poetica*, 333 ff. Cf. Hermes, pp. 45 ff.
16 It is basically oriental in origin e.g. al-Fârâbî (Sellheim, p. 11). G. Eis, *Vom werden altdeutscher Dichtung, Literar-historische Proportionen*, Berlin, 1962, pp. 76 ff.
17 Pabst, p. 42.
18 Of 9 February 1560 (Hans Sachs, *Fastnachtspiele*, trans. and ed. Th. Schumach, Tübingen, 1957, pp. 1 ff.).

5   Eastern Forms of Wisdom

1 *Jātaka* 374 (*Buddh. Märchen*, no. 29, pp. 221 ff.; *Jātaka* 318, ibid., no. 30, pp. 225 ff. has a similar theme).
2 Palmblätter, pp. 40 ff.
3 *Arabian Nights*: Littmann III, 540 ff. (a double of the corresponding story in the *Hist. Septem Sap.*, IV, 262–5); cf. III, 95 (fable).
4 Sellheim, p. 8.
5 Ibid., p. 15.
6 Schabinger, pp. 172 ff.
7 Hermes, pp. 35 ff.
8 Littmann, *Spruchweisheit*, p. 10.
9 Ibid., p. 35.
10 It is interesting that H. Weinrich has, in a linguistic investigation into the 'speech situations' of story telling and 'talking', come to a similar conclusion. (Tempus, *Besprochene und erzählte Welt*, Stuttgart, 1964, p. 293: 'Sayings and proverbs in the gnomic aorist are condensed stories', and p. 205 on the function of the oriental stories within a story: 'In these telling a story is the form in which wisdom ripens to resolution. Talking and story telling are not unrelated; one talks or converses when one is telling a story. Wisdom is not the product of a discursive thought process, it is the flower and fruit of the story'.)

11 Sellheim, p. 9. (The Greek word for proverb is *paroimia* which means 'by way' in the same way as the German 'bi-spel', 'bi-wort'. Cf. Aristotle, *Rhetoric*, III, 11, 1413 a 11–18.)

12 Sellheim, p. 11.

13 Ibid., p. 14.

14 Ibid., p. 11.

15 Thus the prophet himself: Weisweiler, p. 7.

16 Sellheim, pp. 41 ff. (pre-Islamic) cf. *Arabian Nights*: Littmann III, 512–18.

17 Cf. Curtius Rufus VIII, 6 (Alexander the Great).

18 Heller, pp. 10 ff. R. Nicholson, *A Literary History of the Arabs*, Cambridge, 1962, p. 43. On the Lakhmid state of Hira see F. Gabrieli, *Geschichte der Araber*, Stuttgart, 1963, p. 9.

19 Weisweiler, pp. 10 ff.

20 von Grunebaum, p. 214.

21 Hadas, p. 130.

22 M. Grünbaum, *Neue Beiträge zu semitischen Sagenkunde*, Leiden, 1888, p. 240.

23 Loretz, p. 274.

24 Ibid., p. 275.

25 Ibid., p. 313.

26 Ibid., pp. 313 ff.

27 von Grunebaum, p. 216.

28 Buber, p. 514.

6 Everything is Two-sided

1 S. Freud, GW XIII 146. A detailed sociology of self-preservation has been developed by E. Goffman in a follow-up to the symbolic interaction of G. H. Mead; *The Presentation of Self in Everyday Life*, Edinburgh, 1956.

2 Fellowship at table is the most noticeable manifestation of social relations; today, as also in primitive times, political affairs, business matters and working discussions are often held and completed at table.

3 *Felix Krull*, II, 6.

4 Prologue to the *DC*.

7 The Life of the Author

1 'Libellum elegantem': *Speculum Historiae*, XXV, 118. Further testimonia in Schmidt's edition.

2 Gröber, para. 130, p. 232.

3 Ibid., p. 274.

4 *Conversations*: *PL*, 157, 597 ff.; *Legenda Aurea* (Benz, p. 967); further parallels in J. A. de Lasarte, pp. 374 ff.

5 Cf. von Grunebaum, pp. 64 ff.

6 By means of this formula the problem of the 'murder' of God is avoided. Cf. the draft of the so-called 'Absolution' of the Jews of Vatican II—'The Jewish people should never be regarded as depraved or mad, or considered as the murderers of God' (Report in *Frankfurter Allgemeine Zeitung*, 21 November 1964).

7 I.e. godfather.
8 I.e. his godchild.
9 *PL*, 157, 535–8.
10 *PL*, 157, 537–9.
11 Mitscherlich (see n. 5 on p. 164), pp. 43 and 52.
12 Ibid., p. 187.
13 Cf. Steinschneider, pp. 864 ff. Goldziher, pp. 159 ff.; in the West the 'romance' was known through the *Legenda Aurea* (Benz, pp. 943–58) and the middle high German work of Rudolf von Ems.
14 Klapper, no. 2.
15 Sura 18, 90 ff.
16 Littmann III, 704 ff.
17 Tamid 32a/b.
18 III 6 (Pfister, p. 107).
19 Knust, p. 360. Already in Pañcatantra (Benfey Buch I, suppl. 11 and 12).
20 Steinschneider, pp. 978 ff.
21 Individual evidence in Knust, loc. cit.
22 Littmann IV, 208–59.
23 K. Künstle, *Ikonographie der christlichen Kunst*, Freiburg, 1928, I pp. 208 ff.
24 Over it is Masaccio's famous fresco, probably from 1425.
25 Baer (1929), no. 401, pp. 644 ff. This confusion appears to have passed over Spain, as the response of a school child from Toledo to the question 'what is a synagogue?' shows: 'A synagogue is a mosque consecrated to Christian worship' (Ehrenpreis, p. 35).
26 Wüstenfeld, p. 129 (re Mūsā ibn Jūnus Kamāl ad-Dīn, 1156–1242).

8   The Jews in Christian Spain

1 Pp. 933 ff.
2 Pp. 89 ff.
3 Rudy, p. 90; cf. the letter from Jacques Maritain to Jean Cocteau where a similar assumption is made (Rudy, pp. 214 ff.).
4 'Ells se fessen christians, et tot lo brugit seria passat' (Baer (1929), no. 432, pp. 683 ff.).
5 *PL*, 154, 1206–9
6 *PL*, 170, 805–36. Corrections to Migne's text in J. Greven, 'Die schrift de. Herm. quondam Judaeus ...' in *Annalen d. Hist. verins f.d. Niederrhein* 115 (1929), pp. 11–13: cf. Misch, vol. III, 2, 1, pp. 505–22.
7 *Monumenta Judaica*, pp. 150 ff.
8 Hilka, no. 146, p. 121.
9 Baer (1929), no. 361, pp. 547 ff.
10 *Dial. Mirac.*, IX 8.
11 *Libri VIII Mirac.*, 1, 9.
12 Baer (1961), pp. 21 ff.
13 Baer (1929), no. 464, pp. 732 ff.
14 *Monumenta Judaica*, p. 264. Cf. the passages in H. J. Gamm, *Judentums-kunde*, Munich, 1964, pp. 153 ff. That the Jews had something completely

different in mind is shown by the last sentence of the answer of a Rabbi from Bamberg to a question: 'I cannot any longer stay here, the matter is very urgent, for we are faced by expulsion and arrest. The respite granted us by the bishop has already run out, and he won't increase the respite allowed by one hour, let alone a day' (A. Berliner, *Aus dem Leben der Juden Deutschlands im Mittelalter, in neuer Fassung*, ed. I. Elbogen, Berlin, 1937, p. 13). So great was people's interest in spiritual exchange, even in time of need.

15 Letter to his son Marcus (Pliny, *Nat. Hist.*, XXIX, 12 ff.).

16 Ep. 40, 14 (*PL*, 15, 1101 ff.).

17 J. Vogt, 'Kaiser Julian und das Judentum, Studien zum Weltanschauungskampf der Spätantike', in *Morgenland, Darstellungen aus Geschichte und Kultur des Ostens*, part 30, Leipzig, 1939, pp. 73 ff.

18 According to OT, Obadiah 20.

19 *PL*, 20, 733 = 41, 822 ff. Characterization of Jews as serpents became a topos (S. Stein, 'Die Unglaubigen in der mittelhochdeutschen Literatur', thesis, Heidelberg, 1932 (now Darmstadt, 1963), p. 26).

20 *Tancred*, 11, 1.

21 Introductory text of the so-called 'Judenerklärung' or Vatican II (printed in *Frankfurter Allgemeine Zeitung*, 21 November 1964).

22 Ibid.

23 Schnürer, p. 195.

24 von Grunebaum, pp. 227 ff.; Dubnow, pp. 222 ff.

25 Baer (1961), p. 24.

26 Ibid., pp. 40 ff.

27 Rudy, p. 63.

28 Baer (1961), pp. 29 ff. and 36 ff.; Dubnow, pp. 195 ff.; the Christian kings could send such diplomats to Arab courts, because they were adepts at the indirect manners of speech through word-games, quotations from poets and metaphorical descriptions (Graetz, pp. 71 ff.).

29 Baer (1961), p. 61.

30 von Grunebaum, pp. 53 ff., 459, n. 28.

31 Baer (1961), p. 52.

32 E.g. Baer (1929), no. 17.

33 Berliner (see n. 14), pp. 11 ff.

34 *PL*, 149, 337. This work is often found with the *Conversations*, e.g. in 1536: Graesse, *Trésor de Livres rares et précieux*, V, 242.

35 Decree of the Infante Juan dated 11 June 1339 (Baer (1929), no. 293, pp. 426 ff.).

36 *Europäische Geistesgeschichte*, Stuttgart, 1953, p. 281.

37 M. Gudemann, *Quellenschriften zur Geschichte des Unterrichts und der Erziehung bei den deutschen Juden, von den ältesten Zeiten bis auf Mendelssohn*, Berlin, 1891, pp. iii ff.

38 Ibid., pp. xi ff. Cf. M. Gudemann, *Das Jüdische Unterrichtswesen während der Spanisch-Arabischen Periode*, Vienna, 1873.

39 Gudemann, *Quellenschriften*, pp. xiii ff.

40 Ibid., p. xiv.

41 Ibid., p. xvi. Cf. the same author's *Geschichte des Erziehungswesens und*

der Cultur der Juden in Italien während des Mittelalters, Vienna, 1884; *Geschichte des . . . in Frankreich und Deutschland*, Vienna, 1880; *Geschichte des Erziehungswesens under der Cultur der abendändischen Juden*, Vienna, 1880.

42 Berechya ha-Nakdan (Steinschneider, pp. 958 ff., *Monumenta Judaica*, p. 696). An edition of his *Mishle Sahualim* is being prepared by Haim Schwarzbaum (see *Fabula*, 10, 1969, pp. 107–31).

43 L. Zunz, *Zur Geschichte und Literatur*, vol. I, Berlin, 1845, pp. 144 ff.

44 Ibid., p. 441.

45 Ibid., pp. 137 ff. and 156 (source is Mishna, Awot V 1–23).

46 Ibid., pp. 138 ff. ('Join forces with a generous fool rather than a mean wise man.' *DC* on Intelligence. 'To consort with simple men, who have grown up amongst wise men, is better than the company of intelligent men who have been brought up in bad company.')

47 Ibid., p. 141. ('A man who has scarcely enough to keep alive, married a rich wife; he turned her out, because her brothers were good for nothing, and he was afraid that she might produce similar offspring.')

48 Ibid., pp. 135 ff. and 143: *DC* XV, XIX and on Intelligence.

49 Ibid., p. 143. ('Keep the two-fold hope of a single possession before you; a little "of course" is better than a big "perhaps"', *DC* on Riches.)

50 Gudemann, *Quellenschriften*, pp. 3 ff. (based on the ancient Eastern topos of the father's address to the son, of the 'Testament': ibid., p. xxxi).

51 Ibid., p. 56.

52 Ibid., p. 25.

53 Zunz, p. 159

54 F. Heer, *Mittelalter*, pp. 5–27 (exhaustive bibliography on this question, pp. 691–720).

55 See n. 4 on p. 168.

56 *Der Berliner Antisemitismusstreit*, ed. W. Boehlich, Sammlung Insel 6, Frankfurt am Main, 1965.

57 A. and M. Mitscherlich, *Die Unfähigkeit zu trauern*, Grundlagen Kollectiven Verhaltens, Munich, 1967, pp. 145 ff.

58 *Der Berliner . . .* , p. 218.

9   Science and Superstition

1 OT, Genesis 5: 18–24.

2 44, 16.

3 The honorary name of Enoch (Idris from Arab/Hebrew 'darasha' = to study, to investigate, to learn, whence 'midrash' = instruction). German Jews said 'darschen' meaning to hold a lecture in the synagogue: A. Tendlau, *Sprichwörter und Redensarten deutsch-jüdischer Vorzeit*, Schockenbücherei 10, Berlin, 1934, no. 32, pp. 27 ff.

4 von Grunebaum, pp. 416 ff.

5 Knust, pp. 87 f.; Horten, pp. 66 f.

6 Thorndike, p. 214.

7 Khâlid ibn Yazīd (635–704), an Ummayad prince, himself wrote apparently an alchemical tract in 2315 lines. The *Fihrist*, a catalogue of all works,

written in 987 by the bookseller Muhammed an-Nadim (concerns books of which he had been able to acquire information), tells us that his instructor was a man of learning called Morienus. According to the historian of medicine Ibn Abī Uṣaibi 'ah, reported by Wüstenfeld, Morienus came from Greece and not Rome. Here he is mentioned as indulging in medical activities (Wüstenfeld, p. 9). Al-Mas'udi (ob. 956) has recorded the recipe that is to be found in Khâlid's poem for the making of gold, 'that it may be of use to us today'. Cf. n. 28 on p. 177.

 8 *Liber de compositione alchemiae quem editit Morienus Romanus Calid regi Aegyptiorum quem Robertus Castrensus de Arabico in Latinum transtulit*, in the year 1144, Prologue (Thorndike, pp. 214 ff.).

 9 *Dial. Mirac.*, VII 37.

10 Tertullian, *De resur.*, 58.

11 *The Book of the Bee, The Syriac Text*, ed. from the MSS. in London, Oxford, Munich, with an English translation by E. A. Wallis-Budge, Oxford, 1886, chap. XV.

12 Fuller redaction 43, 3 (the so-called *Slavonic Book of Enoch*, ed. G. N. Bonwetsch, fascicle 2, Leipzig, 1922). Further similarities to the *DC*: 42, 6 = Prologue 50, 5 = Ex. XXIX; 61, 3 = 'Life's End'.

13 E. Kautzsch, *Die Apokryphen und Pseudepigraphen des Alten Testaments*, vol. 2, Tübingen, 1900, p. 299 (Ethiopic version, chap. 91, 4).

14 OT, Genesis 5: 23.

15 R. de Vaux, *Das Alte Test. und seine Lebensordnungen*, vol. I, Freiburg, Basle, Vienna, 1960, p. 303.

16 von Grunebaum, p. 417.

17 Ibid., pp. 417 ff.

18 Necromancy (e.g. St Macarius caused a murdered man to appear to attest the innocence of someone wrongly accused: *Vitae patrum*, 2, 37): in folk-etymology 'nigromancia' is explained as Black Magic—Dieffenbach, *Gloss. Med. et Inf. Latin.*, Frankfurt am Main, 1857, s.v.).

19 Cf. Thorndike, pp. 72 ff.; Millás, *Sefarad*, III, pp. 66 ff.

20 *Inferno*, XXVI, 90 ff. F. Friedrich, 'Dante und die Antike, Odysseus in der Hölle, Inferno XXVI', *Gymnasium* 73, 1966, pp. 9–26.

21 *Hist. Septem Sap.*, II, pp. 14 ff.

22 Ibid., I, pp. 21 ff.

23 *Hist. von D. Johann Faust*, *Eint. z. II Teil*, ed. R. Benz, Reclam UB 1515/16 Stuttgart, 1964, no. 18, p. 36.

24 Seven Hedin, *Mein Leben als Entdecker*, Leipzig, 1928, pp. 10 ff. Cf. ATh, 753 A.

25 Neuburger, pp. 173 ff.

26 A. Jores, 'Magie und Zauber in der modernen Medizin', in *Vom ärtzlichen Denken und Handeln, Deutsche Kliniker über die Medizin unserer Zeit*, Stuttgart, 1956, p. 52.

27 *MGH SS*, X, 461 ff. (ATh, 300 A, 313, 313 A, 325, 328, 330). Hermes, pp. 112–17. Cf. The campaign of the humanists against 'godless' physicians (A. Buck, *Grundzüge d. ital. Geistesgesch.*, Uhrach, 1947, pp. 56 ff.).

28 It is Marienus, that legendary pupil of Adfar, for whom such a tract was written. Differences in writing the name are cleared up in a non-

vocalised text. Whence came the name is still unclear. In the fourth century it is found of a Syrian hermit (*RE*, XIV, 1753). Galen is aware of a Greek doctor of this name (*RE*, XIV, 1796, no. 4), and so is the *Fihrist* (Steinschneider, *Die europ. Übers. aus d. Arab. bis Mitte des 17. Jh.*, Graz, 1956, vol. I, pp. 71 ff.).

29 Thorndike, pp. 779–82.
30 Schipperges, p. 149.
31 Thorndike, pp. 777 ff. ('Anguemis', 'Neumich', etc. are bastard forms of Arabic 'nawamis' = leges).
32 Steinschneider, p. 848.
33 *Spec. Astronomiae* 16 (*Opera Omnia* X, 629 ff.); the authenticity is disputed (E. Gilson), *Der Geist d. mittelalt. Philo.*, Vienna, 1950, p. 396, n. 8.
34 Heer, pp. 479 ff.
35 H. Schipperges in *Miscellanea Mediaevalia*, ed. P. Wilpert, vol. I, *Antike und Orient im Mittelalter*, Berlin, 1962, pp. 129–53.

10   Further Information on the Life of the Author

1 Baer (1929), p. 9 and (1961), p. 54 (between 1186 and 1189).
2 Baer (1929), no. 15 (from the year 1121).
3 A. von Weiss, *Hauptprobleme der Zweisprachigkeit*, Heidelberg, 1959, p. 161.
4 Ibid., p. 168.
5 Heer, pp. 478 ff.; that the profession of doctor was hereditary, and that medicine was considered as a basic for all study, appears to be so from Arabic custom (Wüstenfeld, pp. x and 14).
6 J. M. Millás Vallicrosa, 'Un nuevo dato sobre Pedro Alfonso', *Sefarad*, vii, 1947, pp. 136 ff.
7 Even Balthasar Gracián sings his praises: *Handorakel*, no. 67.
8 Baer (1961), p. 59.
9 Ibid., pp. 54 ff. Talmud, Sanhedrin 97b, takes a position contrary to such reckonings.
10 Toledo was the capital city of 'nigromancia' (Caesarius of Heisterbach—Hilka, no. 115, p. 111; *Count Lucanor*, no. 13). The rejection of grammar as the basis of all study in the *DC* and in the *Letter on Study* appears to originate in a particularly Jewish discussion.
11 Neuburger, pp. 317 ff. The Church did not view it favourably. Pope Gregory VII bemoaned the fact in a letter to Alfonso VI, in 1080, that the Jews were a dangerous influence: 'what does the authority that the Jews have over Christians, other than an undermining of the Church and a strengthening of Satan's synagogue? And what is your sympathy for the enemy of Christ other than a denial of Christ himself?' (*Ep.*, IX, 2; Mansi, *Coll. Conciliorum*, XX, 341).
12 Misch, III, 2, 2, p. 995n. 184; Glatzer, pp. 151–5; cf. Wüstenfeld, pp. 109 ff.
13 Ibid., pp. 15 ff.
14 Neuburger, p. 277; Baer (1929), nos 149, 204, 350.
15 Millás, *Sefarad*, III, p. 66.
16 Misch, III, p. 66.

17 An Eastern topos: in *Sayings of the Old Wise Men*, the wise man who withholds his knowledge from others is classed among the 'seven evil things'.

18 'Verba vulgaria': the reference to the 'lingua materna' first comes to life in Petrus Alfonsi (*PL*, 157, 110 ff.). The problem there broached is enlarged upon by Dante in *De Vulg. Eloquentia*, I, 1; John of Salisbury puts Dante's argument in the mouth of his imaginary opponent (*PL*, 199, 833 ff.).

19 Thus already Hippocrates, *De Aere, Aquis, Locis*, c. 2 (Littré, II, 14): If however someone considers this to be mere star-gazing ('meteorologia': this was the prejudice of Socrates too; Plato, *Apology*, 19 B/C), he should alter his opinion that astronomy has only a little to do with the physicians' art (only use of the word astronomy in the whole Hippocratic corpus). For just as the seasons of the year alter, so too does the state of the humours in men.

20 Hippocrates, op. cit., c. 11 (Littré, II, 50–2): 'For if investigations are made as to these rules, one will learn a great deal from them as to how the transition from one season to another is effected.' The proverb that here follows in Hippocrates is introduced by Petrus Alfonsi into the prologue of his astronomical table.

21 The translator of the first phase of the Graeco-Arabic medical texts in Salerno (c. 1015–1087) is now very objectively appraised by Schipperges, pp. 17–54. The text *De Aere, Aquis, Locis* was not translated by Constantine. For these passages see Prognosticon c. 25 (Littré, II, 188) and Aphorisms III, 11–14 (Littré, IV, 490–2): H. Diller in a letter 6 April 1965. The passages from the Aphorisms Petrus Alfonsi would have got from the collection of sayings made by Hunayn (Knust, pp. 64 ff.).

22 The commentary of Macrobius is meant, his Neoplatonic explanation of the *Somnium Scipionis* of Cicero.

23 In the text there follows: ' ... which are called by us "uniones"' ('onions' in English).

24 Cf. the section on Silence in the *DC*.

25 Proverbs 15:32.

26 Cf. the prologue to the astronomical table.

27 MS. B. M. Arundel 270, 40v–45r.; printed by Millás, *Sefarad*, III, pp. 97–101. The critical distance as regards the Eastern tradition of science is also to be seen in Albertus Magnus in his designation of 'Latini' (*Phys.* I, 1, 1; Schipperges, p. 129).

28 von Grunebaum, p. 425.

29 In a hadith (Bukhari 76 bab 45); Opitz, pp. 20 ff.

30 von Grunebaum, p. 425.

31 Millás, *Sefarad*, III, p. 69.

32 Thorndike, p. 68. The astrolabe is what is particularly meant, the instrument which serves to measure angles of the heavenly spheres (see F. Becker, *Geschichte der Astronomie*, Bonn, 1947; pp. 33 ff. for a description). Cf. *Arabian Nights*: Littmann I, 347 ff.

33 What is meant is not the constellation but the date point which is fixed by the 'line of the dragon' which connects the two points of intersection of the moon's path and the ecliptic (Cassel on Judah Halevi, *Kuzari* IV, 25, p. 348 n. 8).

34 The Arabic system works on the basis of a division of a circle into 360 degrees, and a division of the Zodiac into 365 days.

35 Millás, *Sefarad*, III, p. 88. The importance of the correct reckoning of dates for medieval man, who knew no world time, is demonstrated by stories like that of the farmer who on every feast day used to wear red top boots by which folk used to set their calendars (Jacques de Vitry, 2), or that of the person who every day used to bind up a besom, and when he had six ready used to say mass (Wickram, *Rollwagenbüchlein*, no. 47). The Arabs counted the date by piling date stones in a pot (*Arabisch. Märchen* trans. H. Wehr, Goldmann, 1406, Munich, 1963, p. 95). ATh, 1848 A/B. Talmud, Rosh Hashana 24b/25a.

36 Mitscherlich (see n. 5 on p. 164), p. 301.

37 Basically we have here an early witness for the operational conception which is characteristic of modern empirical science. (Cf. K. R. Popper, *The Logic of Scientific Discovery*, New York, 1959.) An important basic fact of this conception is the question that brings together simple standpoints and preliminary decisions under scientific analysis.

38 *De Eodem et Diverso*, Epilogue (Misch, III, 2, 1, p. 459).

39 *Questiones Naturales* (Schipperges, p. 146).

40 He had ordered his royal nephew to occupy himself with Arabic science (Schipperges, p. 145).

41 Schipperges, p. 145.

42 Millás, *Sefarad*, III, pp. 68 ff. When Adelard in *De Eodem et Diverso*, ed. Willner (*Beitr. z. Gesch. d. Phil. d. Mittelalters*, IV, 1,1903, pp. 32 ff.) gave as an example of his advice to seek knowledge in different lands, the doctrine of 'sap', the passage in which he had made use of the current physical metaphor (different knowledge to be gained in different countries—different functions for different organs) (see E. R. Curtius, pp. 146 ff.) ended up being considered not as a simple topos, but as a serious theory of medicine. In this a connection can be seen between him and Petrus Alfonsi. Whether Petrus met Adelard before his journey, or whether he came a second time to England, is not known. The history of mathematics cannot close the gap that lies between Adelard and his sources (A. P. Juschkewitsch, *Geschichte der Mathematik im Mittelalter*, Leipzig-Basle, 1964, pp. 175–86, 220, 340 ff.). Millás appears to have closed with the form of Petrus Alfonsi.

43 'Phlegma' (cf. the characterisation of the doctrine of 'sap' in Hippocrates, *De Nat. Hom.*, c. 7. Littré, VI, pp. 46–8).

44 'Colera rubea' (Hippocrates, op. cit.).

45 The Pleiades and Arcturus also play a decisive role in Hippocrates (*De Aere, Aquis, Locis*, c. 11. Littré, II, p. 52).

46 The Jewish reluctance to use the name of God can here, as often, be seen.

47 This tripartite division of astronomy comes perhaps from Petrus Alfonsi's colleague at the Aragonese court, Abraham ibn Hijja (Millás, *Sefarad*, III, p. 80).

48 MS. B. M. Arundel 270, and MS. C.C.C. Oxford, 283 fol. 143v–144r (Millás, *Sefarad*, III, pp. 101–5).

49 Littmann III, 662; on the question of sources Littmann VI, 726.

50 Hilka, no. 9, p. 66.
51 Schipperges, *Misc. Med.* (see n. 35 on p. 172), p. 130; the Arabs had resigned themselves to it, e.g. to a doctrine on foodstuffs ('Alī ibn Rabban aṭ-Ṭabarī in F. Rosenthal, *The Classical Heritage in Islam*, London: Routledge & Kegan Paul, 1975, p. 187).
52 H. Schipperges, 'Psychosomatische Medizin und ärtzliche Praxis', in *Ärtzliche Praxis*, Munich-Graefeling, no. 23, 5 June 1965, p. 1268.
53 Ibid., p. 1251.
54 Neuburger, p. 192.
55 H. Göpfert in *Fischer—Lexikon Medizin*, I, Frankfurt, Hamburg, 1959, pp. 85 ff.
56 *DC*, the Seven Liberal Arts.
57 Baer (1929), no. 318, pp. 468 ff. (10 April 1378): 'e havets a fer ab gents sobtils et entricades' ('we have to do with a people who are clever and devious').

11 The Medicine of Common Sense

1 This notice is also found rather interestingly in the Brussels MS. of Thietmar of Merseburg, *Chron.* IV 48 (*MGH SS* III, 788, 26 ff.).
2 Thietmar of Merseburg, *Chron.* IV 48 (*MGH SS* III, 788, 26 ff.).
3 Venerable Bede, *History of the Anglo-Saxon Church*, I, 19.
4 *Legenda Aurea* (Benz, p. 195).
5 *PL*, 171, 1537 A.
6 Mark 6: 13.
7 James 5: 14
8 Opitz, pp. 20 ff.
9 E. Stemplinger, *Antiker Volksglaube*, Stuttgart, 1948, p. 186.
10 H. Diller, *Ausdrucksformen des methodischen Bewusstseins in den hippokratischen Epidemien*, Arch. f. Begriffsgesch., 9, Bonn, 1964, pp. 134 ff.
11 Ibid.
12 Sura 12, 82; 3, 115; 35, 9.
13 In Dante, *Inferno*, XVII, 85–7, natural and demoniacal conceptions of sickness are placed alongside each other.
14 von Grunebaum, p. 167.
15 Ibid. For a natural explanation of sickness and healing see Talmud, Awoda Sara 54/55.
16 Buber, p. 186.
17 Ibid., p. 187.
18 OT, Deuteronomy 30: 11 ff.
19 Talmud, Bawa Mezia 59b. The Talmud is obviously also aware of belief in miracles, but a comparison of the wonder stories of miracles of the Christians with the Haggadah, shows that even there psychological interest plays the dominant role. When St Benedict produced corn during a famine (Gregory the Great, *Dial.*, II, 21), the power of God and of his saints were proved thereby. In the story of the woman who had nothing to bake and yet on the sabbath eve heated the stove, the stress is laid on the shame of the poor woman and the heartlessness of

her well-off neighbour, whose disappointment at the miraculous gift of bread, which falls to the lot of the poor woman, makes the psychological point of the story (Taanit 24b/25a). The Jewish theme is not just 'God and Man' but 'Man and his Fellow in the sight of God'. The same story is found together with an erotic motif in the *Arabian Nights*; Littmann III, 720–5.

20 Talmud, Shabbat 88b. (Also in the German *Ma'asse Buch*: *Geschichtenbuch aus dem jüd. dt. Maassegebuch*, selected and trans. L. Strauss, Schockenbuch no. 18, Berlin, 1934, pp. 7 ff.)

21 I, 69–79 (Cassel, pp. 49 ff.). The proverb also at I, 97. See Schoeps, pp. 33–69 on the difference between Jewish and Christian concepts of belief.

22 von Grunebaum, pp. 435 ff., Goldziher, pp. 254 ff. on 'sunna' and 'bid 'a' (renewal).

23 von Grunebaum, p. 425.

24 Misch, III, 2, 2, pp. 996 ff.

25 von Grunebaum, pp. 279 ff.

26 Wüstenfeld, p. 96.

27 Neuburger, pp. 193 ff.

28 von Grunebaum, pp. 422 ff.

29 Galen, 'The good doctor is a philosopher' (W. Ruegg, *Antike Geisteswelt* . . . , Zürich, Stuttgart, 1964, pp. 335 ff.).

30 Plato, *Theaetetus* 174 A ff.

31 As in *DC*, XV and XVI.

32 Schipperges in *Ärtzliche Praxis* (see n. 52 on p. 175), p. 1251.

33 *DC*, Prologue. C. E. Dubler, 'Das Weiterleben der Antike im Islam', in *Das Erbe der Antike*, Zürich, Stuttgart, 1963, p. 83, traces this unitary concept of physical and mental health to Indian influences.

12   The Jewish Experience

1 Talmud, Kettubot 67b. For 400 sous one could buy two times three oxen.

2 Sota 22b. A further catalogue of Pharisees is in Brachot 14b. (On the connection of Pharisees and Mu'atazilites see Goldziher, p. 326 n. 63.)

3 Brachot 28b.

4 Buber, p. 753.

5 Ibid. Cf. Goldziher, pp. 42 and 336 ff. (bigots in Islam).

6 Buber, p. 394.

7 Buber, p. 533.

8 Glatzer, p. 114.

9 *Kuzari* III 73 (Cassel, p. 296). The Jewish estimation of *Kuzari* is based on the fact that there is found a modern rehash of famous religious sayings based on contemporary spiritual stresses: see J. Breuer, *Der Neue Kusari, Ein Weg zum Judentum*, Frankfurt, 1934.

10 E.g. OT, 2 Samuel 17: 7 ff.

11 E.g. Exodus 32: 30.

12 E.g. Micah 7: 2/3.

13 E.g. 2 Samuel 12: 1–23, where David uses a simile to inspect his sin.

14 S. Landmann, *Jüdische Witze*, Munich, 1963, p. 47. This self-criticism is

based on belief, and is especially shown in the finding of fault in oneself rather than in others, and the Jews consider their banishment as consequent upon their faults and therefore defend their persecutors (Schoeps, pp. 52 ff.).

15 No Jew should carry money with him on the sabbath.

16 S. Landmann, *Jiddisch, Abenteuer einer Sprache*, 1964, Anecdote no. 7, pp. 144 ff.

17 ATh, 1617

18 Eruwin 14b.

19 Rabbot 53b; Bawa Mezia 86b; Derech Erez. s. chap. 5.

20 Leviticus 19: 34; Deuteronomy 10: 19. Both passages cited by Schoeps (pp. 25 ff.) on Jewish law relating to aliens.

21 Vol. II: Ihering cites its words in an actual situation: *Should the Jews become Christians? A word to Friend and Foe* by J. Singer, Vienna, 1884, p. 166.

22 Brachot 17a; cf. Gittin 61a.

23 Ecclesiastes 7: 13 (Micah 4: 5: 'For all peoples wander in the name of their God, but we are made to wander in the name of the Lord, our God, for ever and ever').

24 Steinschneider, p. xxiii.

25 Baer (1961), p. 11.

26 A. D. Atiya, *Kreuzfahrer und Kaufleute*, Stuttgart, 1964, pp. 223 ff.

27 Funk, p. 117. The only complete MS. of the Talmud that we have today is the Codex Hebraicus Monacensis 95 and it is to be found in the Bayerische Staatsbibliothek in Munich. In 1342 it came from France, escaped the burnings of the Talmud in Italy in 1554, and came to Germany in 1588. A South German publishing house is preparing a facsimile.

28 This was also the case if a Talmudist by being provided with clothes etc. was for a time left free to study. (Cf. the life story of Solomon Maimons who died in 1800, ed. K. Ph. Moritz, Gustav-Kiepenheuer-Bücherei 16, 1960, pp. 60–2.)

29 II, 2 (Fiebig, p. 6; in the text the actual words are 'handworking activity' for which reason Rudy, p. 63, uses it to refute the thesis of 'Capitalist people').

30 Moses Maimonides, *Schulordnung*, Glatzer, pp. 122 ff. (The citation from the Talmud of the first sentence is in Shabbat 119b.)

31 Levi-Seligmann, pp. xii ff.

32 Shabbat 127b.

33 Sanhedrin 109b. In Greek mythology (Diodorus, IV, 59; Apollodorus, I, 4; Pausanias, I, 38, 5; Hyginus, 38) Procrustes had two beds or one with adjustable boards. The Talmudist changes this in order to underline the simile for the psychology of prejudice, which lies in the fact of having to adopt a simple rigid system of orientation.

34 *Libri VIII Mirac.*, 1, 4.

35 *Das hebräische Denken im Vergleich mit dem griechischen*, Göttingen, 1959.

36 Ibid., pp. 170 ff.

37 Ibid., p. 172.

38 Ibid.
39 Ibid., p. 178.
40 W. Sombart, M. Erzberger *et al.*, *Judentaufen*, Munich, 1912, pp. 128 ff.
41 Heer, pp. 505 ff.
42 Proverbs 30: 24 ff.
43 No. 113 (cf. nos 134, 151, 229).
44 Fitzmaurice-Kelly.
45 Nos 3, 117, 179, 228.
46 Nos 19 and 24.
47 Nos 89, 161, 194, 225, 238.
48 Nos 108, 133, 275.
49 Nos 43, 58, 77, 120, 270, 288. The 'Siete Partidas', the law book of Alfonso the Wise, on which the later Spanish legal system is based, are also full of these rules for the conduct of life (see Fitzmaurice-Kelly).
50 von Grunebaum, p. 291.

PART II

The folklore material for the 34 exempla has been collected by Haim Schwarzbaum, 'International folklore motifs in Petrus Alfonsi's *Disciplina Clericalis*', *Sefarad* XXI, 1961, pp. 267–99 (Exempla I-VI), XXII, 1962, pp. 17–59 (VII-XXVI), XXII, pp. 321–44 (XXVII-XXXIV) and XXIII, 1963, pp. 54–73 (additions and commentary). Therefore we have limited our references to literary parallels. On individual topics cf. A. Wesselski, *Hodscha Nasreddin*, 2 vols, Weimar, 1911, and Stith Thompson, *Motif Index of Folk-Literature*, 2nd edition, 6 vols, Bloomington, 1955–8.

1 Glatzer, pp. 152 ff.
2 The word 'disciplina' is to be explained by reference to Jewish tradition (Hebrew 'musar', Greek 'paideia'), where the basic meaning is 'instruction for life' (cf. in particular Proverbs 1: 2; 1: 8; 3: 11; 15: 5; 23: 13). This is the source used by Petrus Alfonsi, the Hebrew title of which is Mischle (schlomo), a name which typifies the form of oriental instruction for life. In Europe it later became a popular title for 'florilegia' (e.g. *Disciplina populi Dei in nov. text. ex scriptoribus sacris et profanis coll.*, Vienna, 1739). Perhaps there was a polemical element included in the title which was used in Spain to contrast the art of the 'clericia', i.e. the educated, with that of the 'juglaria', the simple form of players (L. Olschki, *Die romanischen Literaturen des Mittelalters*, Wildpark-Potsdam, 1928, p. 27).
3 Cf. the prologue to the *Conversations*, the *Letter on Study* and the astronomical tables. On proemion topics see Curtius, pp. 402 ff.
4 1 Peter 4: 10.
5 Cf. Jesus Sirach 17, 7.
6 Matthew 5: 15.
7 Cf. Cicero, *De Oratore*, 1, 1.
8 Cf. the foreword to the *Libro de los Engannos* (see above, Part One, section 2) and Gracian, *Handorakel*, no. 300.

9 On the meaning of 'philosophus' see Curtius, pp. 207 ff. (In late antiquity and even in Marie de France the poet was called 'philosophus'; in the *Romance of the Rose* 18, 742, to write poetry is 'travailler en philosophie'.)

10 Castigatio: Cicero, *Tusculan Disputations*, IV, 45 (Boner, *Edelstein*, Preface uses it as a loan word: 'Gut bischaft kestigt wilden Mann ... ').

11 'Similitudo': Lausberg, *Handbuch der literarischen Rhetorik*, Munich, 1960, pp. 421 ff.

12 Ecclesiastes 1: 14 ff.

13 Proverbs 1: 7. (Topos: this motif found also in the *Libro de buen amor* of the archpriest of Hita, Juan Ruiz, c. 1283–1350. On tradesman metaphors cf. the example in Klapper no. 69, where converted Arabs demand the stipulated guaranteed 'hundredfold reward' from the bishop (Matthew 19: 29). Edrik = Idris (cf. Part One, section 9, note 3).

14 Socrates appears in the Arab Middle Ages as the model of the wise man, in two forms: more popular is the image of Socrates the ascetic, confused by tradition with Diogenes (Ex. XXVIII of the *DC*), whereas the Aristotelians Al-Kindi (ob. 873) and Ar-Razi (ob. 925/935) viewed him as the man of 'in media virtus' (Misch, vol. III, 2, 2, p. 978). In Hugh of St Victor, *Erud. Didasc.* (*PL*, 176), III, 2 he is the 'discoverer of ethics', and is supposed to have written 24 works on this subject. It is one of those cases where 'a fluctuating tradition is focused by the use of a well-known name' (Aly, p. 245).

15 'Hypocrisis' as pious self-righteousness or hypocrisy is to be distinguished from the external adaptation required by sheer necessity referred to in Qur'an 16, 108 and 3, 27 ('taqijja', 'circumspection') (Goldziher, pp. 203 f.) (R. Strothmann, *EI*, VI, 680 ff.).

16 Ibn 'Arabi (ob. 1240) says: 'I shall keep quiet about my mystical preferences for men shall hold them against me.' Al-Ghazzah (ob. 1111) gives a psychological analysis of 'hypocrisis' in his *Path of the Servant of God* (translated and explained by E. Bannerth, Salzburg, *Wort und Antwort*, 33, 1964, p. 174) where it is determined to take part in the jihad or 'religious war'.

17 The stereotyped introduction to a saying ('alius dixit') is found both in the florilegium style of antiquity, and in oriental usage (Stobaeus, Hitopadeśa, Talmud, Ḥunayn, etc.).

18 On the identification of Bileam (OT, Numbers 22: 5 ff.) and Luqman (Qur'an, sura 31; Littmann, *Arabian Nights*, I, 657 and II, 421) see B. Heller, *EI*, III, pp. 38–41.

19 Cf. ATh, 280 A; Proverbs 30: 25; *Count Lucanor* no. 37.

20 ATh, 670; cf. 1375. In Werner, g. 1. p. 55 the motif is used to blame women—'a cock is content with three times five hens, but a woman is not content with three times five men'. *Born Judas* no. 20.

21 ATh, 893; *GR*, 129; Vincent of Beauvais, *Speculum Historiae*, 15, 6; *Legenda Aurea*, chap. 175; *Count Lucanor* no. 38; Polyaenus, *Strateg.*, I, 40; Palmblätter, pp. 33–7; *Born Judas* no. 164. In the Balaam story (Burchard, pp. 85 ff.) a few good works show themselves to be friends at death. Hans Sachs, *Fastnachtspielregister*, no. 31.

22 Jesus Sirach 6: 7.

23 This experience is voiced by Socrates (*Phaedrus*, III, 9), where he answers

a question as to why he has built his house so small: 'In order that I can fill it with true friends' (on Socrates in the barrel see note 14).

24 Cf. Ovid, *Tristia*, I, 9, 5; Cicero, *Laelius*, 22.

25 B. Heller (*Handwörterbuch des deutschen Märchens* I, 350 ff.) considers the connection of citizenship and friendship to be basic. *GR* 108 and 171 (mentioning Petrus Alfonsi); Boccaccio, *Dec.*, X, 8; Frenzel s.v. 'Titus and Gisippus', Valerius Maximus, IV, 7; *Arabian Nights*, Day 976; *Carm. Cantab.* No. 6; *Legenda Aurea* (Benz, pp. 316 ff. and 972); Hyginus, 257 (Schiller, 'Die Burgschaft'); *Jātaka* 513; Heller, pp. 10 ff.; *Arabian Nights*, Littmann III, 512–18; Wesselski no. 120 (= Sellheim pp. 41 ff.).

26 Feeling the pulse and examining the urine bear witness to the speedy introduction of medical techniques of investigation (Neuburger, p. 169, note 3, 269 and 309; John of Capua, Geissler p. 362, 18 ff.). Cf. the anecdote in Ekkehard's 'Casus St Galli', chap. 123, where the duke who looks at the girl's urine, diagnoses pregnancy in order to put the doctor Notker to the test. ATh. 1641 A.

27 Love sickness: *Arabian Nights*, Littmann III, 433, ff.; von Grunebaum, pp. 397 ff.; cf. Opitz, pp. 21 ff. (psychologically induced conditions are classed as sickness in the Qur'an).

28 Heinrich von Behringen (c. 1300) in his middle high German version made all pretty girls come forward (Howie, pp. 569).

29 This oxymoron is noticed by W. Kayser, *Das sprachliche Kunstwerk*, Bern, 1968, p. 113. Cf. the Tristram romance—'Isot, Isot la blonde/Merveil de tout le monde! /Isot ma dure, Isot m'amie./En vous ma morte, en vous ma vie.'

30 Jesus Sirach 6, 13; al-Mubashshir: 'Why do you ask God to guard you from your friends and not from your enemies? Because I myself can protect myself against my enemies, but not against my friends.' (Cf. St Maximos, *PG*, 91, 761 D.) In the dungeons of the Doge's palace in Venice the proverb was found scratched on a wall: 'Da chi mi fido/ Guardi mi Dio/Da chi non mi fido, mi guardarò io' (Knust, pp. 358 ff.).

31 Cf. Cicero, *Laelius*, 60–78.

32 Cicero, *Laelius*, 44

33 Gracian, *Handorakel*, nos 179 and 231.

34 In Arabic: An emperor said: 'I have more power over what has not been said than over what has; for what I have not said, I can always expose, but what I have once expressed I can no more hide' (Knust, p. 184). Babylonian proverb: 'What you have said, will quickly rebound on you.' (Loretz, p. 123). Proverbs 10: 20; Chaucer, *Canterbury Tales* 2333/34 (Tale of Meliboeus). There is a proverb from Cairo—'The intelligent man buries and is buried, the fool broadcasts everything' (Littmann, *Spruchweisheit*, p. 17).

35 Jesus Sirach 21, 7. The word 'leccator', a germanic word (*'leccare' = lecken, west German 'likkon') was probably introduced into medieval Latin by Isidore of Seville as a synonym for Latin 'gulosus' (greedy person). Martial, *Epigrams*, x 50, 5, 'lector nimium gulosus' = 'literary gourmand'; see Meyer-Lubke, *Romanisches etymologisches Wörterbuch*, no. 5027 s.v. 'lingo'). Thence it came into the vernacular, and built up a

complex of human experiences. Du Cange gives three uses: A feminine ornament ('monile') is explained—'quod munit pectus mulieris ne leccatores possint immittere manum in pectus eius' (cf. the fact that a Paris manuscript of the *DC*, at Ex. IX calls an adulterous woman's lover 'leccator', and refers to her lover with the possessive adjective 'her lover', 'suus leccator'). There is mention of a 'rusticus leccator' who gave himself up to Balduin, Count of Flanders in 1225 (Vincent of Beauvais, *Speculum Historiae*, 30, 127 = *MGH SS* 24.837). Finally negligence in study is termed 'turpiter et leccanter vivere'. What sort of man is meant should be clear.

36 For the magnet stone ('adamas') see Plato, *Ion*, 533 D/E; Thorndike, p. 791 (alchemical qualities); Bachtold-Staubli, *Handwörterbuch der deutschen Aberglaubens*, V, pp. 1480 ff, Berlin-Leipzig, 1932/33. Husbands who did not trust their wives used to put it at night under their pillows. If the wife was innocent, she immediately disarmed her husband, if not she fell straight out of bed; Grimm, *Deutsche Sagen*, no. 459 (the stone preserves matrimonial love); E. Stemplinger, *Antiker Volksglaube*, Stuttgart, 1948, p. 186 (sympathetic magic). For the proverb see Jesus Sirach 13, 15; Cicero, *Cato Major*, 3, 9; for more material from West and East, see Knust, pp. 631 ff. (Yiddish version—'Join up with a parfumier, and you'll smell as nice as he'.)

37 Also in Petrus Damiani, *PL* 144, 258 (Welter, p. 103).

38 'The higher the mountain, the deeper the valley, the bigger the man, the harder he falls' (Knust, p. 646). Cf. Herodotus I, 32 and VII, 10 E.

39 Arabic parallel: Knust, p. 360. Cf. La Fontaine, *Fables*, VIII, 10; cf. also note 19 to Part One, section 7.

40 Gracian, *Handorakel*, no. 275: 'One should never exclude oneself, for by detachment one prejudices the others.'

41 Proverbs 7: 11.

42 'Partes': Seneca, *Epistulae Morales*, 80, 7; what is meant is shown further by *Epistulae Morales*, 47, 16/17. On the acting metaphor, see Curtius, pp. 138–44.

43 Islam holds the view that there is no virtue in getting rid of all one's goods and then begging oneself; let he only who has a superfluity give alms (Goldziher, p. 142).

44 Cf. the description of the 'Spring of life' in Ibn Gabirol (K. Schubert, *Die Religion des nachbiblischen Judentums*, Freiburg-Vienna, 1955, pp. 114 ff.).

45 Common in both East and West: 'No one repents for having kept silent, but for having spoken one repents often' (Knust, p. 330). Talmud, Megilla 18a.

46 Disraeli, *The Infernal Marriage*, 3: 'I am always thankful for my simple habit of always waiting until I am at the door before speaking.'

47 'Do not ask who says it, but what he says' (Knust, p. 645).

48 Ancient Egyptian, c. 2400 B.C.: 'Be not proud of your knowledge, and be not too confident that you are a man of learning' (*Geschichte in Quellen*, no. 5, pp. 19 ff.). Talmud, Tmura 16a.

49 Arabic: 'Whoever is quick to ask questions will attain to knowledge'

(Knust, p. 269). A similar remark re intellectual understanding is found in the tract of the Mishna entitled *Sayings of the Fathers*, V, 7 (Fiebig, p. 29).

50 Cf. Hugh of St Victor, *Erud. Didasc.*, III 14 (*PL*, 176). The elder Jibril, royal physician, and professor of medicine in Baghdad, sat modestly among his students, in order to be able to learn from Ḥunayn (Wüstenfeld, pp. 15 ff.; cf. p. 66 above).

51 Seneca, *Epistulae Morales*, 44, 5, 'Animus facit nobilem'. For the ancient and medieval topos see Curtius, pp. 179 ff.

52 On the poet's role at the Caliph's court, see von Grunebaum, pp. 319–28, and stories in Weisweiler, pp. 26–33 and *Arabian Nights*, Littmann III, 524f. Cf. Curtius, pp. 468 ff.

53 A similar remark is found in the chapter on Evil Company, the second part of which ('et vituperium laus') Schmidt (1827) viewed as a later accretion (unjustly).

54 Aesop Halm, 157; Babrius, 62; Wesselski, no. 130; La Fontaine, VI, 7. Chauvin, IX, 17 sees a reference to matriarchy here. The point of such stories is satirical: whoever approaches social considerations so tactlessly is worthy of blame (Hermes, pp. 34 ff.).

55 On the topos of bemoaning the passage of time, see Curtius, pp. 102–6.

56 Thomas à Kempis, *De Imitatione Christi*, III, 50, 56.

57 The reference is to the most widely spread work of medieval medicine, the pseudo-Aristotelian Diatetic known under the name of the *Secretum Secretorum*. This was well established in the East in the eleventh century and was translated from Arabic into Latin by Johannes the Spaniard with the title *De Observatione Diete* (Schıpperges, pp. 77–80). A manuscript in Groningen (Hilka, no. 48) includes it with the *DC*. A sketch of the 'artes liberales' is first found in a fifteenth-century manuscript (see also Steinschneider, p. 256). On exchange of letters see *Nizāmulmulk*, Schabinger, p. 126; Diogenes Laertius, *Vitae Philosophorum*, V, 27. M. Brocker, 'Aristoteles als Alexanders Lehrer in der Legende', thesis Bonn, 1966 (see the review by K. Bayer in *Gymnasium* 75, Heidelberg, 1968, 3, pp. 293–5).

58 Cf. Werner, no. 85, p. 76.

59 Berthold of Regensburg uses this image to compare pardonable sins (chaff) with mortal sins (stones) (Linsenmayer, p. 343).

60 Santillana names 1454 as the year of the death of Alvaro de Luna 'tan gran eclipse de luna' (see also Fitzmaurice-Kelly).

61 For the history of medieval education: *Artes Liberales, von der antiken Bildung zur Wissenschaft des Mittelalters*, ed. J. Koch, *Studien und Texte zur Geistesgeschichte des Mittelalters*, 5, Leiden, 1959. On the 'artes' in the *DC* see Throndike, pp. 72 ff. and Millás, *Sefarad* III, pp. 66 ff. The translation here follows the text of González (contrary to a conjecture of mine based on the London manuscript in *Der Altsprachliche Unterricht* VI, 5, Stuttgart, 1964, pp. 73–98). Cf. also J. Dolch, *Lehrplan des Abendlandes, Zweieinhalb Jahrtausende seiner Geschichte*, 2nd ed., Ratingen, 1965, p. 131.

62 'Nigromancia': OT, 1 Samuel 28; Bachtold-Staubli, *Handwörterbuch des deutschen Aberglaubens*, VI, pp. 997–1002; Baer (1929), no. 219, 224,

388 (Jews with alchemical leanings); J. H. Huizinga, *The Waning of the Middle Ages*, Penguin, 1972; A. Wesselski, *Die Legende um Dante*, Weimar, 1921, pp. 7–12; Erasmus, *Letters*, trans. and ed. W. Kohler (in German), collection Dieterich 2, Bremen 3, 1956, pp. 67 ff. (exact description of a case of magic); Hermes, pp. 113–18; cf. note 18 in Part One, section 9.

63 Chess allegory; *GR*, 166; at times to play chess was forbidden by theologians (Petrus Damiani, *Epistolae*, I 10). First isolated reference to chess in the West in *Ruodlieb* IV, 187–230.

64 Cf. the catalogue of vices in the NT. Rom. 1: 29–31; 13: 13; I Cor. 5: 11; 6: 9–10; II Cor. 12: 20–1; Gal. 5: 19–21; Eph. 4: 31; 5: 3–4; Coloss. 3: 5 and 8; I Tim. 1: 9–10. The 'industries' are also referred to in the 'Siete Partidas' of Alfonso the Wise (see also Fitzmaurice-Kelly).

65 Proverbs 20: 17 (cf. 9: 17).

66 Gracian, *Handorakel*, no. 70.

67 Cf. Matthew 5: 38 ff.

68 Proverbs 26: 27; Gracian, *Handorakel*, nos 138 and 172; Boner, *Edelstein*, 71, 61—'Wer ab den Galgen lost den diep/Dar nach hat er in niemand hep' ('pendulus' can also mean 'pendulum').

69 ATh, 155; Aesop Halm 976; *Phaedrus*, IV, 18; Babrius 42; *GR*, 174 (emperor instead of wanderer; philosopher instead of fox); Romulus n. 13 (Indian authorship in John of Capua, Geissler, pp. 179 ff. where the serpent is treated as a domestic animal, is confused with Greek). G. A. Megas, 'Some Oral Greek Parallels to Aesop's Fables' in *Humaniora, Festschrift for G. A. Taylor*, New York, 1960, pp. 198 ff. (II, The farmer and the snake). Amongst the Heansen (Bavarian and Alemannic settlers in settled areas), the combination of this with blaming women is found—a fox should have the hens as his reward, but the woman beats him to death, so that as he is dying, he realises the truth of what the serpent said; i.e. that the only thanks one is entitled to in this world, is no thanks (J. R. Bunker, *Schwänke, Sagen und Märchen in heanzischen Mundart*, Leipzig, 1906, n. 48, p. 108). La Fontaine, *Fables*, VI, 13. In the *Arabian Nights* (Littmann II, 249–68) the fox teases the wolf and tells this fable (basis of the Reynard-epos: Gerhardt, p. 353). Ljungman (pp. 23 ff.), traces the literary process. In Turkish: Bayazid is bitten by a dog which makes a similar remark: 'Man acts like a man, and a dog as dogs do' (Chauvin, VIII, n. 113).

70 Stereotyped question in the Pañcatantra, and its Eastern and Western offshoot, the *Hitopadeśa*, *Count Lucanor*, and the *Arabian Nights* (Littmann I, 27; II, 530); cf. Gerhardt, p. 389.

71 ATh, 1661; *GR*, 157; *Cento Novelle Antiche*, no. 53; Petrus Alfonsi exemplifies a practical rule for the conduct of life (Do not wait for a better chance!), whereas a Breslau manuscript stresses the moralising aspect: 'Tell this story to a sinner. "A sinner is like a hunchback, or a one-eyed man, or a mangy one, or a leper, for he indulges in like things. Just as they do, so the sinner puts off turning over a new leaf because of shame, and begins sinning new sins, so that he is led by one sin to another".'

72 The coins mentioned in the *DC* are Carolingian silver coins which were imported into Muslim Spain at an early date. The pound (libra 327 gr.) had 240 denarii of c. 2gr (a half denarius was called an obolus), 20 solidi (each of 12 denarii): H. Prienne, *Sozial- und Wirtschaftsgeschichte Europas im Mittelalter*, Collection Dalp 25, Bern, 1947, pp. 108 ff. and 131.

73 Psalm 1: 1; 140: 2; Proverbs 29: 16.

74 Cf. Wesselski n. 42 and 118 where someone enters a brothel in a hassidic story (Buber, p. 753) the Rabbi hauls those whose souls are endangered out of the brothel. This motif is found in two stories in which the seductive power of music, particularly singing, plays a decisive role which is connected with the motif of the 'blaming of women'. It is to be explained by reference to Jewish tradition, which has been made ironical by means of the twist at the end of Ex. VIII. The rabbinic warning against seduction by music refers to Arabic love songs. The distance that brings Petrus Alfonsi to this rigorous moral attitude, shows his impartial relations with Arabic folklore. See further S. Wittmayer Baron, *Social and Religious History of the Jews*, VII, London and New York, 1965, pp. 205 ff.

75 Proverbs 1: 15; in the Castilian translation there is no addition (González, p. 116).

76 On the peculiar admixture of the presentation of the seductive woman who turns man to destruction, and the 'Come hither' or the voice of the bird of death, see: Bachtold-Staubli, *Handwörterbuch des deutschen Aberglaubens*, II sp. 1073–9 and IV sp. 1188–97, and Thomas Mann, *Felix Krull*, II, 6. This cross-fertilisation is no problem in matters of Eastern composition, as the presentations all depend on each other (H. A. Winkler, *Salomo und die Karina, Veröffentlichen des Orientalischen Seminars der Univ. Tübingen, Abhandlungen zu Orientalische Philologie und zu allgemeiner Religionsgeschichte*, ed. E. Littmann and J. W. Hauer, no. 4, Stuttgart, 1931, pp. 50–7 and 86 ff.). An ancient form of the same thing, is the Siren who lures men to destruction by her singing (Homer, *Od.* XII, 165 ff.; Achilles Tatius, I, 7 ff.); for the medieval topos see Marbod of Rennes, liber X, III, 60 ff. = *PL*, 1963 ff.; an ancient Italian anonymous work deals with nuns in the same way, see Wulff, p. 159.

77 The Castilian translation gives: 'announces the death of the screech owl' (Gonzalez, p. 118).

78 ATh, 247; *Buddh–Märch.*, p. 73 (*Jātaka* 402).

79 Ecclesiastes 25: 16 (medieval topos: Wulff, pp. 38 ff.).

80 Proverbs 7: 22.

81 Proverbs 5: 2 ff., and 7: 6–23. In Boccaccio too, *Dec.* IX, 9, Solomon is the man with knowledge of women.

82 Ovid, *Ars Amatoria*, III 201, calls woman's tricks 'ars'.

83 ATh, 1419 C; *GR*, 122; *Cent Nouvelles Nouvelles*, 16; Heptameron, I, 6; Bandello, I, 23. Ex. IX-XIII were suggested by Vincent of Beauvais, *Speculum Morale*, liber III, pars 9, dist. 5.

84 *GR*, 123; Aristophanes, *Thesmoph.*, 498 ff. (re the 'nest of novelle' in this passage see O. Seel, *Aristophanes oder Versuch über Komödie*,

pp. 115–20; Bédier, *Fabliaux*, Paris, 1895, pp. 89, 280 and 422 ff.

85 ATh, 1419 A/B; *Hitopadeśa* II 9; *Hist. Septem Sap.*, I, no. 14; *Decameron*, VII, 6; in Petrus Alfonsi there is only one lover.

86 ATh, 2300; *KHM*, 86; Aesop Halm 117; *Cento Novelle Antiche*, no. 31; *Don Quixote* I, 20 (Avellanada in chap. 21 wants to outdo the exemplum in which he gets geese to cross a small bridge: see also Fitzmaurice-Kelly). For the coins, see note 72.

87 ATh, 1515; *GR*, 28; *Hist. Septem Sap.*, I, no. 5; *Arabian Nights*, Littmann IV, 292 ff.; *Decameron* III, 6; Hans Sachs, FSR, no. 61; Ljungman (p. 301) traces the literary development; Gunter (*Buddha*, pp. 110 ff.) draws attention to Arabic mediation. Cf. Gerhardt, pp. 316–18.

88 ATh, 1377; *Decameron*, VII, 4; Ljungman, p. 291; for the motif 'Studium of women' see Hermes, pp. 117 ff. The basic idea of Cervantes' story *El Celoso entremeño* is already found in Petrus Alfonsi: 'The novella proves the inefficiency of the computations of a jealous man, and thereby of men in general .... The structure of the story lies in how to present a thought structure through a structure of technical reprimands of precaution' (L. Spitzer, *Zeitschrift für romanische Philologie*, 51/1931, p. 196). Cervantes' desire is to give an 'example and image' of 'how little a man can trust keys, doors and walls, as long as desire is still unchecked'.

89 Proverbs 31: 10–31.

90 ATh, 1617; *GR* 118; *Cento Novelle Antiche*, no. 74 (J. Ulrich, *Anhang*, I, p. 106), *Born Judas*, no. 182; Wesselski, no. 151; Nizāmulmulk, pp. 174 ff. (the two pots) and pp. 183 ff. (p. 187 'There are many other stories'). The trick with the chest is found in *El Cid* too (Romance 44) as feigned possession of gold (Landau, p. 82; Heller, pp. 5 ff.). Till Eulenspiegel, Volksbuch 91.

91 Here the relationships are presumed to be in one city (one manuscript gives here: 'lapides remorebat et locabat ut decebat').

92 Book metaphor: Curtius, pp. 312 ff. Here it is the image of the 'memory bank' (see H. Weinrich, 'Typen der Gedächtnismetaphoren', *Archiv für Begriffsgeschichte*, vol. 9, Bonn, 1964, pp. 23–6.

93 I Cor. 3:2; Hebr. 5:12; medieval topos see Welter, p. 75. On the Christian estimate of the 'sermo humilis' which is founded on that image see Auerbach, *Literatursprache und Publikum in der lateinischen Spätantike und im Mittelalter*, pp. 46 ff.

94 Cf. Talmud, Jewamot 115a; another Jewish version is given by Chauvin ad loc. David while still a child broke the jars in which the owner had ordered honey to be stored. It was noticed that the earth was sticky with honey—the same method of fraud is used in Ex. XV by the defrauded party to regain his money.

95 See also Weisweiler, pp. 125–7 for the idea that judgment will be entrusted to the clever man without charge.

96 Steinhöwel (no. 3) calls it yeast.

97 ATh, 926D; J. P. Hebel, *Der Kluge Pichter*.

98 A necklace: Isidore, *Orig.*, 19, 31 (De ornamentis capitis feminarum, no. 12).

99 I.e. in the sense of predestination ('gadar') (Goldziher, pp. 91 ff.).

100 ATh, 926; I Kings 3: 16–28 (the archetype of all stories of the wise judge: see Hermes, pp. 94 ff.).

101 The whole sections in Chaucer, *Canterbury Tales*, Meliboeus 2498 ff. with a mention of 'Piers Alphonce'.

102 *GR*, 103 ('Do not stray even one footstep from the main path'). *Ruodlieb* V, 457 ff.

103 ATh, 910 B; Talmud, Eruwin V, 1, 53b ('one way is shorter, but long, the other longer, but short'); J. P. Hebel, *Der verachtete Rat* ('one arrives faster at one's goal, when one journeys for a long time').

104 A German sermon of the twelfth century says: 'The way to Hell is broad; that to Heaven narrow' (Linsenmayer, p. 249; Midrash Jalkut Shabas 273b, Levi-Seligmann, p. 68).

105 The 'Golden Rule' is of Greek not Jewish origin (see A. Dihle, *Die goldene Regel, Eine Einführung in die Geschichte der antiken und früh-christlichen Vulgarethik*, pp. 82 ff. It is nevertheless worthy of note that Rabbi Hillel views it as a résumé of the Tora (Talmud, Shabbas 31a).

106 ATh, 1626; *GR*, 106; originally a Arabic; Spies, *Orientalische Stoffe in den Kinder- und Hausmärchen der Brüder Grimm*, p. 12; cf. Klapper, nos 97 and 98. The exemplum really belongs to the groups of comparative religion stories, the most well known of which is the parable of the ring (*GR*, 89; *Cento Novelle Antiche*, 73; *Decameron*, I, 3; Landau, p. 143; a Jewish version in *Born Judas* no. 253, where Landau, p. 64, mentions only two jewels). For the speech of the three 'frauds', Moses, Jesus and Muhammed, see Nizāmulmulk.

107 ATh, 555 (Ljungman, p. 162). Further developments of the adage (Latin and French) in the *Compilacio singularis exemplorum* (ed. Hilka, *91. Jahresbericht der Schlesien Gesellschaft für vaterländische Cultur*, Breslau, 1914, no. 120), e.g. 'Qui captat cuncta, totum predit sive cuncta.'

108 See also Vincent of Beauvais, *Speculum Naturae*, 18, 23.

109 This exemplum belongs to the genus of funny stories that contain an agon against extreme guile and craftiness; most of them originate in Egypt (Herodotus, II, 121; Aly, pp. 67 ff.; ATh, 950; *Arabian Nights*: Littmann III, 524 ff.; IV, 685–776; Weisweiler, pp. 36–41). Nedui is perhaps derived from Arabic 'nadwa' (circle, oval), thus 'buddy' perhaps.

110 Honey pancakes as in Littmann IV, 714 ff.

111 Leviticus 19: 18; Mark 12: 31 (the passage from the OT is noted cited after the Vulgate: 'amicum'—'fratrem').

112 Josephus, *Ant. Jud.* XII, 4, 9; Poggio, *Facetiae* 58 (where the reference to 'cane della scala' gives rise to the pun, 'cane' = dog, and thereby reveals his 'joy in the actualisation of widely spread story material'); Pabst, pp. 65 ff.; Hermes, p. 11.

113 Jesus Sirach 12, 4. 'Liberalitas' is viewed as the middle stage between two extremes in accordance with Aristotelian ethics; *Nicomachean Ethics* II 1106 A/B.

114 Gracian, *Handorakel*, nos 31, 38, 51. 171.

115 Horace, *Epistle* I, 2, 26 ('Semper avarus eget').

116 ATh, 150; Barlaam and Josaphat: Burchard, pp. 60 ff. (the peasant

serves as exemplum for a true servant of God; *GR*, 167 (second counsel: 'You're an idiot and will always remain such!'); *Born Judas* no. 171. Wieland in the *Deutsche Merkur* for 1778 ('Don't believe all that you hear!' 'Don't cry over anything you haven't had! Fool, hang on tightly to what you have in your hand, and don't let go!'); cf. *GR*, 103 and *Count Lucanor* no. 47. A Vatican manuscript puts these three rules in a distich: 'Non nimis amissis doleas nec omne quod audis/credas nec cupias id quod habere nequis.' The formulae used in the French lay approach closest those of the *DC* 'Do not believe all that you are told!' 'Do not cry over that which you never possessed!' and 'Do not throw away what you have in your grasp!' (Lommatzsch, pp. 28 ff.)

117 Cf. Luke 6: 43–5. An Arabic translation of selected passages from Ptolemy styles itself 'Fruit of the Tree' (Steinschneider, p. 527), i.e. the pick of the entire work.

118 ATh, 32; 154 I, II; Aesop Halm 45; *Phaedrus*, IV, 9; *Roman de Renart*, I, 240 (Gerhardt, p. 353; germ-cell already found here); La Fontaine, XI, 6; Gerhardt of Minden (*MLG*, XIIc) phrases the judgment thus: 'Such is life: one falls, another rises, one is successful, the other not. That's the unsettled world.' Bernard of Siena (1380–1444) closes his version with the words: 'O the world is one great staircase; always someone going up or down!' This is the general opinion of the revolution of human affairs: Herodotus, I, 207, 2 (already found in Midrash, Rabbot 33b, bound up with the idea of the well)—'The world is like a bucket in a well; when it's full it's emptied and when empty it's filled.' In the *Arabian Nights* (Littmann II, 249–68) there is a satire on the relationship between a calif and his minister in a story where 'wisdom lessons' are parodied (II, 250: 'Then the sage said:' = *DC* on Concourse with Kings; II, 266: When the fox has climbed out, he tells the wolf the story of the thankless serpent = *DC* Ex. V; see note 69).

119 The wolf will gobble you up! (Aesop Halm 275; Babrius 16) = The devil will carry you off! (ATh, 1186; Ljungman, p. 275; Wesselski, no. 36; Gregory the Great, *Dialogue* III, 20; Chaucer, *Canterbury Tales*, The Friar's Tale, 1299–1664. For a thorough and detailed treatment of this motif, see L. Röhrich, *Der Deutschunterricht*, Stuttgart, 1962, vol. 2, pp. 49–68.)

120 For processes between man and beast see H. Gunkel, *Das Märchen im Alten Testament*, Tübingen, 1921, pp. 26 ff.; cf. the philosophic story of the *Ikhwan assafa* translated by F. Dieterici under the title *Tier und Mensch vor dem König der Genien* (Berlin, 1858) and edited by him (Leipzig, 1881).

121 For the reflection of the moon considered as a cheese see ATh, 34; 121; 1250.

122 Originally Indian: Gunter, *Buddha*, p. 106; John of Capua, Geissler, p. 32; *GR*, 136.

123 Cf. Herodotus, VII, 10e (greatness is dangerous for most people).

124 Jesus Sirach 29, 17. Cf. the passage in the *DC* on the Ant, the Cock and the Dog.

125 Ecclesiastes 10: 16 : Arabic, 'Go not near princes when they are angry,

nor near the sea when there is a storm!' (Knust, p. 375; king joined with sea in Herodotus, VII, 160.) Cf. John of Capua, s.v. 'king', Geissler, pp. 403 ff.

126 The French translation of al-Mubashshir's book of sayings takes into consideration the relationships of Feudalism: 'You must both in war and peace conduct yourself in a knightly manner; for if you save nothing in peace, you will be requited when you need it' (Knust, p. 579). Cf. note 57 (Aristotle's letter to Alexander).

127 2 MSS. read: 'Sed tandem [Hilka conjectures tendente] omnino animo pertinaci ad malum pronus fuit. In illius igitur necem immisericordes et barbaras suscitavit gentes.' The translation follows this text.

128 In al-Mubashshir the speech concerns only land not a king (Knust, p. 234). Steinschneider, p. 258 (*Secretum Secretorum*: cf. note 57) Sacchetti, *Novella* 157.

129 For reception ceremonial see Littmann IV, 213.

130 For similar thoughts in Arabic tradition see von Grunebaum, pp. 554 ff., n. 72. (The caliph al Ma'mun (813–833), is said to have said: 'The man who has the best life, is the one with a large house, a beautiful wife, and adequate fortune, and who knows not us, nor we him.')

131 Jesus Sirach 13, 9 ff.

132 See too Mishna, 'Sayings of the fathers', where consorting with kings is warned against.

133 Ecclesiastes 8: 2 ff.

134 Similar rules for relationships are already found in 2300 B.C. in the book of sayings of Ptahhotep (*Geschichte in Quellen*, no. 5, pp. 19 ff.).

135 Seiler, *Deutsche Sprichwörterkunde*, Munich, 1922, p. 336: 'Whoever works himself to death in his master's service, is carried off by the devil.' Furthermore pointed remarks on royal service in John of Capua, who in his translation of the story of the royal physician Burzoe (VIc), taken from the Pañcatantra and from the Persian translation thereof, says: 'Although he was in royal service, yet he was a wise and good man' (Geissler, p. 18).

136 Cf. the Midrash on table-manners, Derech Erezr., cap. 6, 8, 9 (Levi-Seligmann, pp. 222 ff.), where invitations and acceptance, eating and drinking are treated as in the *DC* (more directly e.g., 'To empty the glass in one gulp is not polite; in three that is affectation, but in two is the right proportion'). Jesus Sirach 31, 12–24. The German passage from al-Ghazzâli's chef d oeuvre (see Goldziher, pp. 181 ff.) has recently been newly edited by H. Kindermann, *Über die guten Sitten beim Essen und Trinken*, Brill, Leiden, 1964. See there for further information on the history of our table customs. No. 46 of the *Compilacio singularis exemplorum* (see note 107) contains some advice on 'conduct at table' (e.g. 'Mensa submota prius ablue, postea pota!'). Cf. the opinions given in Werner, p. 130 under 'Tischregeln'.

137 'Parapsis': Isidore, *Orig*. 20, 4 ('quadrangulum et quadrilaterum vas', i.e. paribus absidiis). Proverbs 23: 1.

138 Genesis 18: 1–8; 19: 1 ff.; ATh, 750; *KHM*, 87; Frenzel, pp. 517 ff.; cf. *Count Lucanor* no. 35 (a poor nobleman who is in need); see also

Nizāmulmulk; Rabbi Levi Jizchak of Berditschew (Buber, pp. 359 ff.) gives the following interpretation: 'Know ye what difference there was between our father Abraham, peace be upon him, and Lot? Why is the story told with such pleasure of how Abraham offered to the angels curds, milk and a tender calf? For Lot too he baked a cake and prepared a meal. Why is it seen as his due that Abraham invites him into his house? He invited Lot in and gave him shelter! But the fact is so: Of Lot it is said: "The angels came to Sodom." Of Abraham however it is said: "He lifted up his eyes and saw that men stood before him." Lot saw angel shapes. Abraham poor dust-covered men, in need of rest and thirsty for refreshment,' Talmud, Shabbas 127a (good treatment of guests as a necessary part of divine service). See also Talmud, Kiddushin 32b, for question of rank in connection with the story of Abraham's hospitality.

139 Cairene proverb: 'Eat your friend's bread, for it will delight him; Eat your enemy's bread, for it will spite him' (Littmann, *Spruchweisheit*, p. 25).

140 Old Arabian: Kabbani no. 180.

141 ATh, 1560, 1561 and 2040; Wesselski, nos 20 and 47; cf. further versions in Hermes, pp. 5 ff.

142 The same thought: Herodotus, VII, 46 3. Cf. Aly, pp. 281 ff.

143 Gregory the Great's *Moralia in Job* were widely read in the Middle Ages.

144 Moses Maimonides, too, is aware of the misunderstandings that are commonly connected with the concepts of happiness and unhappiness (Glatzer, p. 97).

145 *Phaedrus*, IV, 18; Herodotus, III, 40, 2. Cf. John of Capua, Geissler, p. 40, 15 ff., 100, 34 ff.

146 Predestination ('qadar'): Goldziher, pp. 88 ff.

147 On the Islamic conception of Socrates and the interchange with Diogenes see note 14. *GR*, 61. In Ḥunayn, it is Socrates in the barrel, in al-Mubash-shir Diogenes (Knust, pp. 21 and 144). Cf. Cicero, *Tusculan Disputations* V, 32; Plutarch, *Alexander*, 14, 671; Diogenes Laertius, VI, 38; Juvenal, *Satire* 14, 311. Cf. Plato, *Gorgias*, 466 A–471 C and Herodotus, I 30–3; see also Aly, pp. 36 ff.

148 Same method of thinking in Gracian, *Handorakel*, no. 251 and Buber, pp. 538 ff.

149 Jewish proverb: 'The world is a caravanserai, and we are a caravan' (Knust, p. 650). Arabic topos: Littmann IV, 218. Sayings of the Fathers, IV, 16 (Fiebig, p. 25): 'This world is like the ante-room of the next; prepare thyself in the ante-room, so that you may enter the dining room.' Pseudo Plato, *Axiochus*, 365 B 4/5.

150 Job 1 : 21; Clement of Alexandria, *Stromata*, IV, 25 160, 1.

151 Treasures stored up in heaven: Matthew 6: 19–20; Luke 12: 33–4, on which see Strack-Billerbeck, IV, 565 ff. The Barlaam romance (Burchard, pp. 105 ff.): a young man marries a poor maid whose riches are later revealed (cf. the marriage of St Francis to poverty: 1 Celsus 1, 3; 2 Celsus 1, 3).

152 Thief in the night: Matthew 24 : 43. In contrast to the magical signification

in Gregory the Great, *Dialogues*, iii, 22, where the saint rivets the thief to the ground, we have here psychological meaning. Cf. *Count Lucanor* no. 12 (the devil leaves the master thief in the lurch).

153 Life is a dream: a Spanish theme (Gerhardt, pp. 444 ff.). The Hispano-Jewish poet Ibn Chasdai (70 and Steinschneider, pp. 356 ff.) says 'Man's day is a fleeting shadow and his year a dream of the night. Life is a lengthy sleep from which man first awakes at death' (Knust, p. 382). Cf. Pindar, *Pythian Odes*, VIII, 95 ff.

154 Old Arabian: Kabbani, no. 273. On the coins cf. note 72.

155 The MSS. have an interesting medieval conjecture for the unintelligible mango (cattle dealer): 'Quas mango cuidam pretio cupiens emere.'

156 On the common sentiments concerning life in Islam and Christianity (futility, desire for the hereafter), see von Grunebaum, pp. 37 ff.

157 This word was put into the mouth of Muhammed himself (von Grunebaum, p. 167).

158 Werner, q. 224, p. 104.

159 Address of the ancient topos (e.g. *Corpus Inscriptionum Latinorum* 1², 1732: 'Si quaeris, quae sim, cinis en et tosta favilla').

160 *Carmina Med. Aev. Post. Lat.* vol. I, *Initia Carminum et Versuum Medii Aevi Posterioris Latinorum*, Göttingen, 1959, nos 18728 and 19501; cf. *PL*, 145, 968. The formula already found in Arabic proverb poetry in the ninth century came through Spain to Europe in the tenth or eleventh century (K. Künstle, *Ikonographie der christlichen Kunst*, vol. I, pp. 209 ff.). For the accompanying legends see K. Künstle, *Die Legende der drei Lebenden und der drei Toten und der Totentanz*, Freiburg, 1908). How widespread the formula was in Islam can be seen from the parody of 'Umar Khayyam the tent-maker (ob. 1132) 'Last night when full of wine I struck my pitcher on a stone. The pitcher cried: "I was once like you, and you shall be even as I am."'

161 Cf. the story of the city of brass: Littmann IV, 208–59 (denial of the world, p. 235).

162 The golden grave: Quintus Curtius Rufus, *History of Alexander*, X, 31, 9–13. On the transport of the gold Ptolemy says in the Alexander story (chap. 34) 'you have never in all your life killed so many men, as now after your death', *GR*, 61; Otto of Freising, *Chronicles*, II, 25; Hunayn and al-Mubashshir: Knust, pp. 45 ff., 301 ff. and 470 ff. Other Persian and Arabic authors name the wise men at the grave as Plato, Aristotle, Socrates, Hippocrates, Zeno, Pythagoras, Solon, Xenophanes and others (Knust, p. 303). F. Gregorovius (*Geschichte der Stadt Rom im Mittelalter*, vi, 7), records the Roman tradition that Caesar's ashes were kept in the golden ball on the top of the Vatican obelisk. An inscription found there reads: 'Caesar, once you were as great as the world, but now a tiny grave contains you!' Caesar was buried there in order that the world might be subject to him even though dead, as it had been during his life. Cf. *Born Judas* nos 41 and 44.

163 *Born Judas* no. 193; Address to the single soul: Luke 12: 19; *Count Lucanor*, no. 25; Book of Acts in Sayings of the Fathers 11, 1 (Fiebig, p. 6) and Psalm 138: 16. 'Ubi-sunt' topos: Nizāmulmulk; Huizinga, *Waning*

of the Middle Ages (see note 62); Gerhardt, p. 208; Howie, pp. 48, 124; E. Gilson, 'Tables pour l'histoire du thème littéraire "ubi sunt?" in *Les Idées et les lettres*, Paris, 1955, pp. 31–8; J. Engels in *Neophilologus* 44/1960, pp. 221–39 (verse), and pp. 253 ff. The image of the scale is already found in the Egyptian Book of the Dead (*Geschichte in Quellen*, no. 32, pp. 55 ff. and Table I, pp. 48–9).

164 In the French translation of al-Mubashshir's Book of Proverbs 'in genere tuo' is rendered as 'à ton pouvoir'.

165 Ecclesiastes 12: 13–14.

BIBLIOGRAPHY

1 PETRUS ALFONSI AND HIS WORKS

Texts

Petri Alfonsi Disciplina Clericalis, ed. A. Hilka and W. Söderhjelm, Acta Societatis Scientiarum Fennicae, vol. 38, no. 4, Helsingfors, 1911.

Die Disciplina Clericalis des Petrus Alfonsi ... nach allen bekannten Handschriften, ed. A. Hilka and W. Söderhjelm (same text as above without apparatus criticus), Sammlung mittellateinische Texte, Heidelberg, 1911.

Petri Alfonsi Disciplina Clericalis, ed. with notes by F. W. V. Schmidt, Berlin, 1827.

Pedro Alfonso, Disciplina Clericalis, ed. and trans. from Latin, A. González Palencia, Madrid-Granada, 1948.

Pietro Alfonsi, ed. Alberto del Monte, La. Nuova Italia (Primo Scaffale Latino 7), Florence, 1967.

Stücke der Disciplina Clericalis ... in lateinischen Versen der Berliner Handschrift Diez, B28, ed. J. Stalzer, Graz, 1912.

Petri Alfonsi ex Judaeo Christiani Dialogi contra Judaeos, in quibus impiae Judaeorum opiniones ... confutantur quaedamque prophetarum abstrusiora loca explicantur, Migne, *PL*, 157, 535 ff.

Ainaud de Lasarte, J., 'Una versión catalana desconocida de los "Dialogi" de Pedro Alfonso', *Sefarad (Revista de la Escuela de Estudios Hebraicos)*, vol. III, Madrid, 1943, pp. 359–76.

Millás Vallicrosa, J. M., 'La aportación astronómica de Pedro Alfonso', *Sefarad*, vol. III, 1943, pp. 65–105 (texts of *Sententia Petris Ebraei, cognomento Anphus, de Dracone, quam Dominus Walcherus prior Malvernensis ecclesie in Latinam transtulit linguam*, and of the *Epistula de studio artium liberalium praecipue astronomiae ad peripateticos aliosque philosophicos ubique per Franciam*, together with the *Prologus in tabulas astronomicas*).

Background and General

Baer, F., *A History of the Jews in Christian Spain*, vol. I, *From the Age of Reconquest to the Fourteenth Century*, trans. from Hebrew, L. Schoffman, Philadelphia, 1961, p. 59.

González Palencia, A., Introduction to above edition, pp. vii-xl.

Gröber, G., *Grundriss der romanische Philologie*, vol. II, 1, Strasbourg, 1902.

Gröber, G., *Übersicht über d. Lat. Lit. von. d. Mitte d. 6. Jhs. bis zur Mitte d. 14. Jhrs.*, Munich, 1963, sections 114 and 130.

Landau, M., *Die Quellen des Decamerone*, Vienna, 1869, pp. 79–83.

Lexicon für Theologie und Kirche, vol. VIII, Freiburg, 1963, p. 332.

Manitius, M., *Geschichte d. lateinischen Literatur des Mittelalters*, vol. III, Munich, 1931, pp. 274–7.

Pabst, W., *Novellentheorie und Novellendichtung zur Geschichte ihre Antimonie in den romanischen Literaturen*, Hamburg, 1953, pp. 41 ff.

Rudy, Z., *Soziologie des jüdischen Volkes*, Hamburg, 1965, p. 89.

Schipperges, H., *Die Assimilation der arabischen Medizin durch das lateinische Mittelalter*, fascicle 3 of the *Sudhoffs Archiv für Geschichte der Medizin* etc., Wiesbaden, 1964, pp. 146–9.

Steinschneider, M., *Die hebräischen Übersetzungen des Mittelalters und die Juden als Dolmetscher*, Berlin, 1893 (reprinted Granz, 1956), pp. 933–5.

Thorndike, L., *A History of Magic and Experimental Science during the First Thirteen Centuries of our Era*, vol. II, New York, 1923, pp. 68–73.

Vossler, K., *Spanien und Europa*, Munich, 1952, pp. 118–20.

Wulff, A., 'Die frauenfeindlichen Dichtungen in den romanischen Literaturen des Mittelalters bis zu Ende des 13. Jahrhunderts', in *Romanistischen Arbeiten*, ed. C. Voretzsch, Halle, 1914, pp. 63–5.

2 GENERAL BACKGROUND STUDIES

Texts

The Romance of Alexander of the Archpriest Leo, ed. F. Pfister, Sammlung Mittel *lat.* Texte, 6, Heidelberg, 1913.

Baer, F., *Die Juden im christl. Spanien*, Berlin, 1929.

Barlaam and Josaphat of St John Damascene, trans. G. R. Woodward, and Harold Mattingly with a new introduction by D. M. Lang (Loeb Library), 1967.

Born Judas, Der, Legenden, Märchen und Erzählungen, collected by Micha Josef bin Gorion, revised edition by E. Bin Gorion, translated by Rahel bin Gorion, Wiesbaden, 1959.

Buber, M., *Die Erzählungen der Chassidim*, Zürich, 1949.

Buddhistische Märchen, trans. and ed. E. and H. Lüders, Düsseldorf-Cologne, 1961.

Caesarius of Heisterbach, *Historia Mirabilium*, ed. A. Hilka, vol. I, *Public. der Gesellschaft für Rheinische Geschichtskunde* 43, Bonn, 1933.

Fiebig, P., *Pirque aboth*, Der Mischna tractat 'Sprüche der Väter', trans. into German, Tübingen, 1906 (C. Schedl, Sprüche der Väter, Innsbruck-Vienna-Munich, 1968).

Geschichte in Quellen, ed. W. Lautemann and M. Schlenke, vol. I, Altertum, Munich, 1965.

Hilka, A. (ed.). *Historia Septem Sapientum I*, Heidelberg, 1912.

Hilka, A. (ed.), *Historia Septem Sapientum II*, Heidelberg, 1913.

Hitopadeśa, trans. F. Johnson, London, 1925.

Jehuda Halevi, *Kitab al Khazari*, trans. Harting Hirschfeld, London, 1905 (new rev. ed., 1931).

John of Capua, *Works*, trans. from the Hebrew and ed. F. Geissler, Institut für Orientforschung, Berlin, 1960.

Juan Manuel, Don, *Count Lucanor* ... trans. James York, London, 1924

Kabbani: *Altarabische Eseleien* ..., ed. S. Kabbani, Herrenalb, 1965

Klapper, J., *Exempla aus Handschriften des Mittelalters*, Heidelberg, 1911.

Knust, H., *Mittheilungen aus dem Eskurial*, Tübingen, 1879.

Koran, The, trans. A. J. Arberry, Oxford.

Legenda Aurea of Jacobus de Voragine. *The Golden Legend*, trans. and adapted by Granger Ryan and Helmut Ripperger, 2 vols, 1941.

Legenda Aurea, trans. and ed. R. Benz, Heidelberg, n.d.

Levi-Seligmann: *Parabeln, Legenden und Gedanken aus Thalmud und Midrasch*, ed. G. Levi, trans. L. Seligmann, Leipzig, 1863.

Libro de los engaños y los asayemientos de las mugeres, ed. A. Bonilla y San Martin, Barcelona-Madrid, 1904.

Littmann, E., *Arabian Nights*, VI vols, Wiesbaden, 1953.

Littmann, E., 'Morgenländische Spruchweisheit', in *Morgenland*, Leipzig, 1937.

Lommatzsch, E., *Geschichten aus dem alten Frankreich*, Frankfurt am Main, 1966.

Mardrus, J. C., and Powys Mathers, trans. *The Book of the Thousand and One Nights*, 4 vols, London, 1937.

Moses Maimonides, *Rabbi Mosche ban Maimon* ... ed. N. N. Glatzer, Berlin, 1935.

Nizāmulmulk, *Siyāsatnāmā*, trans. into English by K. B. and D. J. Irani, Bombay, 1916.

Palmblätter, *Morgenländische Geschichten*, Leipzig, 1957.

Talmud, The Babylonian, trans. into English under the editorship of I. Epstein, 8 vols, The Soncino Press, 1936

Weisweiler, M., *Von Kalifen* ... *Arabischer Humor aus altarabischen Quellen*, Düsseldorf, 1963.

Werner, J., *Lat. Sprichwörter und Sinnsprüche des Mittelalters*, 2nd ed., P. Flury, Heidelberg, 1966.

Wesselski, A., *Mönchslatein, Erzählungen aus geistl. Schriften d. 13. Jhs.*, Leipzig, 1909.

Wüstenfeld, F., *Geschichte der arabischen Ärzte und Naturforscher*, Göttingen, 1840.

General works

Aly, W., *Volksmärchen, Sage und Novelle bei Herodot und seinen Zeitgenossen*, 2nd rev. ed., Göttingen, 1969.

van Caenegem, R. C. and Ganshef, F. L., *Kurze Quellenkunde des westeuropäischen Mittelalters* ..., trans. from Dutch, M. Gysseling, Göttingen, 1964.

Chauvin, V., *Bibliographie des ouvrages arabes ou relatifs aux arabes publiés dans l'Europe chrétienne de 1810 à 1885*, vol. 8 Liège-Leipzig, 1904 *(Historia Septem Sapientum)*, and vol. 9, 1905 *(Disciplina Clericalis)*.

Comparetti, D., *Researches Respecting the Book of Sindbad*, Publications of the Folk-Lore Society, IX, London, 1882.

Curtius, E. R., *European Literature and the Latin Middle Ages*, trans. by W. R. Trask, London: Routledge & Kegan Paul, 1953.

Dubnow, S., *Die Geschichte d. jüd. Volkes in Europa . . . bis zum Ende der Kreuzzüge*, Berlin, 1926.

Ehrenpreis, M., *Das Land zwischen Orient und Okzident, Spanische Reise eines Juden*, Berlin, 1928.

Fitzmaurice-Kelly, J., *History of Spanish Literature*, Milford, 1922.

Frenzel, E., *Stoffe der Weltliteratur, Ein Lexicon dichtungsgeschichtlicher Längsschnitte*, Stuttgart, 1963.

Funk, S., *Die Entstehung des Talmuds*, Leipzig, 1910.

Gerhardt, M. I., *The Art of Story-Telling, A Literary Study of the 1001 Nights*, Leiden, 1963.

Goldziher, I., *Vorlesungen über den Islam*, reprint of the 2nd ed., Darmstadt, 1963.

Graetz, H., *Geschichte der Juden . . . bis Maimunis Tod* (vol. VI of *Geschichte der Juden*), Leipzig, n.d.

von Grunebaum, G. E., *Medieval Islam*, 2nd ed., Chicago, 1953.

Gunter, H., *Buddha in der abendländ. Legende?*, Leipzig, 1922.

Hadas, M., *Hellenistic Culture*, Columbia, 1959.

Heer, F., *Mittelalter, Kindlers Kulturgeschichte*, Zürich, 1961.

Heller, B., *Die Bedeutung des arabischen Antar-Romans für die vergleichende Literaturkunde*, Leipzig, 1931.

Hermes, E., *Die drei Ringe, aus der Frühzeit der Novelle*, Göttingen, 1964.

Horten, M., *Die Philosophie des Islam*, Munich, 1923.

Howie, M. D., 'Studies in the use of exempla with special reference to Middle High German literature', thesis, London, 1923.

Judentum im Mittelalter, Beiträge zum christlich-jüdischen Gespräch, ed. P. Wilpert and W. P. Eckert, Miscellanea Medievalia vol. IV, Berlin, 1966.

Levy, Reuben, *The Social Structure of Islam*, Cambridge, 1957.

Linsenmayer, A., *Geschichte der Predigt in Deutschland*, Munich, 1886.

Ljungman, W., *Die schwedischen Volksmärchen, Herkunft und Geschichte*, Berlin, 1961.

Loretz, O., *Qohelet und der alte Orient, Untersuchungen zu Stil und theologischen Thematik des Buches Qohelet*, Freiburg, Basle, Vienna, 1964.

Misch, G., *Geschichte der Autobiographie*, vol. III, *Das Mittelalter*, Frankfurt am Main, 1959–62.

Monumenta Judaica, 2000 Jahre Geschichte und Kultur der Juden am Rhein . . ., ed. K. Schilling, Cologne, 1964.

Neuburger, M., *Geschichte der Medizin*, vol. III, part 1, Stuttgart, 1911.

Opitz, K., *Die Medizin im Koran*, Stuttgart, 1906.

Schnürer, G., *Kirche und Kultur im Mittelalter*, vol. II, Paderborn, 1929.

Schoeps, H. J., *Israel und Christenheit, jüdisch-christliches Religionsgespräch in neunzehn Jahrhunderten*, Munich and Frankfurt, 1961.

Sellheim, R., *Die klassisch-arabischen Sprichwörtersammlungen, insbesonderen die des Abū ' Ubaid*, The Hague, 1954.

Spies, O., *Der Orient in der deutschen Literatur*, 2 vols, Kevelaer, 1951–2.

Spies, O., *Orientalische Stoffe in der Kinder- und Hausmärchen der Brüder Grimm*, Walldorf (Hessen), 1952.

Welter, J. Th., 'L'exemplum dans la littérature religieuse et didactique du moyen âge', thesis, Paris, 1927.

EARLY EDITIONS OF THE
DISCIPLINA CLERICALIS

Some years ago, in a paper published by the Bibliographical Society, E. P. Goldschmidt remarked on the difficulty of tracking down the works of many of the most popular works of the Middle Ages, as many of them were to be found masquerading under false authors, no authors at all, or in anonymous collections. In view of the fact that the *Disciplina Clericalis* of Petrus Alfonsi enjoyed such enormous popularity in medieval times, witness the large number of manuscripts listed in Hilka and Söderhjelm's editio major, it has seemed interesting to the present writer to attempt to track down at least some of its earliest appearances in print, as it would seem unlikely that such a popular work should pass from view on the appearance of the printing press. The following account is, for the purposes of this note, kept very brief.

The most commonly printed author of the 'fabulists' was Aesop, whose works in the Latin translations, by Laurenzo Valla and Rinucius, were often printed and widely circulated—there are approximately one hundred incunabular editions of Aesop in Latin, Greek (three only), and the various vernaculars. Most of these editions, some of them selections from the Aesopic corpus, had selections from other fabulists included. The most popular were Avian, Poggio, and Petrus Alfonsi, though the last is found under the names of Adelphonsus, Aldephonus and Doligamus-Doliganus-Adulphus, and combinations of these. Only one complete edition of the *DC* seems to have been published—the Textus Summularum which was printed in Alost in Flanders in 1478 (Hain-Copinger 2982). All the others seem to be selections only.

Germany produced the most editions. Before 1500 there appeared in Ulm, Augsburg, Magdeburg and Basle seventeen editions of Aesop with selections from the other fabulists, all with the German translation made by Steinhöwel, the earliest being that produced in Ulm in 1476/77 by Johann Zainer—'. . . der fabel Aviani auch doligami Adelfonsi [etc.]'. A French translation by Julien Macho was published in Lyons in 1480, and between 1480 and 1500 there were five more editions of this. This same Macho also published a Dutch translation in 1485. From the English point of view, however, the most interesting item is the translation made by Caxton of the fables of Aesop and the other fabulists, Avian, Petrus, and Poggio, from the German edition of 1480 published at Ulm by Anton Sorg. This Caxton published in 1484. Caxton's versions were reprinted in 1889 by J. Jacobs.

197

As pointed out above, the complete text seems to have been printed only once before F. W. V. Schmidt's edition of 1827, but it must be remembered that a great many of the MSS. which transmit the *DC* to us do so only in a selected form. The *Sententiae*, as the *DC* was often called, was freely excerpted, and obviously the most famous and popular tales are those most commonly found.

Note: reference should be made to vol. I of the *Gesamtkatalog der Wiegendrucke*, nos 351–75, where details of all the above mentioned editions may be found, except for the 1478 Textus Summularum, a description of which can be found in Brunet's *Manuel du libraire et de l'amateur de livres*, vol. I, col. 199.

INDEX

Note: The majority of authors referred to in the notes are not included in the index.

199